What Every Cybersecurity Professional Must Master

Prabhat K. Andleigh

ISBN : 9798234926071

Dedication

This book is dedicated to my parents, the Late Dr. H.S. Andleigh and the Late Mrs. Mohini Andleigh and my sister Mrs. Pramila Mathur who have been my support and inspiration.

Acknowledgements

I would like to start by acknowledging my mentor and dear friend Mr. Peter Purushotma who I have known for 30 years when he became an investor and advisor in my startup on a skills-based search engine that was later used by Monster for resume analysis. Most recently, Peter has been an advisor to the Chairman and CEO of Genpact Headstrong, a global consulting and IT services company with a specialized focus in capital markets. Prior to that he was President for Advanced Technologies at HCL America. Peter had been a key figure in the growth of HCL in Singapore and is highly respected in the nation because of his ongoing advocacy and advice to senior leaders in the IT industry, the technical university, as well as the IT leaders in the government.

I would like to express my sincere gratitude to Mr. Rajeev Koolath, who has been a mentor, former supervisor at Charles Schwab, and a lasting source of professional inspiration. Rajeev led Enterprise Architecture at Charles Schwab as Managing Director and later served as CTO for the Americas Region at DXC Technology. He currently serves as Global CTO for BFSI at GlobalLogic, a Hitachi Group Company, where he continues a distinguished career of technology leadership across global enterprises. He also serves as an Advisory Board Member for AI/ML at DevNetwork and for CX & AI at the University of Colorado. Rajeev's guidance has played an important role in shaping my perspective and in the development of this work.

I would like to further acknowledge my dear friend and colleague for my full stint of over 7 years at Charles Schwab, Mr. Johnson Michael. Currently Director ISO - Developer Experience at Capital One Bank, Johnson was the Senior Director for Security Architecture at Charles Schwab. We were the two complementary architects at Charles Schwab, and sitting side by side for most of our stints worked together and collaborated on many projects.

Another key person I would like to acknowledge is Mr. Sudhir Mohan, a consulting CEO for the last 10 years. Prior to that he was the CTO at Quixey where I reported to him and he gave me the opportunity to work actively on public cloud (AWS) application design and operations. I also worked closely with him in his role as Senior Director of Search at Yahoo! when I headed the Search development and operations team in Yahoo! India. He has been a great friend, mentor and guide since then.

Last but not the least, I would like to acknowledge my wife, Jennifer Chen Andleigh whose love and patience throughout the last six months of writing this book allowed me to focus completely on this effort.

About the Author
Prabhat K. Andleigh

Phone and WhatsApp: (760) 445-0010
Email: pandleigh@gmail.com
LinkedIn Profile: https://www.linkedin.com/in/prabhat-andleigh-61a7498/

Prabhat's core achievements over the last 12 years are delivering world-class broad-based enterprise on-premises and cloud-based cybersecurity architecture, design and implementation in hands-on as well as in leadership mode, while acquiring broad in-depth security, risk and compliance experience at major financial organizations such as Wells Fargo Bank and Charles Schwab Corporation. He has evaluated, run production level proofs of concept on, and implemented a wide range of cybersecurity tools.

Prabhat is CISSP (Certified Information Systems Security Professional) certified by ISC2 in 2017 and GDPR certified in 2018.

Most recently, as Enterprise Cybersecurity Governance Analyst at Wells Fargo Bank, and as a Member of a cyber security governance team validating compliance of cloud-native applications and cloud services, he validated cloud-native applications and services against the security requirements documented for Cloud Cybersecurity Framework principles (derived from NIST and CSA CCM).

For more than 7 years at Charles Schwab Corporation, as Principal Enterprise Security Architect, Prabhat worked on the architecture and design of cloud-native applications and on-premises to cloud migration of enterprise applications. He has extensive experience in enterprise security architecture in areas including infrastructure vulnerability management, identity and access management (IAM), risk management for on-premises applications and for deployment to public clouds (AWS and GCP), data security, security policy standards, audits and compliance, and access authorization.

Prabhat has authored and published in 2024 a comprehensive 300+ page book being sold on Amazon as a paperback titled "Enterprise Data Security Around the World". In addition to cybersecurity and data security, it covers laws, regulations, standards (including NIST, FISMA, GDPT, COBIT, CCM, etc.) and best practices around the World.

With over 25 years industry experience, Prabhat has over 15 years of architecture and design experience in areas including logging and monitoring analytics using machine learning; big data analytics based on Cassandra, Hadoop, and MongoDB; and healthcare EMR and group practice management information systems based on HIPAA standards. He has also worked on many major technology modernization transformation assessments and planning for multi-billion-dollar corporations.

Preface

Cybersecurity and Data Security have grown into very large, rapidly growing fields with high demand and strong, long-term employment prospects. The rapid adoption of Artificial Intelligence (AI) and Generative AI (GenAI) has transformed the cybersecurity and data security landscape with malicious actors using the AI and Gen AI capabilities to mount cyberattacks. AI and GenAI also provide the technologies for mitigating these attacks.

There is intense competition, a severe talent shortage, and high turnover for organizations, finding candidates with specialized skills to counter rapidly evolving threats. Organizations are looking for professionals who can hit the ground ruining and contributing with these skills immediately on projects.

On the other hand, for professionals, the AI bots driven resume selection and the resulting highly focused skills-based hiring as opposed to what used to be capability and maturity-based hiring has become a major challenge. They need to master a wide range of technologies and related tools to survive the AI driven questions during interviews. And even when they start a new job, they are expected to be masters in these new technologies almost from day one once onboarding has been completed.

The comments from Ella described in Peter Purushotma's foreword summarize the core value of this book for cybersecurity professionals quoted again here: "She found it comprehensive and illuminating, noting that it clarified concepts she already understood while introducing her to new ideas and emerging areas. She believes it will serve as an excellent resource for students and for professionals seeking to deepen their knowledge or advance in their careers." Peter further went on to say that "for students like Ella, and for new professionals establishing themselves in the field, this book provides both knowledge and confidence".

Also important to note is that this book is based on the author's own interviewing experience over the last year or so. This book is focused on the professionals looking for reference material to prepare for interviews in this emerging challenge of skills-based hiring rather than experience and capability-based hiring, and the use of AI bots for resume evaluation and selection out of hundreds of resumes presented for each job. It is intended to help candidates present the best skills and capability profile during the interview and from day one. The content is the gist of the extensive research on the technologies and tools that the author had mastered during his deep cybersecurity stints at Charles Schwab and Wells Fargo.

Foreword by Peter Purushotma

The recent cyberattacks on Singapore unsettled me in a way I did not anticipate. I have always regarded my home country as disciplined, technologically advanced, and exceptionally well-prepared for any form of emergency. Learning that a sophisticated group such as UNC3886 had successfully infiltrated national systems challenged that long-held confidence. It underscored a sobering reality: if a nation with Singapore's formidable cybersecurity defenses can be targeted, then no nation is entirely beyond reach.

What concerned me most was the realization that the attackers were driven not by financial motives but by alleged geopolitical objectives. Their demonstrated ability to penetrate elements of Singapore's critical infrastructure made the threat feel immediate and tangible. At the same time, the National Security Ministry's success in attributing the attack to a specific APT actor strengthened my respect for Singapore's cybersecurity institutions. Their diligence and technical expertise reaffirmed that the story of cybersecurity is ultimately one of human vulnerability, resilience, and the necessity of global cooperation in a world where digital threats transcend borders.

I shared these reflections with my granddaughter, Ella, who is studying International Relations with a particular interest in transnational cybersecurity threats, AI, and GenAI. I asked her to review Prabhat's new book and offer her perspective on its relevance for her generation. She found it comprehensive and illuminating, noting that it clarified concepts she already understood while introducing her to new ideas and emerging areas. She believes it will serve as an excellent resource for students and for professionals seeking to deepen their knowledge or advance in their careers.

For students like Ella, and for new professionals establishing themselves in the field, this book provides both knowledge and confidence. I am certain it will help current and future cybersecurity practitioners in Singapore and around the world rise to the challenge of protecting critical infrastructure, ensuring that attacks like those that unsettled me become far less likely.

It is a privilege to write this foreword. I have known Prabhat Andleigh for thirty years, ever since 1996 when I first recognized the groundbreaking nature of his résumé-search innovation and became an advisor. Over the decades, our friendship has grown through many conversations about emerging technologies. His dedication is exemplary — not only in mastering new skills and technologies, but also in sharing his insights through the many books and articles he has authored.

Prabhat's work in this book demonstrates why the future of technology depends on intelligence and integrity together. Cybersecurity, at their intersection, is essential for safeguarding corporate assets and national resilience. It is a vast and complex domain, and a book such as this brings critical knowledge together in one authoritative and accessible volume

---- Peter Purushotma, most recently Advisor to Chairman and CEO of Genpact Headstrong

- https://www.linkedin.com/in/peter-purushotma-a1938/

Foreword by Mr. Rajeev Koolath

Some professionals do more than handle their responsibilities well—they improve the people and teams around them. Prabhat Andleigh is one of those professionals.

When Prabhat served as Senior Director of Enterprise Architecture, focused on cyber and information security, on my team at Charles Schwab, what stood out most was not only his expertise but his constant drive to learn and improve. He kept up with emerging threats, changing standards, new frameworks, and the growing role of AI in security. Just as important, he shared what he learned generously. Our team meetings were stronger, and our architecture reviews more effective, because Prabhat came prepared and kept everyone informed. This book reflects that same approach.

Throughout my career, I have believed enterprise architecture should enable progress, not slow it down. At its best, it connects innovation, practical solutions, and business value. Within that framework, cyber and information security architecture is essential. Weak security creates risk across the entire organization. It is not easy to find professionals who truly understand cybersecurity—not just the tools, but the principles and relationships behind them. When someone with that level of understanding is part of your architecture team, the quality and resilience of the organization improve in measurable ways. I saw that directly with Prabhat.

This book is the kind of resource the profession needs. It starts with the fundamentals: identity and access management, cloud security, network security, and data loss prevention. The material is clear and practical, useful both for experienced professionals and for those entering the field. From there, it moves into more advanced topics, including AI and GenAI in cybersecurity, current standards and regulatory frameworks, and zero-trust architectures that are quickly becoming standard practice for serious enterprises.

I was especially interested in the sections covering AI-driven cybersecurity. AI presents both opportunity and risk in this space. The same capabilities that help defenders can also be used by attackers at speed and scale. Prabhat addresses these issues thoughtfully and with the right level of balance.

Whether you are preparing for an interview, starting a new role, or building a stronger overall understanding of cybersecurity, this book will be valuable. It is the kind of reference you keep close at hand and return to often.

Prabhat, once again, you have found a way to help others improve. That is high praise, and well deserved.

--- Rajeev Koolath, CTO | Technology Executive | AI Researcher & Builder

- Linked-In Profile: https://www.linkedin.com/in/rkoolath/

Foreword by Mr. Johnson Michael

With over two decades of experience as a cybersecurity and technology leader, and a strong collaborator with the author of this book, Prabhat Andleigh, on enterprise security architecture, cloud security, application security, risk management, standards and policies, and threat modeling. I can confidently comment on the extreme value of this book to every information security professional.

This book is a very exhaustive list of everything a cyber security professional should know. The chapters for each domain have sufficient details included to get the professionals started on their own journey of researching technologies and developing expertise in information security and its derivatives of cybersecurity, application security, data security and data loss prevention, cloud security, network security, mobile device security, threat intelligence, endpoint and APU security, IoT security and operational technology security. A quick scan of job descriptions for cybersecurity professionals shows all of these technologies are described as required or nice to have in prospective candidates at various levels from cybersecurity engineers to architects. This book is expressly targeted to preparing candidates for interviews as well as preparing them to hit the ground running on their new jobs.

Some other key areas covered in excellent detail include international cybersecurity and data security regulations and what role they play for all sizes and types of organizations and what cybersecurity professionals need to know how to apply them, both in preparation for interviews as well as in their day-to-day jobs in this space.

AI and GenAI have taken the world by storm with massive investments in these areas. They have also become a haven for malicious actors and hackers as individuals or as groups and state actors holding organizations hostage for ransomware. The chapter on these topics not only covers the range of attack methodologies based on AI and GenAI but also how these attacks can be mitigated.

For over seven years at Charles Schwab central architecture team, Prabhat and I worked side by side, very often jointly, on all aspects of cybersecurity architecture and design, standards and policies, best practices, and protection from threats and vulnerabilities. Prabhat's focus throughout was deep on architecture and design and documenting guidance to services teams and operations on ensuring their adherence to best practices, as well as evaluating and onboarding many cybersecurity tools.

I can say from first-hand experience that this book is grounded on sound direct experience with these technologies enhanced with extensive research in all aspects to provide a comprehensive perspective to prepare cybersecurity professionals.

--- Johnson Michael, Director, ISO – Developer Experience, Capitol One

- https://www.linkedin.com/in/johnsonmichael/

Table of Contents

1 -- What is Cybersecurity

Cybersecurity is the practice of protecting digital systems, networks, and data from digital attacks, damage, or unauthorized access. It involves using technologies, processes, policies, and procedures to safeguard an organization's corporate and sensitive information, prevent cyberattacks like ransomware, phishing, and data exfiltration and ensure the confidentiality, integrity, and availability of data.

Cybersecurity protects a wide range of digital assets, including computer networks, cloud environments, data center and on-premises servers, devices, programs, and sensitive data. It is designed to prevent and mitigate threats like data breaches, malware injections, unauthorized access, and ransomware attacks, which can lead to financial loss, disruption of business, and damage to reputation.

Cybersecurity is a comprehensive practice that uses a combination of physical security measures, software tools (like firewalls and antivirus programs), and organizational policies to create a multi-layered defense, known as Defense In-Depth. Cybersecurity measures must be designed to prevent attacks from happening, detect them in real-time, and respond rapidly in real-time when an incident occurs to mitigate lasting damage to the organization's data assets and business.

Cybersecurity, as a comprehensive solution has many dimensions or domains described in the following section.

Cybersecurity Domains

The following list of the key cybersecurity domains is the foundation for understanding the full scope of cybersecurity for organizations. In addition to these domains, an understanding of Cybersecurity Tools and their evaluation, acquisition, and implementation is really critical for an overall understanding of cybersecurity

The chapters in this book are organized around deep dives into each of these domains.

1. Identity and Access Management
2. Cloud Security
3. AI and GenAI in Cybersecurity
4. Security Standards, Regulations, & Frameworks
5. Data Security Standards & Regulations
6. Data Loss Prevention
7. Application Security

8. Network Security
9. Cyber Threat Intelligence
10. End-point Detection Response (EDR)
11. Wireless Security and MDM
12. Internet of Things (IoT) Security
13. Operational Technology Security

Figure 1-1 : Common Cybersecurity Domains

The previous graphic describes the key highlights of these domains. The following provides a brief introduction to each of these domains to highlight their importance to cybersecurity.

Identity and Access Management: Identity and Access Management (IAM) is a framework of policies, processes, and technologies that ensures that only authorized and authenticated individuals can access resources that they are permitted to access at approved times such access is permitted. IAM is designed to manage and secure digital identities to control who can access systems and data, prevent unauthorized access, and ensure the confidentiality and integrity of information.

Cloud Security: With the continuing shift to active use of public clouds for many financial and business applications, it has become crucial to protect sensitive data, applications, and infrastructure in the clouds from cyber threats like breaches, malware, and unauthorized access. Cloud security covers identity management in the clouds, granular access control, enlarged perimeter security, governance and risk management, and continuous monitoring.

AI and GenAI in Cybersecurity: Artificial Intelligence (AI) is a technology that enables computers and machines to simulate human intelligence and solve problems especially when it is combined with other technologies such as sensors, geolocation, and robotics. Generative AI (GenAI) is the most recent major development in the overall realm of AI. It is a specific subset of AI that uses programs to process large data sets to detect patterns and then create new content derived from the existing content. Both of these technologies are being actively used by malicious actors. They can also be used to protect networks and systems from attacks.

Security Standards, Regulations, & Frameworks: Cybersecurity and data security regulations, such as NIST in the US and ISO/IEC in Europe and the rest of the world, are standards set by regulatory bodies or governments worldwide, that guide organizations on protecting the confidentiality, integrity, and availability of data. The frameworks based on them essentially aim at safeguarding the information assets.

Data Security Standards & Regulations: Data Security Standards: such as the General Data Protection Regulation (GDPR) in Europe and subsequent regulations derived from GDPR and enacted within the United States and other nations in almost all continents, enforce specific rules for data handling and processing, often with penalties for non-compliance. These regulations and standards are designed to ensure data confidentiality, integrity, and availability (the CIA triad) and protect sensitive data from cyber threats, prevent costly data breaches, and comply with legal obligations.

Data Loss Prevention: Data loss prevention (DLP) includes all tools, technologies, and initiatives for preventing loss of data due to unauthorized access and exposure of confidential and highly confidential data (collectively sensitive data) that should be accessible only to authorized users with proper permissions, privileges, and justification to access the data. DLP technologies use data classification labels and tags, content inspection techniques, and contextual analysis to identify sensitive data and determine protection actions. They also provide centralized policy management that drive these actions. DLP solutions can be described as Enterprise DLP, Integrated DLP and Cloud-Native DLP. Furthermore data encryption at rest, in transit and even is use are other technologies used for data protection.

Application Security: Application Security (or AppSec) is the practice of securing software applications from vulnerabilities throughout their lifecycle, from development to deployment and beyond. It focuses on identifying, mitigating, and preventing security risks that attackers could exploit to gain unauthorized access or cause harm. It protects applications from threats like SQL injection, XSS (Cross-site Scripting), buffer overflows and data breaches by fixing vulnerabilities before they can be exploited, using methods like secure coding, penetration testing, WAFs (Web Application Firewalls) and RASPs (Runtime Application Self-Protection technologies).

Network Security: Rigorous use of network security helps in threat prevention by blocking threats from entering the network. Organizations can achieve this by using tools like firewalls, intrusion detection/prevention systems, and antivirus software. Furthermore, good access control in managing who can access network resources through user authentication (IDs, passwords, biometrics) and authorization policies prevents unauthorized access and risks to the assets. It is also important to protect the sensitive data in transit and at rest through encryption and access restrictions, maintaining its integrity and confidentiality. Continuously monitoring the network traffic is essential to identity and block suspicious activity using both manual an automates procedures to respond to incidents.

Cyber Threat Intelligence: Cyber Threat intelligence (CTI) is the processed, analyzed, and contextualized information about cyber threats. It includes potential attackers, their motives, their tactics, techniques, and procedures (TTPs), and the tools used by them. This information can help organizations proactively defend against attacks like ransomware or phishing. Organizations can become proactive rather than being reactive in implementing a preventative security posture to manage the threat. Threat intelligence is much more than raw data; it is actionable knowledge that enables better decision-making, risk management, and faster incident response.

End-point Detection Response (EDR): Observability and Vulnerability are two key technology areas for ensuring cybersecurity protection in an organization's environments. Observability is the technology that helps the security team gain deep insights into their system's internal state from its external outputs such as logs, metrics, events and traces and collected endpoint activity information. Vulnerability management, on the other hand, is the continuous process of identifying, assessing, prioritizing and remediating vulnerabilities across the organization's systems to prevent breaches. Vulnerability management uses insights from their observability tools in real time.

Wireless Security and MDM: Protection of wireless networks and Mobile Device Management (MDM) are key to protecting data from unauthorized access, theft, or damage. It is important that many end-user devices are connected through wireless networks and are targets for malicious actors to intercept and exfiltrate data. Wireless security implemented to protect wireless networks and data from unauthorized access, theft, or damage, employs methods like encryption (WPA2/WPA3), authentication, and firewalls to secure radio-transmitted data, preventing attackers from eavesdropping on, accessing, or damaging the network. Using Virtual Private Networks (VPNs) to create secure "tunnels" for data, is essential for protecting information over public Internet.

Internet of Things (IoT) Security: The IoT refers to a network of these physical objects—"things"—embedded with sensors, software, and technologies that enable them to connect, collect, and exchange data with other systems and devices over the internet. These interconnected "smart" devices, range from home appliances and medical devices to industrial machinery. They facilitate automation, remote monitoring, and increased efficiency. Security of IoT systems is the practice of protecting internet-connected and their networks from cyber threats, unauthorized access, and data breaches

Operational Technology Security: Operational Technology (OT) consists of hardware and software designed to detect or cause direct changes in, and controlling industrial equipment. OT priorities focus on system safety, reliability, and availability, in addition to data security. OT includes Industrial Control Systems (ICS), Supervisory Control and Data Acquisition (SCADA), and Distributed Control Systems (DCS) that automate tasks too dangerous or precise for manual operation.

Who Are Facing Challenges That This Book Is Designed For

This reference book is ideal for all cybersecurity professionals preparing for interviews and helping them gain widespread knowledge rapidly to answer any questions that come up during interviews. It is also ideal for professionals entering this important field of cybersecurity in helping them get a head start in the intricacies of the cybersecurity solutions in very succinct discussions.

As a seasoned cybersecurity professional over the last 15 years, I as the author, built up a vast library in Confluence based on my learnings and this reference book is a fine-tuned extraction and summarization from my library. I expect it will be a valuable resource for all cybersecurity professionals who will find answers in their quest for knowledge across this vast field in one place. I am confident that you will enjoy reading it as much as I enjoyed writing it.

2 – Identity and Access Management

Identity and Access Management (IAM) is a framework of policies, processes, and technologies that ensures that only authorized and authenticated individuals can access resources that they are permitted to access at times such access is permitted. IAM is designed to manage and secure digital identities to control who can access systems and data, prevent unauthorized access, and ensure the confidentiality and integrity of information.

IAM systems can be deployed on-premises or through a cloud-based subscription model or deployed in a hybrid model. They can be home-grown or provided by a third-party vendor.

IAM is primarily concerned with processes and technologies used to manage digital identities from their creation to their eventual retirement within an organization. This encompasses all stages of a user's or entity's interaction with an organization's systems and resources, from initial onboarding to final deprovisioning. Identity Lifecycle Management (ILM) is a crucial component of Identity Governance and Administration (IGA) and is essential for maintaining security, ensuring compliance, and streamlining operations.

IAM Basics

Key functions and the terms used as the basics of IAM include the following

- **Administration**: for managing user identities, creating accounts for new employees (provisioning), updating roles as a user's job changes, and deleting accounts when an employee leaves (deprovisioning). This process is part of Identity Lifecycle Management.
- **Authentication:** verifies the user's identity to ensure they are who they claim to be through the use of passwords, biometrics, passkeys, multi-factor authentication (MFA), or single sign-on (SSO).
- **Authorization:** determines what specific resources an authenticated identity is allowed to access based on a user's role (RBAC – Role Based Access Control), or attributes (ABAC – Attribute Based Access Control) such as job title, department, location, security clearance.
- **Privileged Access Management:** is and extra protection layer of authentication and authorization capability that elevates the rights and privileges of specific users to perform critical functions or access sensitive data.

- **Auditing:** monitoring user activity to track who is accessing what, where, and when to identify abnormal activity and ensure compliance with security policies and regulations.
- **Password management**: a software application that securely stores and manages the organization's login credentials (usernames, passwords, etc.)
- **Identity Lifecycle Management**: is about managing digital identities in a secure, efficient, and compliant manner throughout their entire journey within an organization, from initial creation to final retirement.
- **Identity Governance and Administration (IGA):** a framework that manages and monitors digital identities and their access to organizational resources, ensuring that only authorized identities have the appropriate access at the appropriate times. It encompasses policies, processes, and controls to manage user access, ensure compliance with regulations, and align with security and risk management practices
- **Identity Management**: assignment of access based on a digital identity (what differentiates one identity from another) and ensures authorized individuals (users, devices, or systems) have the right access to resources at the right time. It manages the entire digital identity lifecycle —creation, maintenance and deletion.
- **Access Control**: determines what resources an authenticated identity is permitted to access across the organization's extended network perimeter and the application running within the networked environments.
- **Single Factor Authentication (SFA)**: requires a single factor consisting of username and password only for authenticating a user identity.
- **Multi-factor Authentication**: Requires in addition to the password another form of authentication such as one of 1) who your are – biometrics, 2) something you know - secret password or PIN, 3) something you have – token or smartphone.
- **Single sign-on (SSO)**: an authentication method that allows users to log in once and access multiple applications and websites without needing to re-enter their credentials for each one
- **Federated Identity**: allows users to access multiple applications and resources across different domains or organizations using a single set of credentials
- **Identity analytics**: a security practice that uses data analysis and machine learning to understand and manage risks associated with user identities and access rights

With an IAM framework in place, information technology (IT) managers can control user access to critical information within their organizations. Systems used for IAM include single sign-on systems, two-factor authentication, multifactor authentication and privileged access management. These technologies also provide the ability to securely store identity and profile data as well as data governance functions to ensure that only data that is necessary and relevant is shared.

The following lists the most important concepts and practices for IAM:

- How entities are identified
- How roles are defined (Role-based Access Management)
- Assigning levels of access to roles – Role Design
- Protecting the system and sensitive data

Identity Lifecycle Management (ILM)

Identity Lifecycle Management (ILM) is the comprehensive process of creating new digital identities, provisioning access to necessary resources, setting up initial configurations for users or entities, managing changes as user roles change, and eventually deprovisioning identities. The core practices of ILM include.

- **Onboarding Identities:** the process of verifying and integrating an individual's identity into the organization's identity management system to allow the identity owner to access the organization's networked resources. This process is crucial for security and includes collecting, verifying (through documents, biometrics, or knowledge-based questions), and registering a person's unique information to grant the person access to an application, service, or the organization itself.
- **Identity Provisioning**: is the automated process of creating, managing, and deactivating user identities and their access permissions across multiple systems and applications. Provisioning coordinates data from multiple sources including the organization's human resources database, and tools such as Active Directory or Azure Entra ID and other cloud identity management systems (known as Identity Providers). This process ensures that user accounts and access rights are correct throughout their lifecycle.
- **Offboarding Identities and De-provisioning**: involves the secure removal of access when a user or entity leaves the organization, including disabling accounts, revoking permissions, and deleting the identity. It is the automated revoking of access when an employee or workforce member's role changes or the member leaves the organization.
- **Ongoing Identity Management**: includes managing user roles, permissions, and access rights as they change or evolve within the organization.
- **Identity Management Automation**: ILM often relies on automation to streamline processes like onboarding, offboarding, and access management, reducing manual effort and potential errors.
- **Policy Enforcement**: ensures that access is granted based on predefined policies and that access rights are regularly reviewed and adjusted, promoting the principle of *least privilege.*
- **Improved Compliance**: ILM helps organizations comply with regulatory requirements related to data privacy and security by ensuring that access is controlled and monitored.

Privileged Access Management (PAM)

Privileged Access Management (PAM) is a security strategy and a set of tools. It is a security framework for controlling, monitoring, and auditing privileged access to on-premises and cloud resources. Service accounts, managed through PAM, are used to escalate privileges to access specialized resources such as sensitive data and production environments. This ensures that developers do not have access to sensitive data or production without privileged authorization and oversight. Service accounts are also used for identities that applications and workloads use to interact with cloud services without human intervention. Service accounts are a type of account that PAM is designed to manage.

Privileged accounts provide users custom accounts with elevated access rights such as admin and service accounts, system processes and secure access to data. Access is controlled such that only authorized users and systems can use privileged accounts and resources.

PAM ensures controlling access and enforcing policies and controls such as MFA and least privilege access to limit access to only the resources that the user or account is permitted to view and/or edit. All PAM access requests need to be monitored and tracked along with monitoring sessions, logging privileged activities, insights into user behavior, and threats. Session management is used to monitor and record privileged sessions to track user activity during that session to ensure that the user accessed only the permitted resources and performed only the permitted functions.

Password Management is an important aspect of PAM including securely storing and managing privileged credentials in a vault. Privileged accounts aren't necessarily "stored" in a single location; rather, the credentials (like passwords and keys) for these accounts are securely stored in a *Privileged Access Management (PAM) vault,* such as a *CyberArk Privilege Cloud* or a *Google Cloud PAM vault.* This vault acts as a secure control point, isolating sensitive credentials from the underlying systems and platforms they protect. To access systems and apps users "check out" the secret from the vault through the PAM system. The PAM system monitors and records every instance of privileged access.

Components of PAM:

The key components of PAM include:

- **Secure Vaults** - for storing privileged credentials like passwords, API keys, and SSH keys in a centralized, encrypted, and secure vault.
- **Password Rotation:** Automatically rotates credentials at regular intervals,
- **Least privilege, JIT Access, MFA**, session monitoring and recording, session isolation, automated workflows, DevSecOps integration, auditing, and Zero Trust.

Key Services for PAM

The following describes the key services associated with PAM.

- **Auditing and Reporting**: Providing detailed logs and reports on privileged access activities.

- **Risk assessment** -- to understand critical assets and data in the cloud and identify all privileged accounts and their associated risks. The best practice is to grant only the necessary access to the user and escalate privileges when required.
- **Implement Just-In-Time (JIT) access and least privilege** -- to dynamically provision permissions for specific times and tasks, aligning with Zero Trust principles.
- **Automate discovery and access workflows** -- automating routine tasks such as credential discovery and rotation, access requests management and approval of workflows, and threat response actions.
- **Enforce multi-factor authentication (MFA)** – blocks account compromise attacks by requiring a second form of authentication.
- **Enforce RBAC controls** – PAM requires role-based privilege escalation
- **Continuously monitor and audit all privileged sessions** – including automating audit logs of all access requests, grants, and session activities.
- **Align PAM with Zero Trust principles** -- to secure hybrid/multi-cloud environments.

PAM Controls on API

API security requires controlled access to the API. All accounts, both human and service accounts, that have elevated privileges or access to critical on-premises and cloud APIs need to be identified. This includes API keys, service accounts, and any credentials used by applications or automated processes to interact with cloud services.

Service accounts in the context of API services are specialized accounts used by applications, services, or virtual machines (VMs) to interact with APIs, rather than by human users. Instead of traditional username/password combinations, service accounts often use methods like key files (e.g., JSON key files), client certificates, or client secrets for authentication. Service accounts are granted specific permissions or roles, determining which API resources they can access and what actions they can perform. service accounts typically do not have a user interface for login or direct human interaction. They are automatically created when a cloud service is activated but have to be managed by administrators.

Just-in-Time PAM

Implementing Just-in-Time (JIT) access requires granting temporary access only when a user requests elevated access to a specific resource or system. This is done by evaluating the request against policies and access rules (identity, role, justification). JIT elevated privileges expire automatically.

JIT can also be implemented with public clouds. For example, it can be implemented as JIT with AWS IAM Identity Center, or integrate with an IdP (e.g. MS Entra ID) and enforce the Least Privilege by granting temporary, role-based permissions only when needed. JIT is important to securely manage credentials, enable MFA for privileged accounts, utilize tools such as AWS IAM Access Analyzer to monitor privilege escalation and use. A SCIM (System for Cross-domain Identity Management) an open standard protocol designed to automate the exchange of user identity information between IT systems, can be used for provisioning and managing user accounts in cloud applications. For example, to automate provisioning users and groups from your IdP to AWS.

Tools for JIT process include PAM Solutions (e.g. Beyond Trust); MFA, ABAC and RBAC supported IAM solutions; Cloud Infrastructure Entitled Management (CIEM); CSPM tools, SIEM, and ITDR (Identity Threat Detection and Response)

- Specific tools for JIT access include Tenable Cloud Security (CNAPP), Azure AD Privileged Identity Management (PIM), AWS Identity Center, StrongDM, Apono, Delinea, and Securden.

PAM in Clouds

Implementing PAM in the public clouds depends on the cloud services available and potential integrations with third party tools required for the implementation.

AWS:

In AWS, Privileged Access Management (PAM) is not a single, defined service like IAM or EC2. Instead, it's a set of practices and tools used to secure, manage, and monitor privileged access to AWS resources. AWS provides various services and features that can be combined to implement a PAM solution. AWS Console does not explicitly define PAM. Ways to implement PAM in AWS:

- Navigate to the IAM console in the organization's AWS account. Select "Access Analyzer" under "Access reports" on the left-hand panel. Click "Create Analyzer" and provide a name for it.
- Use Role-Based Access Control (RBAC).
- Secure Privileged Accounts and Credentials: use MFA, strong passwords, and disable root access,
- Create emergency access keys for root user only when absolutely necessary and delete them when not required any more.
- Monitor and Audit Privileged Activity: AWS CloudTrail to log all API calls and monitor privileged activities. Forward Cloud trail logs to Cloud Watch for detailed auditing and alarm.
- Enforce broad security invariants, that is, security conditions that should always be true.
- Discover privileged accounts: human users, service accounts, and apps with elevated permissions.
- Understand their roles and responsibilities: Determine what each privileged account is authorized to do and why. Reduce attack surface by removing accounts no longer needed.
- Eliminate unnecessary privileged accounts:

Azure

Azure leverages a "just-in-time, just-enough" access model, where users only receive the necessary permissions for a limited time, minimizing the risk of unauthorized access. This is achieved through features like role-based access control, temporary role assignments, and approval workflows.

PAM in Azure, primarily defined and managed through Microsoft Entra Privileged Identity Management (PIM) and Microsoft Purview Privileged Access Management, focuses on managing access to roles within Azure Active Directory (Azure AD renamed as Entra ID), Azure resources, and other Microsoft Online Services. Microsoft Purview PAM, on the other hand, focuses on managing access at the task level, particularly within the Microsoft 365 environment. To requests access, a user submits a request, often through a portal or interface.

- Approval Process: The request is routed to designated approvers based on pre-defined policies.
- Temporary Role Activation: If approved, the user's role is activated for a specific duration.
- Session Monitoring: Azure monitors the user's session for activity and logs all actions.
- Role Expiration and Deactivation: when the time limit expires, the user's access is automatically revoked.

GCP

(PAM) in Google Cloud Platform (GCP) allows for temporary and auditable elevation of user privileges. It works by enabling administrators to create entitlements, which define specific roles and permissions that can be temporarily granted to users for a set duration. These grants can be set up with or without approval requirements and justifications, and all actions are logged for auditing purposes. Privileged Access Manager (PAM) is a feature within GCP and is directly integrated into the GCP Console.

- Administrators define entitlements, which act as templates for granting temporary access.
- Entitlements specify the roles that can be granted, the users or groups eligible to request those roles, and whether approvals or justifications are required.
- Entitlements can be scoped at the organization, folder, or project level.
- Users who need elevated privileges can request a grant against an existing entitlement.
- Requests can be justifications for the access and may require approval from designated approvers.
- If approval is required, the request remains pending until approved or denied, and automatically expires
- When a request is approved (or automatically granted), the specified roles are temporarily assigned.
- The granted roles are automatically removed when the grant duration expires.
- All entitlement and grant events are logged in Cloud Audit Logs, providing a detailed history of privileged access.

Common PAM Systems:

Selecting a robust on-premises and cloud PAM solution integrated with your existing identity provider is critical for good PAM design. Common PAM systems include:

- BeyondTrust -- can be deployed in cloud, hybrid, or on-premises environments to manage privileges across an organization's entire infrastructure. A modern PAM platform integrates cloud PAM , CIEM, and IGA capabilities
- CyberArk – privileged accounts are stored in centralized vaults called "Safes". It also manages automatic rotation of credentials, and can verify credentials against remote systems.
- OKTA -- Okta provides dedicated Privileged Access Management (PAM) capabilities through its Okta Privileged Access (OPA) offering, which extends core identity and governance controls to privileged resources, integrating seamlessly with its broader Workforce Identity Cloud to secure servers, secrets, and SaaS accounts with features like credential vaulting, just-in-time access, and session monitoring
- GCP IAM and PAM -- temporary, approved access to privileged roles, with logs tracking
- AWS – AWS Systems Manager, which offers Session Manager for just-in-time access and auditing, and supports PAM solutions found on the AWS Marketplace such as. CyberArk.
- Azure – tools like Microsoft Entra ID Privileged Identity Management (PIM)

Behavioral analytics

Behavioral analytics is the process of analyzing user data to understand the user behavior, intentions, and patterns across digital platforms like websites and apps. It can range from user behavior tracking on accessing the types of data, when it is accessed, and how the user uses it if that can also be tracked. It uses data such as page views, clicks, and navigation paths to provide insights that help businesses improve products, enhance customer experience, and increase engagement and conversions. It can also be used for cybersecurity purposes by tracking typical user actions in terms of login habits, data accessed, roles used by the user, etc. Behavior analytics facilitates organizations in making data-driven decisions, personalize user experiences, and identify trends or cybersecurity related anomalies.

Behavioral analytics in cybersecurity uses machine learning (ML) and artificial intelligence (AI) to monitor and analyze user and system activity patterns to detect deviations from an established "normal" baseline. This approach helps identify potential security threats that traditional, signature-based security measures might miss.

Behavioral analytics operates through a continuous cycle that consists of:

- **Data Collection**: The system aggregates large amounts of data from various sources, including network traffic, application logs, endpoint activities, and authentication systems.
- **Baseline Modeling**: ML algorithms analyze this historical data to build dynamic profiles and baselines of typical, legitimate behavior for each user, device, and application (sometimes referred to as User and Entity Behavior Analytics, or UEBA).

- **Anomaly Detection**: Current, real-time activity is continuously compared against these baselines. Deviations—such as a login from an unusual location or an employee accessing files outside their normal role—are flagged as anomalies.
- **Risk Scoring and Response**: Anomalies are assigned a risk score based on context and potential impact. High-risk events trigger alerts for security teams, or in advanced systems, automated responses like temporary account lockouts or network disconnection may be initiated to mitigate immediate risks.
- **Insight generation:** The analysis generates insights into what users are interested in, what their pain points are, and what actions lead to a desired outcome, like a purchase or in the case of cybersecurity their typical usage and application and data access patterns such as times of day or location.

The key benefits from a cybersecurity perspective include some of the following:

- **Detection of Unknown Threats**: It can identify new (zero-day) attacks and advanced persistent threats (APTs) that do not match known signatures.
- **Insider Threat Identification**: It is highly effective at spotting malicious activity by authorized users (employees, contractors) who misuse their legitimate access. Any deviation from normal usage patterns can trigger an anomaly analysis.
- **Reduced False Positives**: By understanding the context of normal behavior, the system identifies legitimate usage and minimizes irrelevant alerts, allowing security teams to focus on genuine threats.
- **Proactive Stance**: It enables organizations to detect and respond to threats in their earliest manifestations.

Some examples of where behavioral analytics is being used include the following:

- E-commerce: Optimizing website layouts, improving product recommendations, and personalizing the shopping experience.
- Product development: Understanding what features users like and dislike to guide future product improvements.
- Marketing: Optimizing campaigns by understanding what users are clicking on, ignoring, or searching for.
- Cybersecurity: Detecting anomalies and potential security threats by identifying unusual activity patterns on a network or application.
- Customer service: Proactively anticipating user needs and personalizing service to improve customer satisfaction and retention.

MFA (Muli-factor Authentication)

Muli-factor Authentication (MFA), Single-Sign-On (SSO), Federated Identity and Privileged Access Management are the core building blocks of Identity and Access Management.

While Single Factor Authentication (SFA) requires user ID and password only, unfortunately, SFA has a high probability of being compromised so for accessing sensitive data a more robust solution is required, Multi-factor Authentication (MFA) provides a more robust authentication solution by requiring factors additional to the user ID and password. The additional authentication factors can consist of one of 1) who you are – biometrics, 2) something you know - secret password or PIN, 3) something you have – token or smartphone. It makes accounts significantly harder to hack, because even if a malicious actor has the password, they are not likely to have the other required factor to gain access.

MFA is implemented through the use of authenticator applications or hardware tokens. It is important to balance security with user experience by offering multiple verification options and prioritizing phishing-resistant methods like biometrics or FIDO2 keys.

FIDO2 Keys are physical security devices (like USBs or NFC tags) or built-in device features that enable passwordless, phishing-resistant logins using public-key cryptography which replace traditional passwords with secure cryptographic key pairs tied to a user's device and a physical gesture (like a tap or PIN). Phishing-resistant factors can include biometrics (fingerprints, facial recognition), hardware security keys, or passkeys. Integrating the MFA solution with the overall IAM solution is a best practice approach.

Ping Identity and OKTA are the most common tools used for MFA.

Ping identity

Ping Identity specializes in identity management solutions. The components of the Ping Identity solution include the following:

- PingID - Enables MFA using mobile apps, biometrics, and one-time passwords. PingID Uses a pairing key (or QR code). It can be mobile or desktop app. It requires the enrollment of the user on the target device. Once enrolled, the PingID service automatically calls the mobile device to authenticate. When a user logs in the PingID service, it automatically calls the user device or the app, if the device is setup with the PingID mobile a, the app automatically pushes a notification to the smartphone.
- PingAccess: Provides role and attribute-based access control that protects web applications and APIs by applying security policies to client requests. Access requests are either routed through a PingAccess gateway to the target site or intercepted at the target web application server by a PingAccess agent.
- PingFederate: this is an enterprise-grade federation server that centralizes user authentication and enables Single Sign-On (SSO) across cloud, mobile, and on-premises applications. It acts as a bridge between identity providers (such as Active Directory) and service providers (such as Salesforce, or any other app). PingFederate offers SSO, API security, and provisioning capabilities. An enterprise federation server and identity bridge facilitates user authentication and single sign-on (SSO) for employees, partners, and customers. It connects various systems, including applications, third-party authentication sources, and identity management systems, enabling seamless access across the enterprise. Token mediation allows a PingAccess gateway to use a PingFederate token generator to exchange

the PingAccess token or an OAuth bearer token for a security token used by the foreign authentication system.

- PingOne Identity Access is cloud-based and works with PingFederate by creating a secure, hybrid, or multi-cloud identity architecture. PingFederate acts as a central hub, authenticating users against local directories (e.g., AD) and federating that identity to PingOne to leverage cloud-native services like MFA, risk-based authentication (such as PingOne Protect which provides threat intelligence), or SaaS application access. PingFederate connects to PingOne, allowing user data to stay on-premises typically in AD while accessing cloud applications. PingFederate acts as an Identity Provider (IdP) for PingOne, forwarding auth requests. PingOne then provides services like PingOne MFA or PingOne Protect, sending risk assessments back to PingFederate. PingFederate uses PingOne's threat intelligence to make risk-based access decisions.

OKTA Tools

Okta is a platform for identity and access management that offers secure identity verification, single sign-on (SSO), and multi-factor authentication (MFA). The core components of OKTA include the following:

- OKTA Identity Governance (OIG) -- enables access controls that limit user access only to the resources they need for their role or a project on a time-bound basis, reducing the risk of lateral movement if a phishing or other social engineering attempt is successful.
- FastPass is a phishing-resistant, passwordless, Zero Trust authenticator that eliminates the need to use passwords.
- Okta Adaptive MFA -- is context-aware and dynamically adjusts authentication requirements using techniques such as behavior detection which analyzes user behavior patterns and creates profiles of typical patterns based on previous activity. These can include location, device, time of day for typical logins, etc.
- Okta Identity Threat Protection with Okta AI -- leverages security signals from various security solutions, including email security vendors
- Okta Verify -- integrates with mobile device management (MDM) and endpoint detection and response (EDR) tools and captures device signals during sign-in to make policy-based access decisions.
- Okta Device Access – extends MFA access to desktops, can work without internet.
- OKTA Privileged Access -- protects critical resources by eliminating standing access, securing shared accounts,

Both Ping and Okta have multifactor authentication features, but Ping has more support for features like fingerprint verification.

Single Sign-On (SSO)

Single sign-on (SSO) is an authentication method that allows users within a single identity management system to log in once and access multiple applications and websites without needing to re-enter their credentials for each one.

Common technologies used for SSO) include protocols like SAML 2.0, OAuth 2.0, Open ID Connect (OIDC) and Kerberos which define how authentication and authorization information is exchanged. These are implemented using a variety of software solutions such as BeyondTrust, OKTA, Microsoft Entra ID, JumpCloud, CyberArk, and OneLogin.

Federated Identity Solutions

Federated identity is a method of linking a user's identity across multiple separate identity management systems. It allows users to quickly move between systems while maintaining security.

Identity federation enables users to access multiple applications and systems with a single set of credentials by sharing identity information across different domains. This is achieved through trust relationships between organizations and identity providers, allowing users to authenticate once and access various applications without repeating the login process. It simplifies user experience and reduces the need for managing multiple logins.

Identity federation, therefore, is a system of trust between two parties for the purpose of authenticating users and conveying information needed to authorize their access to resources. In this system, an identity provider (IdP) is responsible for user authentication, and a service provider (SP), such as a service or an application, controls access to resources.

Identity Federation vs. SSO

Identity federation and Single Sign-On (SSO) are both about simplifying user login, but they differ in scope. SSO enables single authentication within a single organization or domain, while federation extends this concept across multiple organizations. Essentially, SSO handles logins within an organization, while federation handles logins across different organizations.

SSO allows users to access multiple applications within a single organization using a single set of credentials. For example, an employee might use the same username and password to access their email, HR portal, and other company applications. SSO relies on a centralized identity provider within the organization, while FIM requires trust relationships to be established between different organizations.

Federated Identity Management (FIM) extends the concept of SSO to multiple organizations, enabling users to access applications across different domains using a single set of credentials. This is often seen when a user can log into a third-party application (like Salesforce) using their existing company credentials. FIM is used for accessing third-party applications or resources across different organizations. So, FIM can be seen as a broader concept that includes SSO as a specific case within a single organization's context.

Identity federation involves:

- **Authentication** to confirm users are who they say they are.
- **Authorization** to confirm users should have permission to specific resources.
- **Access control** to grant users permission to each downstream system.

Identity federation *services* are a category of identity management solutions that propagate users' digital identities to web applications, cloud servers, and other back-end systems. They establish communication with Identity Providers (IdPs) which store and manage the user identities checked through authentication, authorization, and access control, and service providers.

Identity federation services are typically layered on top of legacy identity management solutions — like Microsoft Active Directory (AD) — to push traditional user identities to non-Windows or cloud-based IT resources.

How Identity Federation Works

The key terms that are relevant for identity federation include:

- **Identity Providers (IdPs):** These are organizations or systems that store and manage user identities.
- **Service Providers (SPs):** These are applications, services, or systems that users want to access. These can be web-based solutions that could be anything from an email platform to a CRM, to an ERP, or more privileged resources like remote servers, databases, and network equipment.
- **Trust Relationship:** A federation agreement is established between IdPs and SPs, allowing the IdP to authenticate users and the SP to rely on the IdP's authentication.
- **Authentication:** When a user attempts to access an application, the SP redirects the user to the IdP for authentication.
- **Authorization:** Once authenticated, the IdP sends information about the user's identity and permissions to the SP, which then grants access accordingly.

The following figure illustrates the Federated Identity pattern when a client application needs to access a service that requires authentication.

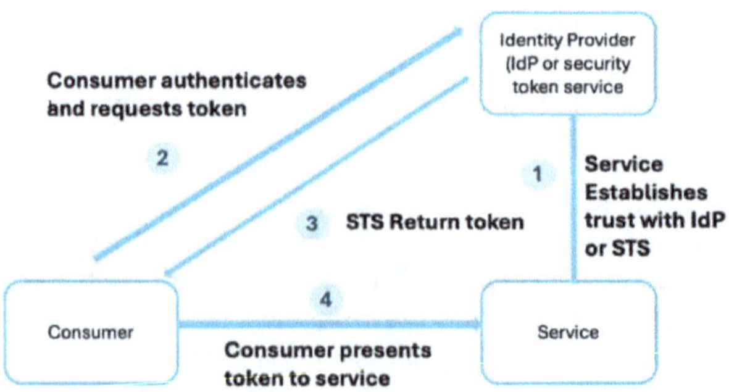

Figure 2-1 : Federated Identity Pattern

The authentication is performed by an IdP that works in concert with an STS. The IdP issues security tokens that provide information about the authenticated user. This information, referred to as claims, includes the user's identity, and might also include other information such as role membership and more granular access rights.

When someone attempts to access a service provider (SP), the SP looks to the IdP to confirm the user's identity, establish mutual trust, and then send the appropriate user information to finalize the login process.

The key Technologies used for Identity Federation include:

- SAML 2.0 **(Security Assertion Markup Language):** A standard for exchanging authentication and authorization data between parties. It uses Extensible Markup Language (XML) to communicate with other systems.
- OAuth 2.0**:** An open standard for delegation of access rights. It is an authorization framework ideal for APIs.
- Open ID Connect (OIDC)**:** An open standard for user authentication and access, it is an interoperable authentication protocol that's based on OAuth.

Federated Identity and Authentication

Seven so-called "laws of identity" sit beneath federated identity systems.

1. **User control and consent:** Users give permission to share data, and they have at least some say in how shares happen.
2. **Minimal disclosure:** The smallest amount of identifying information is shared, and it's stored securely and deleted quickly.
3. **Justification:** Only those who can prove they need access can get it.
4. **Directed identity:** Protection of identity is paramount, and users should be assigned private identifiers for that purpose. Companies work together to build a more permanent view of someone working across platforms.
5. **Competition:** Many identity providers should be supported, as competition breeds better performance.
6. **Human integration:** A real person has a place in the process, reducing the risk of computer-to-computer hacks.
7. **Consistency:** The users have a simple, consistent experience among platforms.

Implementation Steps for Federated Identity

The following steps are required for setting up federated identity:

- Set up the identity provider.
- Implement the authentication platform.
- Integrate the FIM solution with the identity provider, the authentication platform, and each of the major service providers.
- Make sure that there is a button on each application that gives end users the choice to sign in with a federated IdP on the login page.

- Ensure meaningful trust has been established among all service providers.

Federated Identity in the public Clouds

How FIM works in the three public clouds depends on the cloud-native services available.

Azure Identity Federation

Azure Identity Federation enables secure access to Azure resources from external workloads (like GitHub Actions, Kubernetes, or Google Cloud) without managing long-lived secrets or passwords. It works by establishing a trust relationship between an external identity provider and Microsoft Entra ID (previously Azure AD), where the external service exchanges its own token for a temporary Azure access token.

The trusted identity providers include corporate directories, on-premises federation services, other security token services (STS) provided by business partners, or social identity providers that can authenticate users who have, for example, a Microsoft, Google, Yahoo!, or Facebook account.

Token Exchange is the process where an external token is exchanged for an Azure AD access token, provided the issuer and subject match pre-configured federated identity credentials.

Key Components of Azure Identity Federation include the following:

- Trust Relationship: A federated credential is created on a Microsoft Entra ID Application or User-Assigned Managed Identity, defining which external issuer (OIDC provider) is trusted.
- OpenID Connect (OIDC): The authentication mechanism that enables secure, secret-less authentication between Azure and external providers.
- The external workload (e.g., a CI/CD pipeline) requests a token from its provider.
- The workload sends this external token to Microsoft Entra ID.
- Microsoft Entra ID validates the token's claims (issuer, subject, audience) against the pre-configured trust.
- Upon successful validation, Microsoft Entra ID issues a temporary Azure access token.
- No Secrets are required because authentication is based on OIDC tokens rather than static credentials (client secrets), the risk of credential leakage is eliminated.

AWS Identity Federation

Uses two AWS services to federate your workforce into AWS accounts and business applications: AWS IAM Identity Center (successor to AWS SSO) or AWS Identity and Access Management (IAM).

AWS IAM Identity Center makes it easy to centrally manage federated access to multiple AWS accounts and business applications and provide users with single sign-on access to all their assigned accounts and applications from one place. AWS IAM Identity Center can be used for identities in the AWS IAM Identity Center's user directory, your existing corporate directory, or external IdP.

AWS IAM Identity Center works with an IdP such as Okta Universal Directory or Azure Active Directory (AD) via the SAML 2.0 protocol. AWS IAM Identity Center seamlessly leverages IAM permissions and policies for federated users and roles to help you manage federated access centrally across all AWS accounts in your AWS organization. With AWS IAM Identity Center, permissions can be based on the group membership in the IdP's directory, and access is controlled for users by simply modifying users and groups in the IdP.

AWS IAM Identity Center also supports the System for Cross-domain Identity Management (SCIM) standard for enabling automatic provisioning of users and groups from Azure AD or Okta Universal Directory to AWS. AWS IAM Identity Center makes it easy to implement attribute-based access control (ABAC) by defining fine-grained permissions based on user attributes defined in the SAML 2.0 supported IdP. AWS IAM Identity Center allows selecting ABAC attributes from the user information synchronized from the IdP via SCIM or pass multiple attributes, such as cost center, title, or locale, as a part of a SAML 2.0 assertion. Permissions can be defined once for the entire AWS organization, and then granted, revoked, or modified for AWS access by simply changing the attributes in the IdP. With AWS IAM Identity Center, permissions can also be assigned based on the group membership in the IdP's directory, and then the access can be controlled for users by simply modifying users and groups in the IdP.

AWS IAM Identity Center can serve as an IdP to authenticate users to AWS IAM Identity Center integrated applications and SAML 2.0 compatible cloud-based applications, such as Salesforce, Box, and Microsoft 365, with a chosen directory. AWS IAM Identity Center can also be used to authenticate users to the AWS Management Console, AWS Console Mobile Application, and AWS Command Line Interface (CLI). For identity source, Microsoft AD or AWS IAM Identity Center's user directory can be used.

Google's Federated Identity Process With OAuth

OAuth 2.0 can be used for Identity Federation in GCP. The following describes the steps:

1. **Pull OAuth credentials from Google's API.** Choose data, such as a client ID and client secret, that both Google and your company know.
2. **Grab an access token from the Google Authorization Server.** Users will need a token from Google to complete web requests for access.
3. **Compare the access scopes.** Users grant access to data, and it must be confirmed that the request matches the willingness of the users to share.
4. **Send the token to an API.** Users are ready to gain access, as long as the token is included in an HTTP authorization request header.

Key Concepts for Implementing an Identity Federation Solution

Basic requirements every organization should consider for identity federation:

1. Security and compliance. Many organizations have to comply with GDPR, CCPA, and uphold other standards like SOC 2 and PCI. They need to look for solutions with extensive logging, automated notifications for suspicious activity, and reporting capabilities.

2. Integrations. If it can't natively integrate with their platforms, databases, and existing IT infrastructure, they have to build their own custom integrations, which take time to develop and may have security gaps.
3. Intuitiveness. If it's not easy for end users to adopt, they simply won't use it. And if users have to memorize passwords, organizations are basically asking for some kind of security or compliance incident because the users may not comply.
4. Scalability. This is especially important for mid-market and enterprise companies looking to expand to new markets and geographies. Finding an FIM tool that complements existing IT or MSP tech stack is a boon — that way, everything can be controlled and updated in one place.

AD (Active Directory)

Active Directory is a directory service implemented by Microsoft for Windows domain networks for authentication and authorization. An AD domain controller authenticates and authorizes users in a Windows-domain network by enforcing security policies for all computers.

Active Directory uses Light Weight Access Protocol (LDAP) versions 2 and 3, Microsoft's version of Kerberos, and DNS. Kerberos is an open standard and provides interoperability with other systems which use the same standard. The protocol offers strong authentication for clients and servers using secret-key cryptography.

AD simplifies user account management by providing a centralized platform to create, modify or delete users across the entire network. Active Directory checks the submitted username and password and determines whether the user is a system administrator or a non-admin user. Furthermore, it allows the management and storage of user information, provides authentication and authorization mechanisms, and establishes a framework to deploy other related services such as Certificate Services, Active Directory Federation Services (ADFS), Lightweight Directory Services, and Rights Management Services.

AD DS (Active Directory Domain Service) authenticates users before they can access resources on the network, ensuring only authorized individuals have entry to specific parts of the system. It stores directory data, like usernames, passwords and phone numbers, which help streamline operations within an organization.

Other Active Directory services (excluding Active Directory Light-Weight Directory Service or LDS) and most Microsoft server technologies rely on or use Domain Services. Examples of this include Group Policy, Encrypting File System, BitLocker, Domain Name Services, Remote Desktop Services, Exchange Server, and SharePoint Server. Active Directory Certificate Services (AD CS) establish an on-premises PKI (public key infrastructure). It can create, validate, revoke and perform other similar actions, such as public key certificates for internal uses of an organization.

Active Directory Federation Services (AD FS) is an SSO service. With an AD FS infrastructure in place, users may use several web-based services (e.g. internet forum, blog, on-line shopping, webmail, etc.) or network resources using only one set of credentials stored at a central location, as opposed to having to be granted a dedicated set of credentials for each service. AD FS uses many popular open standards to pass token credentials such as SAML, OAuth, or OIDC.

Components of AD

The key components of AD organized hierarchically include the following:

- **Forests**. A collection of multiple trees that share a common schema but do not form a contiguous namespace.
- **Domain Trees**. A group of one or more domains organized hierarchically in a contiguous namespace and connected via trust relationships.
- **Domains.** A logical group where all objects—such as computers and users—reside under specific administrative control.
- **Organizational units (OUs).** A container object within a domain containing other objects like users, groups and computers.

Group policies, another major component of AD is a collection of settings that define how computers and users operate within an organization. The Group Policy feature in AD enables admins to control how systems operate and what users can do on those systems. From setting up firewall rules to disabling USB ports on endpoints for enhanced security--everything becomes easier with group policies in place.

The objects held within a domain can be grouped into organizational units (OUs). OUs can provide hierarchy to a domain, ease its administration, and can resemble the organization's structure in managerial or geographical terms. OUs can contain other OUs—domains are containers for OUs also in this sense. Microsoft recommends using OUs rather than domains for structure and simplifying the implementation of policies and administration. The OU is the recommended level at which to apply group policies, which are Active Directory objects formally named group policy objects (GPOs),

Active Directory offers security features like access control lists (ACLs), and encryption and auditing capabilities to protect sensitive data and resources.

Managed Service Accounts (MSA) have complex passwords that AD manages automatically. The AD domain controller rotates the passwords regularly, so the risk of passwords for service accounts being weak, stale or exposed is reduced. By eliminating manual password changes the likelihood of human error is minimized. So, too, is the risk of service disruptions due to password changes.

LDAP (Light Weight Directory Access Protocol) Authentication is an authentication protocol mainly used to access directory services. A user cannot access information stored within an LDAP database or directory without first authenticating (proving they are who they say they are). LDAP authentication involves verifying the entered credentials, such as username and password, by making a connection with directory services. The directory services that support LDAP authentication include OpenLDAP, Microsoft Active Directory, Azure Active Directory, FreeIPA Directory, etc.

The graphic below shows an LDAP Example:

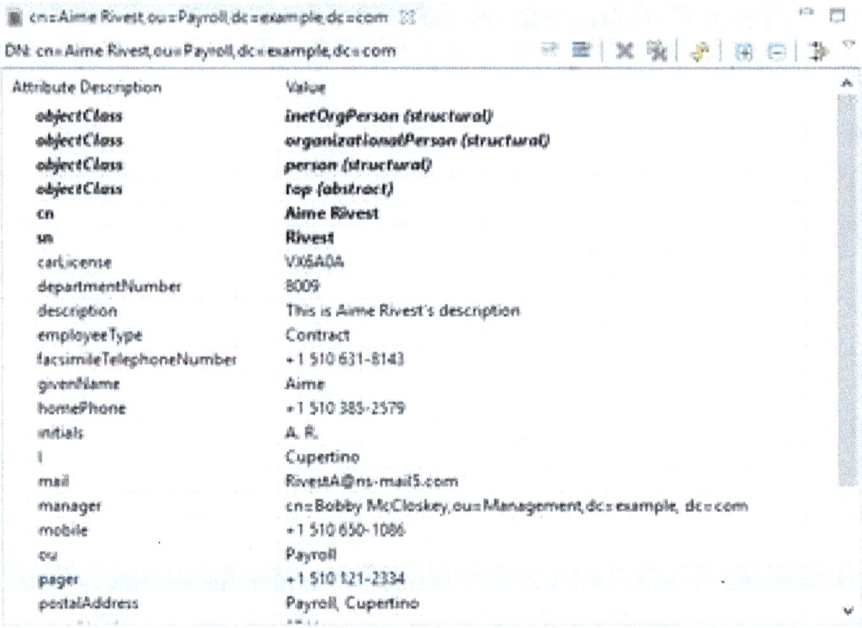

Figure 2-2 : Example of an LDAP Entry

The following lists a sampling of the typical attributes found in LDAP Version 3:

- DN - Distinguished Name, the name that uniquely identifies an entry in the directory
- sn - surname
- dc - domain component
- ou - organizational unit (or user group) to which the user belongs. There may be more than one of these.
- cn - common name
- RDN - Relative Distinguished Name, an attribute that will make the entry unique in its hierarchy when combined with its parent's Distinguished Name
- objectClass - the type of the entry. There may be more than one of these.

LDAP, in a sense, is an IdP and authority for organizations by helping store and verify credentials in their network. Upon request and authentication, those credentials give users the ability to retrieve information and gain functionality from their software application.

Authentication and Authorization Technologies

The following sections describe the most common technologies used for authentication and authorization. These are the foundations that you as a cybersecurity professional need to develop expertise on.

Auth0

Auth0 is a cloud-based identity and access management platform that helps developers quickly and securely add authentication and authorization to their applications. It simplifies the process of user login by handling complex security tasks, so that organizations can focus on building their products instead of managing their security infrastructure. Key features include social login (a type of SSO using existing, verified credentials from social networking or identity providers like Google, Facebook, Apple, or LinkedIn), single sign-on (SSO), and multi-factor authentication.

For authentication Auth0 verifies a user's identity through the username and password, social logins, or passwordless options. For authorization it manages what authenticated users are permitted to access within an application through native role-based access control (RBAC) or attribute-based access control (ABAC) through integrating with policy engines or by managing attributes in an access token and having your API check them.

Auth0 provides SDKs and APIs to easily integrate into various programming languages and frameworks that facilitate organizations to customize the login experience with their own branding and domain.

The key features or Auth0 include:

- **Universal Login**: a customizable and pre-built login page that can be integrated into applications.
- **Social Login**: enables users to log in with their existing social media accounts (e.g., Google, Facebook).
- **Single Sign-On (SSO):** which allows users to log in once and access multiple applications without re-entering their credentials.
- **Multi-Factor Authentication (MFA):** for an extra layer of security beyond a password, using methods like a code from a mobile device or a biometric scan.
- **User Management**: tools for managing user profiles, roles, and permissions from a central dashboard.
- **Security**: Handles the complexity of security, including protection against common attacks, and offers compliance with standards like HIPAA.

Note that while Auth0 is a commercial identity management platform, which is a product that provides authentication and authorization services OAuth2.0 is an open-standard protocol used for authorization. Auth0 uses OAuth 2.0 along with other protocols like OIDC and SAML, to secure applications, making OAuth the framework and Auth0 the service implementing it.

SAML 2.0

Security Assertion Markup Language (SAML) 2.0 is a standard for exchanging security information, primarily used for single sign-on (SSO) which allows a user to log in once and access multiple applications within the organization's network. It works by enabling trust between an Identity Provider (IdP) where a user authenticates and a Service Provider (SP) which provides the application or service.

When a user logs in, the IdP sends a SAML Assertion (a security token as an XML document) to the SP, confirming the user's identity and authorization.

SAML works through trust establishment between the IdP and SP through an exchange of SAML metadata. The IdP when requested (typically by the user's browser), authenticates a user and generates a SAML assertion which contains information about the user's identity and authorization. The assertion is sent to the SP via the user's browser which is validated by the SP to grant user access.

SAML works with Active Directory as the IdP and can also work with Microsoft Entra ID as the IdP. The steps below show how SAML works with Microsoft Entra ID.

In Microsoft Entra ID, SAML (Security Assertion Markup Language) is used to enable single sign-on (SSO) for applications, allowing users to authenticate once and access multiple applications without needing to re-enter their credentials. Microsoft Entra ID acts as the IdP and the application acts as the SP.

How SAML Works

The flow diagram below shows these key steps.

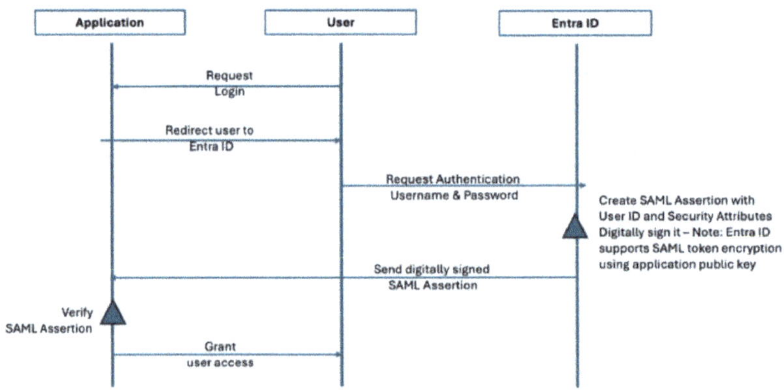

Figure 2-3 : Flow Diagram for SAML Use

The following describes the key steps shown in the diagram for the operation of a SAML assertion:

1. User Initiates Login: to access an application that is configured to use SAML for SSO with Microsoft Entra ID.
2. Redirection to Entra ID: The app redirects the user's browser to Microsoft Entra ID for authentication.
3. User Authenticates: with their Microsoft Entra ID credentials (username and password, or other configured authentication methods).
4. SAML Assertion is Created: After successful authentication, Microsoft Entra ID creates a SAML assertion (an XML token) containing user information and security attributes.
5. Assertion is sent to the Application: The SAML assertion is digitally signed and sent back to the application (SP)

6. User Gains Access: The application verifies the SAML assertion and grants the user access based on the information it contains.

The following terms describes some key aspects of SAML 2.0.

- Token Encryption: Microsoft Entra ID supports SAML token encryption which encrypts the SAML assertion using the SPs public key, and the app (SP) decrypts it with its corresponding private key.
- Claims Customizing: Microsoft Entra ID allows administrators to customize the claims included in the SAML assertion, controlling what information is passed to the application.
- Application Proxy: Microsoft Entra Application Proxy can be used with SAML SSO to provide remote access to on-premises apps, allowing users to access them securely from anywhere.
- Federation: Microsoft Entra ID can federate with other identity providers using SAML, enabling users to access applications using their credentials from other organizations.
- SAML Request Signature Verification: Entra ID can enforce the signing of SAML requests
- SAML Authentication Requests (samlp:AuthnRequest): Sent from SP to the IdP to start authentication (unique ID, version, destination, issuer, digital signature and NameIDPolicy.
- SAML Responses (samlp:Response): Sent from the IdP back to the SP after successful user authentication (response ID, version, issue instant, issuer, status, and the SAML Assertion)
- SAML Assertions (saml:Assertion): XML structures: authentication & authorization information, nested within a SAML Response (information about the user (Subject) and authentication event (AuthnStatement), attribute statements with user details and authorization decision statements.
- SAML Metadata: XML documents describing the capabilities and endpoints of a SAML entity (IdP or SP) to establish trust (Entity ID, public keys for signing and encryption, and URLs for SSO & SLO)

While SAML primarily uses XML for its messages and metadata, there are scenarios where JSON is used, particularly for configuration and communication with certain tools or APIs.

Open ID Connect (OIDC)

Open ID Connect (OIDC) is an authentication protocol that verifies a user's identity, allowing them to access multiple applications using a single set of credentials. It builds upon OAuth 2.0, adding an identity layer to enable user authentication and information exchange. OIDC works by delegating authentication to an Identity Provider (IdP), which issues an ***ID token*** and ***access token*** to the app (Relying Party),

The following describes the key concepts used in OIDC including the underlying OAuth usage..

1. User Request: user attempts to access a protected resource on a relying party (application).

2. Redirection to IdP: the application (SP) redirects user to IdP (AD, Entra ID, Google, Facebook, etc.) for authentication.
3. Authentication at IdP: user logs in at IdP using the credentials (username/password, social login, etc.).
4. ID Token (a JWT token) and Access Token Issuance: IdP authenticates the user and issues an ID token (containing username, authentication process, claims like the issuer, subject, audience, and timestamps for issuance and expiration, etc.) and an access token.
5. Access Granted: app verifies the ID token and grants the user access to the resource.
6. Client Secret: A secret key used by the application to authenticate with the identity provider.
7. Token Endpoint: RP (Client App) URI for exchanging authorization code for access token.
8. Authorization Endpoint: IdP used by application to initiate the authentication process.
9. Discovery Endpoint: URL provides information about IdP's endpoints and configuration details.

The flow diagram below describes the steps on how OIDC authentication is achieved:

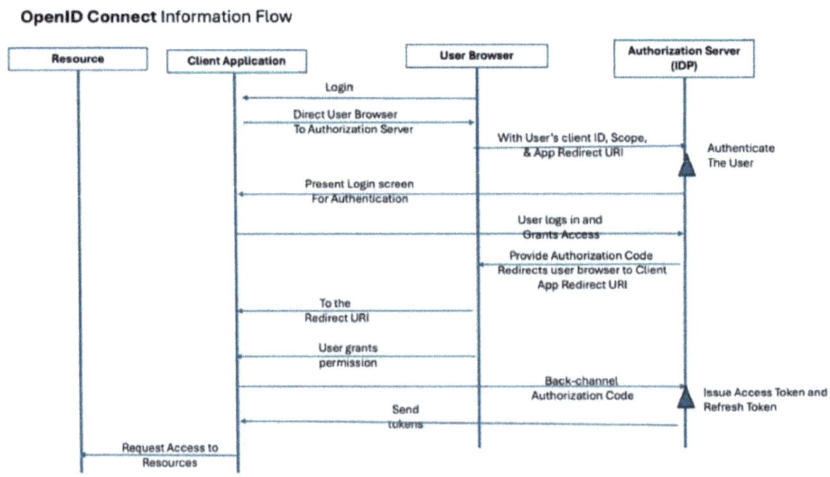

Figure 2-4 : Flow Diagram for OIDC Use

Using OIDC with EntraID

This requires configuring an application registration in Entra ID, setting up an OIDC IdP in the app, then using OIDC protocol to exchange information between the app and Entra ID during the sign-in process. This registration provides the application with a unique client ID and other information for interacting with Entra ID.

Note: OIDC and SAML2 can be used together in an application or environment to cater to different needs. For example, some users might authenticate via SAML, while others use OIDC.

OAuth2.0

OAuth 2.0 is an authorization framework that allows third-party applications to access resources on behalf of a user without requiring the user's credentials. It works by granting limited access to resources through access tokens, not sharing usernames and passwords.

The key concepts used in OAuth 2.0 include the following:

1. **Resource Owner (User):** The user who owns the data or resources.
2. **Client (Application):** The third-party application requesting access to the user's resources.
3. **Resource Server**: The server that hosts the protected resources. It is not an Identity Provider (Idp).
4. **Authorization Server**: IdP server that issues access tokens to the client after verifying the user's authorization.
5. **The Authorization Flow**: allows an application to access resources on behalf of a user without the user having to share their credentials directly with the application
6. **Access Token**: grants the client limited access to specific resources on the resource server.
7. **Refresh Token**: can be used to obtain a new access token without requiring user interaction.
8. **Scopes**: Define the specific resources and permissions that the client is requesting access to
9. **Authorization Sever**: Issues access tokens and manages user authentication and consent.
10. **Resource Server:** Hosts the protected resources that the application wants to access.
11. **Client (Application, the SP)**: The application requesting access to resources.
12. **User (Resource Owner):** The individual who owns the protected resources

The key steps in the authorization flow include the following:

- **User Authorization Request**: The application directs the user's browser to the authorization server's authorization endpoint. This request includes the application's client ID, requested scopes (defining what the application wants to access), a redirect URI (where the user will be sent back after authorization), and other parameters.
- **User Authentication**: The authorization server authenticates the user (e.g., through a login form). If the user is already authenticated, the server may present a consent screen, allowing the user to grant or deny the application's requested access.
- **User Authorization**: if the user grants access, the authorization server redirects the user's browser back to the application's redirect URI. This redirection includes an authorization code and any local state the application previously provided.

- **Access Token Issuance**: if the user grants permission, the application, using a backchannel (server-to-server communication), sends the authorization code, its client credentials, and the redirect URI to the authorization server's token endpoint. The authorization server verifies the authorization code, client credentials, and redirect URI. If valid, it issues an access token (and potentially a refresh token for later use) to the application.
- **Resource Access:** The application can now use the access token to make requests to the resource server, which provides access to the protected resources.
- **Token Refresh (Optional)**: access tokens have a limited lifetime. When they expire, the client can use a refresh token (if provided) to obtain a new access token without needing user interaction.

The flow diagram below depicts the steps used for OAuth 2.0 authorizations:

OAuth 2.0 Information Flow

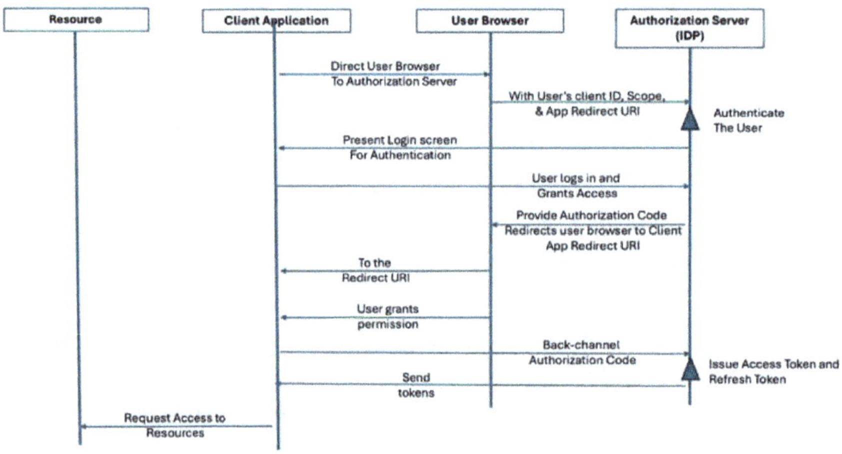

Figure 2-5 : Flow Diagram for OAuth 2.0 Use

3 – Cloud Security

With the continuing shift to active use of public clouds for many financial and business applications, it has become crucial to protect sensitive data, applications, and infrastructure in the cloud from cyber threats like breaches, malware, and unauthorized access.

Organizations required to comply with security standards (such a GDPR, HIPAA, PCI-DSS, CPRA, etc.) and other regulations need to implement security measures in their cloud environments to ensure that they are in compliance. Not only do they avoid fines, by doing that but also maintain the trust of customers who have entrusted them with their confidential and sensitive data thereby preventing loss of reputation.

Adhering to rigorous security standards compliance protects against sophisticated attacks such as ransomware, phishing, and DDoS, which exploit cloud vulnerabilities. It prevents downtime and ensures operations can continue even after security incidents.

Cloud Security Alliance (CSA)

The Cloud Security Alliance (CSA) Cloud Controls Matrix (CCM) provides fundamental security principles, controls, and the controls' criteria to guide cloud service providers (CSPs) and cloud service customers (CSCs) seeking secure implementation, assessment, and management of cloud services security risks. The CSA CCM provides a detailed controls framework aligned with CSA's Security Guidance, which states that "the most important security consideration is knowing exactly who is responsible for what in any given cloud project".

The Cloud Security Alliance's Cloud Controls Matrix Version 4 (CCM v4.0), published in 2021, includes core security and privacy controls and additional components. These include the CCM Implementation Guidelines, the Consensus Assessment Initiative Questionnaire (CAIQ), and the CCM Controls Auditing Guidelines2. The CCM v4.0 also includes useful supporting information for CCM controls. This information includes typical SSRM control ownership assignments and control scope and applicability information, such as architectural relevance, and mappings to other industry-accepted security frameworks (e.g., ISO/IEC, AICPA, NIST, FedRAMP). These works are regularly reviewed and enhanced by the CSA team.

The CCM now includes a comprehensive structure for delineation and proactive management of the cloud shared security responsibility model (SSRM), with transparency and accountability across the cloud ecosystem.

Security Measurements Required for Cloud Environments

The following graphic highlights the security measures required for the cloud environments.

Derived from source : Jerry Archer, SVP and CEO , Sallie Mae

Figure 3-1 : Security Guiding Principles in the Cloud

Cloud Security Posture Management

Cloud Security Posture Management (CSPM) is the automated process of continuously monitoring cloud environments (IaaS, PaaS, SaaS) to identify, assess, and remediate security risks, misconfigurations, and compliance violations, ensuring adherence to best practices across multi-cloud and hybrid setups to prevent breaches and improve overall security posture. CSPM tools provide visibility, automated threat detection, and remediation workflows, helping teams manage complex cloud infrastructures efficiently.

A CSPM tool finds common issues like publicly exposed storage buckets, overly permissive access, or default settings. It discovers assets, identifies shadow IT, and offers insights across complex hybrid and multi-cloud environments (AWS, Azure, GCP). It monitors security posture by providing continuous visibility and a measure of the cloud security health. CSPM tools can automatically fix detected issues or provide prioritized steps for manual resolution. They also help in ensuring compliance) with regulatory standards (such as, NIST, ISO 27001, PCI DSS, HIPAA) and internal standards and policies.

The tools can be integrated with DevOps and DevSecOps to help development teams to embed security early in the development lifecycle.

Leading CSPM Tools) include:

- Wiz: A leading Cloud Native Application Protection Platform (CNAPP) with strong CSPM features.
- Sysdig Secure: Offers comprehensive cloud-native security, including CSPM.
- Palo Alto Networks Prisma Cloud: Provides broad visibility, threat detection, and compliance.
- Microsoft Defender for Cloud: Native to Azure, offering deep integration and multi-cloud protection.
- SentinelOne: Offers CSPM for Azure and other cloud environments.

Cloud Access Security Broker (CASB)

Cloud Access Security Brokers (CASBs) are security policy enforcement points that sit between enterprise users and CSPs. They extend security measures to the cloud, enforcing policies and providing visibility into cloud application usage.

- **Visibility**: Offer a comprehensive view of all cloud services in use (both sanctioned, and unsanctioned known as Shadow IT) within an organization.
- **Compliance:** Helps organizations meet regulatory standards like GDPR, HIPAA, and PCI DSS by enforcing policies aligned with these mandates.
- **Data Security**: Applies encryption, access controls, and security policies to protect data in transit, at rest, and in use.
- **Threat Protection**: Provides defenses against cloud-based threats like malware, ransomware, and unauthorized access attempts through behavioral analytics, anomaly detection, and integrations with threat intelligence feeds.

How CASBs work

CASBs operate through discovery, classification, and remediation

- **Discovery:** Identifies all cloud applications being used, including shadow IT.

- **Classification**: Assesses the risk associated with each identified cloud service based on data sensitivity and security measures.
- **Remediation**: Enforces appropriate security policies to manage and mitigate risks, including access control, data loss prevention (DLP), and real-time threat protection.

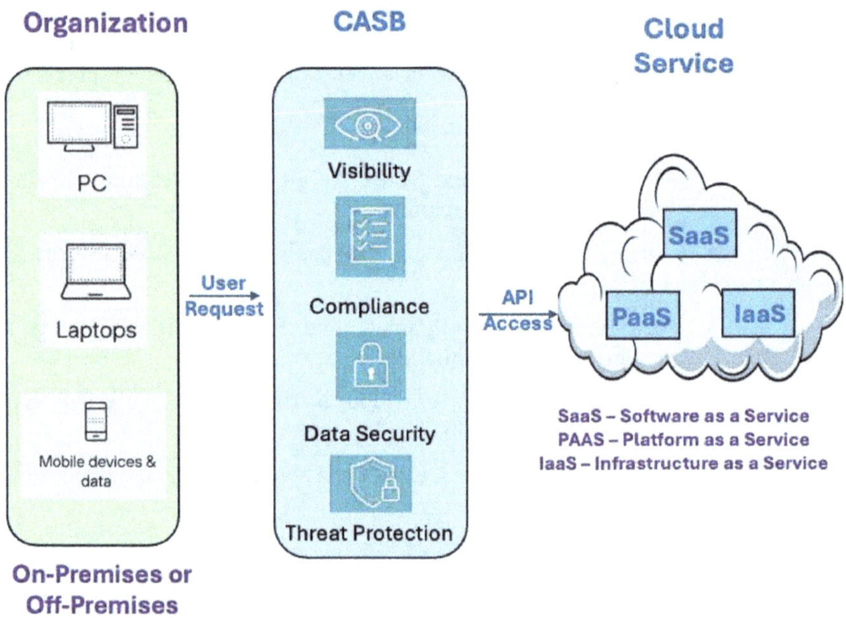

Figure 3-2 : CASB configuration

Deployment models

CASB is deployed using three primary models:

- **API-based**: Integrates directly with cloud service providers (CSPs) using their application programming interfaces (APIs) for monitoring and control without impacting user experience.
- **Proxy-based**: Routes user traffic through the CASB to enforce security policies in real-time, either as a forward or reverse proxy.
- **Hybrid**: Combines API and proxy-based approaches for comprehensive security coverage that balances real-time protection with seamless integration.

Leading CASB tools

- **Netskope**: Known for its deep visibility into cloud traffic and real-time threat protection.
- **Microsoft Defender for Cloud Apps**: Offers strong integration with the Microsoft ecosystem and focuses on detecting sensitive information sharing.

- **Palo Alto Networks Prisma Cloud**: Provides a suite of tools for securing cloud services, including features like cloud security posture management (CSPM) and enterprise DLP.

Cloud Identity and Access Management (IAM)

Cloud Security IAM (Identity and Access Management) is the framework of policies and technologies that controls who (users, services) can access what (resources, data) in a cloud environment and what they can do in the cloud which is acting as the new perimeter for security. It ensures least privilege, and enforces Zero Trust principles like continuous verification. It manages digital identities, authenticates users, authorizes actions via roles/permissions, and governs access for humans, applications, and machines, preventing unauthorized access and breaches.

The primary functions of Cloud IAM are:

- Authentication -- which verifies user identity (using passwords, MFA, and biometrics).
- Authorization -- which is used to assign permissions (roles) to identities, defining what they can access and do.
- User provisioning -- which consists of creating, updating, and deleting user accounts and access rights.

The other functions governed by Cloud IAM include:

- Identity Governance) concerned with monitoring and auditing access for compliance.
- Single Sign-On (SSO): Using one login for multiple cloud services.
- Privileged Access Management (PAM): Securing high-risk, critical accounts.

Cloud IAM becomes critical in the cloud because the network perimeter has been extended to include the cloud environments making Cloud IAM the primary defense. Cloud IAM is also the foundation for Zero Trust for continuously verifying every access request. Zero Trust minimizes cyberattack risks by limiting potential damage from compromised accounts and use of strict controls.

Cloud IAM terms in the cloud environments include the following:

- Principal: The identity (user, service, workload) requesting access.
- Resource: The cloud asset (VM, database, storage) being accessed.
- Role: A collection of permissions granted to a principal for a resource.

In essence, Cloud IAM ensures the right principals get the right access to the assets in the cloud environments.

AWS Identity Management

When a user logs in with their Amazon Web Services (AWS) ID and password to sign into the AWS console, they get the tree menu to select and use a service. The request for authorization is then sent by the service to check their identity in the list of authorized users, and determines what policies are enforced to control access level. Alternately, a request can be made by another AWS account to a trusted account.

The steps for a user authentication and authorization for AWS include:

- A human user or application uses their sign-in credentials to authenticate with AWS.
- Authentication is provided by matching the sign-in credentials to a principal (an IAM user, federated user, IAM role, or application trusted by the AWS account.
- A request is made to grant the principal access to resources
- Access is granted in response to an authorization request.

AWS checks each policy that applies to the context of the request. If a single permissions policy includes a denied action, AWS denies the entire request and stops evaluating. This is called an *explicit deny*. Because requests are *denied by default*, AWS authorizes a request only if every part of the request is allowed by the applicable permissions policies.

The following figure shows the key components or AWS IAM.

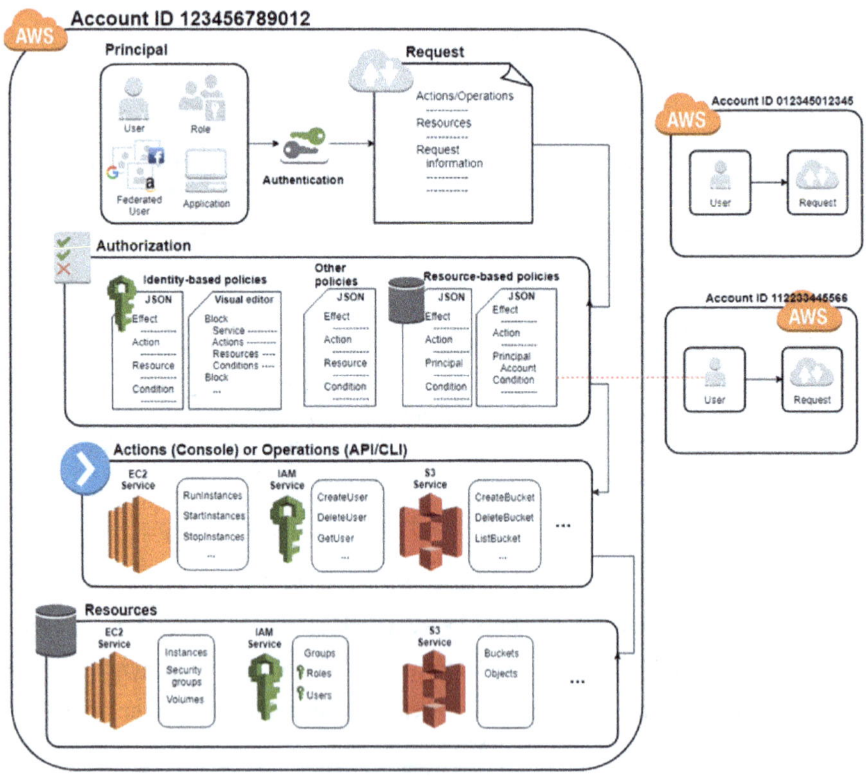

Source: Amazon Web Services Documentation

Figure 3-3 : Amazon Web Services Architecture

- To authenticate from the console as a root user, the user must sign in with their email address and password.

- As a federated user, they are authenticated by their identity provider and granted access to AWS resources by assuming IAM roles. Note that AWS uses multiple, flexible identity provider (IdP) options rather than a single provider. The primary, native choices are AWS IAM Identity Center (formerly SSO) for workforce identities and Amazon Cognito for customer applications. AWS also supports external, third-party SAML 2.0 or OIDC providers like Okta, Microsoft Entra ID (Azure AD), and Google Workspace.
- An IAM user provides their account ID or alias, and then their username and password.
- To authenticate workloads from the API or AWS CLI, they might use temporary credentials through being assigned a role or they might use their long-term credentials by providing your access key and secret key.

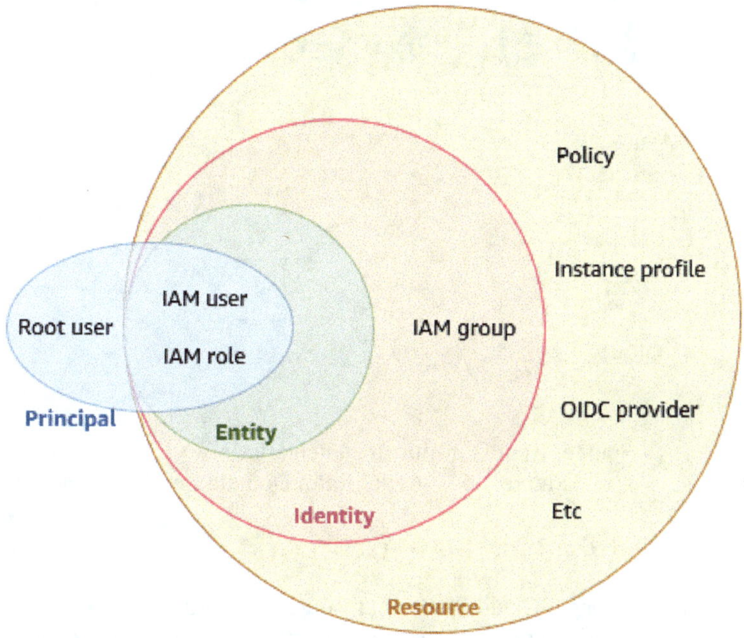

Figure 3- 4 : AWS Architecture for Authentication and Authorization

Azure Identity and Access Management (IAM)

Azure IAM is now part of the Entra ID platform. It ensures secure access via authentication (verifying identity) and authorization (managing permissions). Access Control (IAM) is a menu option found within specific Azure resources, resource groups, or subscriptions used to manage role assignments. Role based Access Control (RBAC) is provided for predefined roles like owner and reader or custom roles which define granular permissions.

Azure IAM can be reached through the Azure Portal by selecting a specific resource (e.g., virtual machine, storage account) for a specific resource group or subscription.

Microsoft Entra Domain Services (formerly Active Directory Domain Services) is a managed PaaS (Platform as a Service) that stores identity information in a hierarchical structure and provides traditional Active Directory features such as domain join, group policy, LDAP, and Kerberos/NTLM authentication in the cloud. The Azure resource management hierarchy consists of Management Groups at the top level, Subscriptions, Resource Groups, and Resources at the lowest level as described in the following diagram.

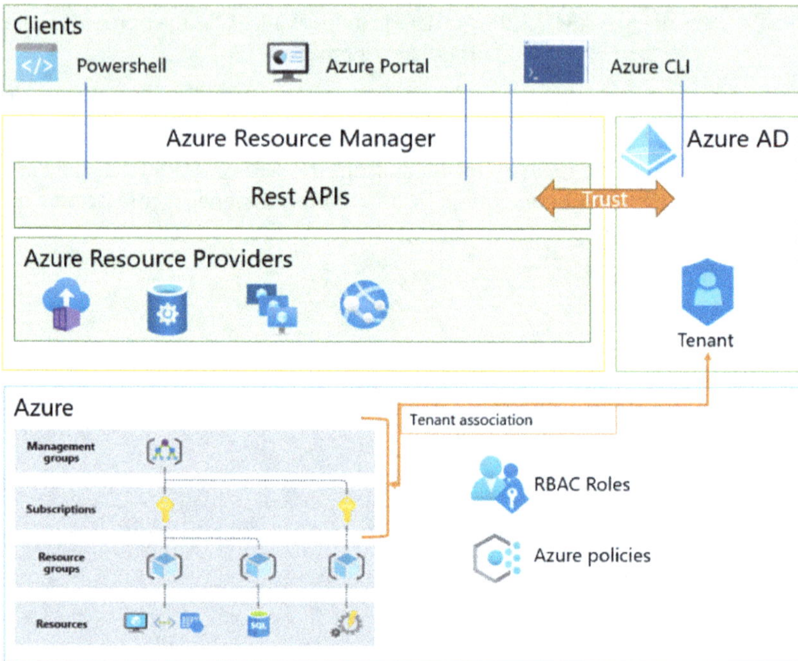

Source: Azure On-line documentation
Figure 3-5. : Azure Entra Domain Services Resource Model

Google Cloud Platform (GCP) IAM

In the Google Cloud Platform, resources are organized hierarchically, where the Organization node is the root node in the hierarchy, Folders under the organization (may be optional group projects (such as by departments), the Projects are the children of the organization under Folders, and the other resources are the children of Projects. Each resource has exactly one parent.

Cloud IAM allows setting policies at the Organization level where the organization represents the company. Cloud IAM roles granted at this level are inherited by all resources under the organization.

Projects within GCP represent a trust boundary within the organization such as departments. Services within the same project have a default level of trust. For example, App Engine instances can access Cloud storage buckets within the same project. Cloud IAM roles granted at the project level are inherited by resources within that project. When setting policies at the project level, it is important to use audit logs to track project-level permission changes.

At the lowest level, the Resource level, resources inherit the policies of the parent resource. If a policy is set at the resource level, it is in addition to the policies inherited from the project, the folder and the organization levels.

In addition to the existing Cloud Storage and BigQuery ACL systems, additional resources such as Genomics Datasets and Pub/Sub topics support resource-level roles so that certain users can be granted permission to a single resource.

Policy Inheritance

Policies set at the organization level are automatically inherited by all its child projects. Similarly, policies set at the project level are automatically inherited by all its child resources. The effective policy for a resource is the union of the policy set at that resource and the policies inherited from its parent. This policy inheritance is transitive; in other words, resources inherit policies from the project, which inherits policies from the organization. Therefore, the organization-level policies also apply at the resource level.

The Cloud IAM policy hierarchy follows the same path as the GCP resource hierarchy. A change at the resource hierarchy, cause the policy hierarchy changes also. For example, moving a project into an organization will update the project's Cloud IAM policy to inherit from the organization's Cloud IAM policy. Child policies cannot restrict access granted at the parent. For example, if the Editor role is granted to a user for a project, and the Viewer role is granted to the same user for a child resource, the user still has the Editor role for the child resource.

When using Cloud IAM, a best practice is to follow the principle of least privilege. The principle applies to identities, roles, and resources. The smallest scope should always be selected that's necessary to reduce exposure to risk. Granting everybody the Owner role on the entire organization is not good practice because intentional hacks or accidental mistakes could expose and bring down all apps. Security teams need to be specific and deliberate

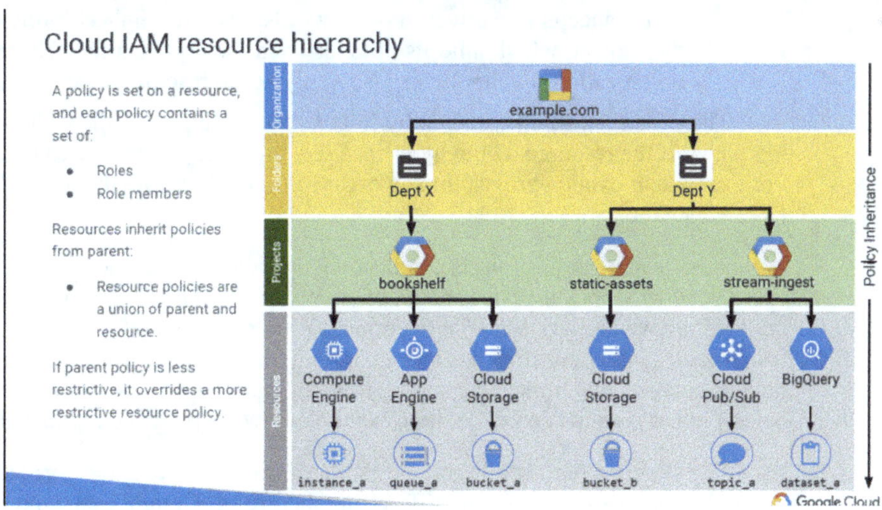

Figure 3-6 : GCP IAM Resource Hierarchy

GCP IAM

Google Cloud Platform resources are organized hierarchically, where the Organization node is the root node in the hierarchy, folders (optional) may group projects, the projects are the children of the organization (potentially under folders), and the other resources are the children of projects. Each resource has exactly one parent.

Cloud IAM allows security teams to set policies at the following levels of the resource hierarchy:

- Organization level: The organization resource represents the organization. Cloud IAM roles granted at this level are inherited by all resources under the organization.
- Folder level: An optional logical grouping mechanism in the Google Cloud resource hierarchy used to organize projects and resources under them, for example, by department, team, or environment.
- Project level: Projects represent a trust boundary within the organization. Services within the same project have a default level of trust. For example, App Engine instances can access Cloud storage buckets within the same project. Cloud IAM roles granted at the project level are inherited by resources within that project. When setting policies at the project level, be sure to use audit logs to track project-level permission changes.
- Resource level: In addition to the existing Cloud Storage and BigQuery ACL systems, additional resources such as Genomics Datasets and Pub/Sub topics support resource-level roles so that a user can be granted certain permissions to a single resource. Resources inherit the policies of the parent resource. If a policy is set at the organization level, it is automatically inherited by all its child projects, and if a policy is set at the project level, it is inherited by all its child resources. The effective policy for a resource is the union of the policies set at that resource and the policies inherited from its parent. This policy inheritance is transitive; in other words, resources inherit policies from the project, which inherits policies from the organization. Therefore, the organization-level policies also apply at the resource level.

The Cloud IAM policy hierarchy follows the same path as the GCP resource hierarchy. If the resource hierarchy is changed, the policy hierarchy changes also. For example, moving a project into an organization will update the project's Cloud IAM policy too.

A large number of projects can become unwieldy to manage at scale. This is why Cloud IAM includes the concept of an organization node. The organization node sits above projects and is in the organization's root node for Google Cloud resources. If an organization has a Google for Work account, when the organization node is enabled, any project created by users in that domain will automatically belong to the organization node; it prevents shadow projects and rogue admins.

The Organization Admin role gives the admin visibility and control over all of the organization's resources on GCP. Using the Project Creator role, who can create projects, regardless of whether they have policies on individual projects, can be restricted. The project roles can also be applied at the organization level and can be inherited by all the projects in the organization. For example, the security team admin can assign the networking team the Network Admin role at the organization level so they have permissions to manage all the networks in all the projects in your company.

Personal/trial accounts have no "organization," and organization features are hidden in the UI. The account with Organization Owner role is empowered to modify all projects within the organization. Changes to the organization itself still occur only through Google Sales

Cloud Native Security Services

All public CSPs provide a set of security-related services that can be used within their own environments and benefit for tight integration within their own environments, The following sections list the services in the AWS, Azure and GCP.

AWS Cloud-Native Services

Amazon AWS provide a broad range of services. The following lists the services most applicable to cybersecurity.

Identity and Access Manageemnt

- ***AWS IAM***: Controls access to AWS resources, enabling you to manage users, groups, roles, and permissions.
- ***Amazon Cognito***: Adds user sign-up, sign-in, and access control to web and mobile applications.
- ***AWS Single Sign-On (SSO)***: Manages access to multiple AWS accounts and cloud applications.

Data Protection:

- ***AWS KMS:*** Enables encryption of data at rest and in transit using encryption keys.
- ***Secrets Manager***: Helps to manage, retrieve, and rotate database credentials, API keys, and other secrets throughout their lifecycles. Credentials are centrally stored and managed along with API keys, and other secrets. AWS Identity and Access Management (IAM) permissions policies should be used to manage access to the secrets. Secrets should be rotated on demand or on a schedule, without redeploying or disrupting active applications. Secrets should be integrated with AWS logging, monitoring, and notification services. It is best practice to securely store and manage access to secrets such as passwords, API keys, and database credentials.
- ***Macie***: a data security service that uses machine learning (ML) and pattern matching to discover and help protect the organization's sensitive data. It uses machine learning to discover and protect sensitive data.
- ***AWS Shield:*** Provides DDoS protection for the applications.
- ***AWS WAF***: Protects web applications from common web exploits.
- ***AWS Firewall Manager***: Simplifies the creation and management of firewall rules across your AWS resources.

Compliance and Governance:

- ***AWS Config***: Tracks and evaluates the configuration of the organization's AWS resources.
- ***AWS CloudTrail***: Records AWS API calls for auditing and compliance.

- ***AWS Artifact***: Provides access to AWS security and compliance reports.

Threat Detection:

- ***Amazon Guard Duty***: Continuously monitors for malicious activity and unauthorized behavior in the organization's AWS environment.
- ***Amazon Inspector***: Automates security assessments for the applications.
- ***AWS Security Hub***: Provides a central view of the organization's security alerts and findings across AWS services.

Other Security Services:

- ***AWS CloudHSM***: Provides hardware-based key storage for cryptographic operations.
- ***AWS Certificate Manager (ACM)***: Manages SSL/TLS certificates for the organization's applications.
- ***AWS Trusted Advisor***: Provides recommendations for improving security, performance, and cost optimization.

Azure Cloud Native Security Services

Azure services are a broad range of cloud-based products and services offered by Microsoft Azure. These services enable users to build, deploy, and manage applications and services in the cloud, providing infrastructure as a service (IaaS), platform as a service (PaaS), and software as a service (SaaS) options. Azure services cover areas like computing, storage, networking, databases, analytics, AI, and more.

Azure security services include identity and access management, network security, data protection, threat protection, and security management and monitoring. Azure offers a comprehensive suite of security tools and features to protect the organization's cloud infrastructure and applications. These services work together to provide a layered security approach, helping security teams manage and mitigate risks effectively.

Identity and Access Management:

- ***Azure Active Directory (Azure AD and now renamed as Entra ID)***: Provides identity and access management, including single sign-on, multi-factor authentication, and role-based access control.
- ***Azure Identity Protection***: Helps detect and respond to identity-based risks.
- ***Azure Privileged Identity Management (PIM):*** Provides just-in-time access to privileged roles, minimizing the risk of unauthorized access.

Network Security:

- ***Azure Firewall***: A managed, cloud-based network security service that protects the organization's Azure Virtual Network resources.
- ***Azure Virtual Network***: Enables you to create isolated networks within Azure, controlling access to your resources.
- ***Network Security Groups (NSGs)***: Allow you to filter network traffic to and from Azure resources.

Data Protection:

- ***Azure Key Vault:*** Securely stores and manages cryptographic keys, secrets, and certificates.
- ***Azure Storage Encryption***: Encrypts data at rest and in transit, protecting it from unauthorized access.
- ***Azure Disk Encryption***: Encrypts the disks used by the organization's virtual machines.

Threat Protection:

- ***Azure Sentinel***: A cloud-native SIEM (Security Information and Event Management) and SOAR (Security Orchestration, Automation, and Response) solution that provides intelligent security analytics and threat intelligence.
- ***Azure Defender*** (part of Microsoft Defender for Cloud): Offers threat protection for the organization's Azure resources, including virtual machines, databases, and containers.
- ***Azure Security Center***: Provides a centralized view of the organization's security posture and helps security teams to identify and remediate security vulnerabilities.

Security Management and Monitoring:

- ***Azure Monitor:*** A centralized log management and monitoring solution that helps the security team to track the health and performance of the organization's Azure resources.
- ***Azure Policy***: Helps the organization manage and enforce organizational standards and assess compliance at scale.
- ***Azure Security Baseline***: Provides a set of recommended security configurations for the organization's Azure resources.

GCP Cloud Native Security Services

Google Cloud Platform (GCP) offers a vast list of services categorized by AI/ML, Compute, Storage, Databases, Analytics, Networking, Developer Tools, Security, and more, including core offerings like Compute Engine, Google Kubernetes Engine (GKE), Cloud Storage, BigQuery, Vertex AI, and managed services for databases (Cloud SQL, Bigtable) and data processing (Dataflow, Dataproc), all designed to build and run applications, analyze data, and manage infrastructure. Here is a breakdown of key services that can apply to cybersecurity by category:

Compute & Containers

- ***Compute Engine***: a secure, customizable Infrastructure as a Service (IaaS) for creating and running virtual machines (VMs).
- Google Kubernetes Engine (GKE): Managed Kubernetes.
- ***Cloud Run***: Fully managed, serverless compute platform that allows you to run stateless, containerized applications directly on Google's infrastructure
- ***App Engine***: Fully managed, serverless Platform-as-a-Service (PaaS that allows developers to build, host, and scale web applications and mobile backends without managing the infrastructure.

- ***Cloud Functions***: Serverless functions (now known as Cloud Run).

Storage & Databases

- ***Cloud Storage*** (GCS): Object storage, a scalable, and secure managed service for storing, accessing, and managing unstructured data (files, images, videos, backups).
- ***Cloud SQL***: Managed relational databases (MySQL, PostgreSQL, SQL Server).
- ***Cloud Bigtable***: NoSQL database. designed for large-scale analytical and operational workloads. It handles billions of rows and columns, providing single-digit millisecond latency for heavy read/write traffic
- ***Cloud Datastore/Firestore***: Managed NoSQL document database.

Data Analytics & Big Data

- ***BigQuery***: Serverless data warehouse that enables fast, SQL-based analysis of massive, petabyte-scale datasets. It decouples storage and compute, allowing for independent scaling and cost efficiency, while featuring built-in machine learning.
- ***Dataflow***: Stream & batch data processing.
- ***Dataproc***: Managed Spark & Hadoop.
- ***Pub/Sub:*** Scalable asynchronous messaging service that decouples service producers (publishers) from service consumers (subscribers), allowing systems to communicate by broadcasting events without direct, synchronous connections.
- ***Looker / Looker Studio***: Business intelligence.

AI & Machine Learning

- ***Vertex A***I: Unified ML platform that enables users to build, tune, and deploy generative AI, predictive models, and conversational agents (via Agent Builder) using tools like Gemini, for applications ranging from search to data analysis.
- ***AutoM***L: Train custom models without the need for coding. It provides end-to-end workflow for building, training, and deploying machine learning models. It enables non-experts to create AI models with minimal coding.
- ***Prebuilt APIs***: ready-to-use AI Powered services such as Vision AI, Natural Language AI, and Translation AI.

Networking

- VPC (Virtual Private Cloud): A virtual network, it is a secure, global software-defined network to host compute engine VMs, GKE clusters, and other resources.
- ***Cloud Load Balancing***: Distribute traffic.
- ***Cloud CDN***: Content Delivery Network.
- ***Cloud DNS***: Managed DNS.

Developer Tools & DevOps

- ***Cloud Build:*** Serverless CI/CD.
- ***Cloud Source Repositories***: Private Git repos.

- ***Cloud Deploy***: Managed continuous delivery.

Security & Identity

- ***IAM (Identity & Access Management):*** securely define the identities and what access roles they have; manages permissions.
- ***Cloud Armor***: DDoS & WAF protection.
- ***Cloud KMS***: Key Management Service that enables creating, managing, rotating and destroying cryptographic keys for data protection.

Privileged Access Management (PAM) in Clouds

Cloud PAM is a cybersecurity strategy to secure, control, and monitor privileged accounts (such as admins, service accounts, and APIs) that access sensitive data and systems in dynamic cloud environments. The tools used for Cloud PAM include identity-based access, just-in-time (JIT) access, session monitoring, and automation to prevent breaches and ensure compliance. It adapts traditional PAM to cloud challenges like rapid scaling and ephemeral resources, focusing on identity rather than just network perimeters. Cloud PAM secures high-value identities including human identities such as admins, service accounts, and non-human identities (NHIs) with elevated permissions in AWS, Azure, GCP, et.. Key features include:

- Implement Just-in-Time (JIT) Access: Grant temporary access only when a user requests elevated access to a specific resource or system. Evaluate request against policies and access rules (identity, role, justification). Expire automatically.
- Tools for JIT process include PAM Solutions (e.g. Beyond Trust); MFA, ABAC and RBAC supported IAM solutions; Cloud Infrastructure Entitled Management (CIEM), CSPM, SIEM, ITDR
- Specific tools for JIT access include Tenable Cloud Security (CNAPP), Azure AD Privileged Identity Management (PIM), AWS Identity Center, StrongDM, Apono, Delinea, and Securden.

AWS:

In AWS, Privileged Access Management (PAM) is not a single, defined service like IAM or EC2. Instead, it's a set of practices and tools used to secure, manage, and monitor privileged access to AWS resources. AWS provides various services and features that can be combined to implement a PAM solution. AWS Console does not explicitly define PAM. The following describes implementing PAM in AWS:

- Navigate to the IAM console in the AWS account. Select "Access Analyzer" under "Access reports" on the left-hand panel. Click "Create Analyzer" and provide a name for it.
- Use Role-Based Access Control (RBAC):
- Secure Privileged Accounts and Credentials: MFA, strong passwords, disable root access,
- Create emergency access keys for root user only when absolutely necessary, and delete them

- Monitor and Audit Privileged Activity: AWS CloudTrail to log all API calls and monitor privileged activities. Forward Cloud trail logs to Cloud Watch for detailed auditing and alarm.
- Enforce broad security invariants. Security conditions that should always be true.
- Discover privileged accounts: human users, service accounts, apps with elevated permissions.
- Understand their roles and responsibilities: Determine what each privileged account is authorized to do and why. Reduce attack surface by removing accounts no longer needed.
- Eliminate unnecessary privileged accounts.

To implement (JIT) with AWS IAM Identity Center, integrate the organization's IdP (e.g. MS Entra ID) and enforce the Least Privilege by granting temporary, role-based permissions only when needed. Securely manage credentials, enable MFA) for privileged accounts, utilize AWS IAM Access Analyzer to monitor. Use SCIM to automate provisioning users and groups from the organization's IdP to AWS.

Azure

Primarily defined and managed through Microsoft Entra Privileged Identity Management (PIM) and Microsoft Purview Privileged Access Management. PIM focuses on managing access to roles within Azure Active Directory (Azure AD), Azure resources, and other Microsoft Online Services. Microsoft Purview PAM, on the other hand, focuses on managing access at the task level, particularly within the Microsoft 365 environment. User Requests Access: submits a request, often through a portal or interface. Key concepts for Azure PAM include:

- Approval Process: The request is routed to designated approvers based on pre-defined policies.
- Temporary Role Activation: If approved, the user's role is activated for a specific duration.
- Session Monitoring: Azure monitors the user's session for activity and logs all actions.
- Role Expiration and Deactivation: time limit expires, the user's access is automatically revoked.

Azure leverages a "just-in-time, just-enough" access model, where users only receive the necessary permissions for a limited time, minimizing the risk of unauthorized access. This is achieved through features like role-based access control, temporary role assignments, and approval workflows.

GCP

(PAM) in Google Cloud Platform (GCP) allows for temporary and auditable elevation of user privileges. It works by enabling administrators to create entitlements, which define specific roles and permissions that can be temporarily granted to users for a set duration. These grants can be set up with or without approval requirements and justifications, and all actions are logged for auditing purposes. Privileged Access Manager (PAM) is a feature within Google Cloud Platform (GCP) and is directly integrated into the GCP Console.

- Administrators define entitlements, which act as templates for granting temporary access.
- Entitlements specify the roles that can be granted, the users or groups eligible to request those roles, and whether approvals or justifications are required.
- Entitlements can be scoped to the organization, folder, or project level.
- Users who need elevated privileges can request a grant against an existing entitlement.
- Requests can justifications for the access and may require approval from designated approvers.
- If approval is required, the request remains pending until approved/denied, automatically expires
- When request approved (or automatically granted), the specified roles are temporarily assigned
- The granted roles are automatically removed when the grant duration expires.
- All entitlement and grant events are logged in Cloud Audit Logs, providing a detailed history of privileged access.

GCP JIT (Just-in-Time) access is implemented by granting ephemeral, time-bound IAM roles to users via a Java-based application, usually deployed on App Engine or Cloud Run. It uses Identity-Aware Proxy (IAP) for secure access, requiring users to request access via a web interface, often with justifications or peer approval, which then automates temporary group membership or IAM binding modifications

4 – AI and GenAI in Cybersecurity

Artificial Intelligence (AI) is technology that enables computers and machines to simulate human intelligence and solve problems especially when it is combined with other technologies such as sensors, geolocation, and robotics. AI can perform tasks that would otherwise require human intelligence or intervention. Some examples of AI include digital assistants, GPS guidance, autonomous vehicles, and a variety of sensors and other applications that encompass machine learning and deep learning. These disciplines involve development of algorithms that simulate the neurological processes of the human brain and, like a human being, are capable of learning from available data to produce intelligent classifications of the information that is being processed.

Modern AI

Prominent AI approaches during the second half of the 20th century were Expert Systems and Fuzzy Logic with Prolog and Lisp being the top choices as programming languages along with C/C++.

The term "Data science" was coined in early 2008. Later in 2012, the real breakthrough happened in artificial intelligence, the utilization of a Graphical Processing Unit (GPU) for the training of the neural network architecture. AI requires high-speed computing power due to the advanced mathematical calculations. Later in 2015, Facebook's leader of AI, Yann LeCun, pushed hard on deep learning and its possibilities. The switch from CPU (central processing unit) to GPU has literally changed the game and has revolutionized technology and redefined computing power and parallel processing.

Major AI breakthroughs are happening in the deep learning space. Neural networks are voracious users of an enormous amounts of data. For example, to train a model to recognize a cat, it is required to feed approximately 100,000 cat and non-cat images to get the perfect classification of a cat that is roughly equivalent to the recognition by the human eye. Other areas of future AI research include significant advancements in the fields of "unsupervised learning" and "reinforcement learning."

Yoshua Bengio, Geoffrey Hinton, and Yann LeCun laid the foundations for modern AI. Today we see a significant use of AI in the workplace as part of our day-to-day employment activities, a sign that we can expect more automation in the future as the current generation of developers and users find more innovative uses of AI technology.

With accessibility and increasingly dramatic development of quantum computing technology, many more discoveries and efficiencies are likely to be made in the scope of AI. The emergence of quantum computing is likely to also create significant challenges and threats for society.

These powerful new technologies have given rise to the exciting new developments in the realm of Generative AI.

GenAI Prompt

A prompt is a natural language text that requests GenAI to perform a specific task. For a good GenAI prompt, the user needs to be specific and provide specific context while asking single questions. The prompt can be used to brainstorm, experiment, and iterate on the results.

For example, ChatGPT prompts are instructions or queries you enter in the GenAI interface to get responses. A prompt consists of keywords and phrases meant to generate a reply. You feed ChatGPT a question or instruction and it will respond as though in a conversation.

Machine Learning (ML) Models and Large Language Models

ML models are computer programs or mathematical algorithms trained on datasets to identify patterns, make predictions, or classify information without being explicitly programmed for every scenario. By analyzing data, these models learn to identify relationships and automatically improve their performance in tasks like image recognition, natural language processing, and forecasting. These models are like neural networks or decision trees and use parameters learned from the data and those set by the developers to drive the analysis. Models can be unsupervised learning where the model figures out the hidden patterns or structures within unlabeled data, supervised learning where models use labeled data to predict future outcomes, or reinforcement learning where the models learn from trial and error.

Large language models (LLMs) are a specialized sub-set of ML models which use algorithms to analyze massive datasets to understand and generate human language. Like ML, LLMs use neural network-based algorithms and are capable of handling unstructured data.

AI vs. Generative AI (GenAI)

Generative AI (GenAI) is the most recent major development in the overall realm of AI. It is a specific subset of AI that uses programs to process large data sets to detect patterns and then create new content derived from the existing content. GenAI can be used to create new content such as text files, audio, images, video and even code. The human language components of GenAI applications are built on top of LLMs (large language models) which have been trained on vast amounts of content gathered from all kinds of sources used for human interactions. These include the internet, books, emails, text messages, website content such as images, videos, and so on.

AI primarily monitors and analyzes behavior patterns. Using these patterns to create a baseline, AI can detect unusual behaviors and restrict unauthorized access to systems. AI can also help to prioritize risk and instantly detect the possibility of malware and intrusions before they begin. It has already been introduced in a large number of vulnerability scanning products to detect and prevent cyberattacks.

GenAI takes this content analysis to the next level by using the existing content to create new content that is predictive and simulative in nature. Cybercriminals are increasingly using GenAI capabilities to mount new cyberattacks that are highly intelligent and designed to defeat defense mechanisms implemented by cybersecurity defenders. Such attacks include a variety of identity-based attacks and the ability to rapidly discover security misconfigurations of endpoints.

While misuse of GenAI allows cybercriminals a powerful new arsenal for cyberattacks, GenAI also offers exciting potential to enhance cybersecurity through automation, advanced analysis, and improved user identity experiences. By using particular risk profiles and usage patterns, GenAI is able to customize and rapidly adapt security measures through automation for individual users and devices.

Many new GenAI models have emerged during the last few years. Most well-known closed-source GenAI models such as GPT-3, GPT-4, GPT-5, ChatGPT, Claude, OpenAI, Google Gemini, and PaLM are available for deployment via cloud APIs. This approach can be further refined by *prompt* engineering — this could include templates, examples, or the organization's own data to better inform the LLM output.

How Malicious Actors Use LLMs

With the brief history of AI and GenAI in the previous section, let us turn to another significant development in the use of these new-found intelligence processing techniques, the emergence of sophisticated AI-driven cybersecurity threats.

LLMs offer various ways for hackers to carry out their malicious acts. Traditional phishing campaigns can be made more lethal by using a LLM to help clean up the language or remove obvious errors to make them look authentic; improperly crafted messages with grammatical mistakes and spelling errors are commonly used to identify fake messages. The technology can also be used to make the content of the messages unique and more customized to issues relevant to the target.

Another use of an LLM is to create code for the attack. This could allow for making a realistic landing page, without having to know how to use a programming or scripting languages. For example, a hacker can take a screenshot of a website of a bank and the LLM will create the code for it.

What this means is that there will need to be new approaches for dealing with social engineering attacks.

Publicly available and open source LLMs potentially lack adequate security against prompt injection vulnerabilities and attacks. A threat actor can take control of the LLM and force it to produce malicious outputs because of the implicit confusion between the control and data planes in LLMs.

AI-Driven Cyberattacks

AI-driven cyberattacks offer several advantages to attackers, making them potentially more dangerous and difficult to defend against. Attackers are increasingly using advanced machine learning algorithms to identify vulnerabilities, predict patterns and exploit weaknesses.

Easy availability of AI tools and technologies are making it increasingly easier for hackers to launch AI-driven cyberattacks. The efficiency and rapid data analysis enhance hackers' capability to gain a tactical advantage, leading to rapid intrusions and exploiting weaknesses which they can use to modify or destroy protected data.

AI based cyberattacks are focused on attack methods driven through content analysis. These are machine-invoked and adaptable to defensive configuration changes performed by the cyber defenders who are overwhelmed and unable to counter the real-time changes, vulnerability analysis of the endpoints by the hacker's systems and the adaptability of AI-driven attacks.

These AI-driven cyberattacks use AI to automate and enhance the capabilities of traditional cyberattacks, making them more sophisticated, targeted, and challenging to detect. AI-powered cyberattacks use machine learning to analyze a human or machine target and find techniques most likely to compromise an organization. These could include generating an email based on your workforce members' social media profile or using small bits of information to predict the most likely vulnerabilities in a target system and launch an attack. Cybercriminals can train robots to socially engineer targets at human or superhuman levels of performance that can potentially defeat the most sophisticated defenses.

Cybercriminals and Malicious Actors Are Now Using GenAI

Cybercriminals and malicious actors are already using GenAI to launch more sophisticated attacks. Their use of the technology will continue rising because it effectively brings speed, insight, automation, and imitation to their cybercrime weapons. GenAI based cyberattacks are focused on attacks that enhance analysis of large volumes of content by creating new content based on the analysis, such as, deepfakes and phishing emails. These are applied in the following ways:

- *Phishing and Social Engineering*. GenAI generates personalized content that closely imitates legitimate communication, tricking the recipients into divulging sensitive information or downloading malware. This can be achieved by using the ability to create in seconds very convincing phishing emails, generated using GenAI for performing the research required without significant effort by the cybercriminals. GenAI-powered tools like ChatGPT have given threat actors the ability to quickly craft convincing and targeted phishing emails that earlier used to require considerable sophistication and resources.
- *Chatbot phishing scams*, where chatbots engage in seemingly harmless conversations with potential victims, subtly gathering information about personal details or login credentials.
- *Deepfakes*. Audio or video powered by GenAI can impersonate individuals, manipulate public opinion, or conduct sophisticated social

engineering attacks. Deep Fake Technology allows a threat actor to use AI-powered software to mimic the voice of an organization's executive to request employees to perform unauthorized transactions that can cause financial loss or sensitive data exfiltration for follow-on targeted attacks. A common exploit is impersonating IRS or FBI agents.

- *Malware Development*. GenAI can create malware that adapts and evolves to evade detection by traditional antivirus and malware detection tools.

Exploiting Vulnerabilities. GenAI can analyze individuals' email and other communications, systems, and software for vulnerabilities to launch more targeted attacks. They can discover software vulnerabilities and cybersecurity misconfigurations using GenAI algorithms through a series of automated vulnerability scans while evading intrusion detection

How AI and GenAI are Being Misused for Cyberattacks

Large Language Models (LLMs) represent a transformative breakthrough in artificial intelligence. These models, built on advanced neural architectures like transformers, comprehend and generate human-like text, enabling them to process vast amounts of linguistic content with remarkable accuracy and coherence. Their prowess in understanding, interpreting, and generating text has propelled their utilization across various domains. Modern LLMs excel in several key functionalities crucial for cybersecurity including natural language understanding, anomaly detection, text generation and analysis, and adaptive learning.

LLMs can generate convincing spear-phishing emails to gain initial access, that are followed up by AI-produced malware to exploit vulnerabilities and escalate an attacker's privileges. Attackers are leveraging GenAI to craft highly convincing deepfakes capable of deceiving even the most vigilant individuals and defensive systems.

AI and GenAI Driven Cybersecurity Threats

AI and GenAI driven cyberattacks are rapidly growing challenges and threats to society. They involve using advanced machine learning algorithms to identify vulnerabilities, predict patterns and exploit weaknesses. The efficiency and rapid data analysis advance a hackers' capability to gain a tactical advantage, leading to rapid intrusions or destruction.

AI and GenAI driven Cyberattacks

AI and GenAI driven cyberattacks offer several advantages to attackers, making them potentially more dangerous and difficult to defend against. Attackers are increasingly using advanced machine learning algorithms to identify vulnerabilities, predict patterns and exploit weaknesses.

Easy availability of AI tools and technologies are making it increasingly easier for hackers to launch AI-driven cyberattacks. The efficiency and rapid data analysis enhance hackers' capability to gain a tactical advantage, leading to rapid intrusions and exploiting weaknesses which they can use to modify or destroy protected data.

AI and GenAI driven based cyberattacks are focused on attack methods driven through content analysis. These are machine-invoked and adaptable to defensive configuration changes performed by the cyber defenders who are overwhelmed and unable to counter the real-time changes, vulnerability analysis of the endpoints by the hacker's systems and the adaptability of GenAI-driven attacks.

These AI and GenAI driven cyberattacks use AI and GenAI to automate and enhance the capabilities of traditional cyberattacks, making them more sophisticated, targeted, and challenging to detect. GenAI-powered cyberattacks use machine learning to analyze a human or machine target and find techniques most likely to compromise an organization. These could include generating an email based on the organization's workforce members' social media profile or using small bits of information to predict the most likely vulnerabilities in a target system or personnel to launch an attack. Cybercriminals can train robots to socially engineer targets at human or superhuman levels of performance that can potentially defeat the most sophisticated defenses.

Attacks Against Defensive AI systems

Cybercriminals can deliberately confuse or even "poison" artificial intelligence (AI) systems to make them malfunction such as modifying the input data used to build the LLMs or attacking the models developed from the LLMs. There are no easy foolproof defense mechanisms that cyber defenders can employ against such sophisticated AI driven attacks against their own AI-driven protections. One of the key risks of AI-powered cyberattacks is their ability to learn and adapt to new defenses. Traditional cybersecurity solutions, even most AI-driven solutions, often rely on known patterns and signatures to detect and block attacks but can be defeated by these sophisticated enhancements.

Automated Hacking

GenAI can automate aspects of hacking, allowing cybercriminals to launch large-scale attacks that are more complex and difficult to detect and counter.

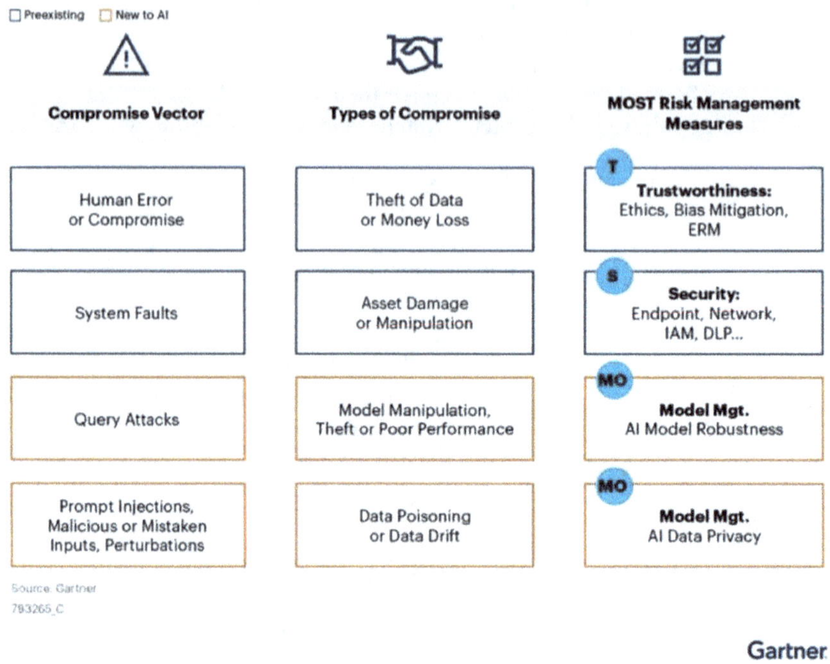

Source: Gartner

Figure 4-1. New Attack Surfaces for Cyber Attacks

Gartner further describes use cases of GenAI that a malicious actor can use as described in the following graphic.

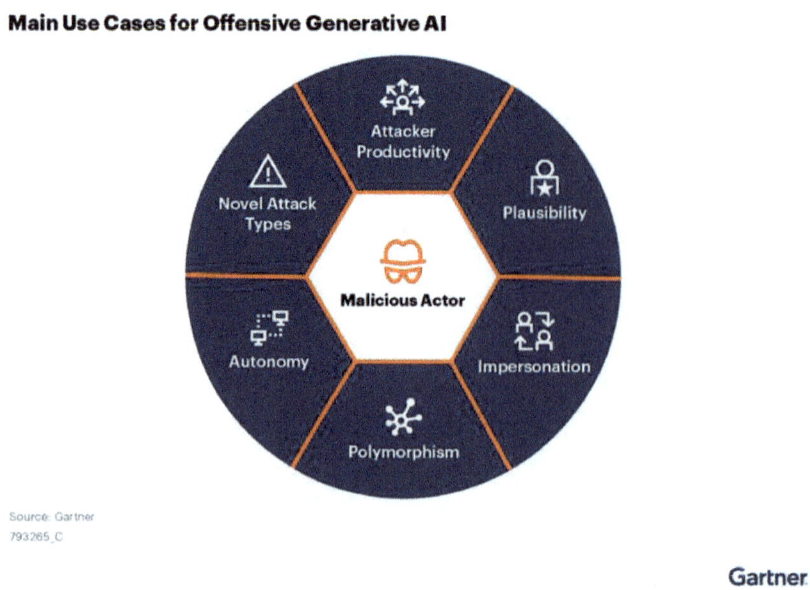

Source: Gartner

Figure 4-2 : Main Use Cases for Offensive Generative AI

Attackers have started to exploit the generative content capabilities of the technology to craft better malicious and fraudulent content at scale and low cost.

There are already lots of threat research examples of ChatGPT crafting more believable phishing lures, customized with public domain knowledge. The following briefly describes how GenAI is misused by malicious threat actors.

- *Attacker Productivity* – GenAI can help the attackers create more attacks more rapidly by upskilling and being able to create correct code, automation through chaining a variety of tasks, and scalability to achieve a faster kill chain or discover more vulnerabilities.
- *Plausibility* – Cybercriminals can use GenAI to discover and curate content from multiple sources to increase their trustworthiness and make them look real and friendly, and then lure other fraudulent content (e.g., through brand impersonation).
- *Impersonation* -- GenAI can create more realistic human voice/video (deepfakes) that appear to be from a trusted source and could undermine identity verification and voice biometrics.
- *Polymorphism* -- Polymorphic malware is a sophisticated class of malicious software designed to mutate its code while preserving its core functionality. It achieves this by employing various obfuscation techniques that alter its appearance with each iteration, making detection and analysis a daunting task for even the most advanced security systems.
- *Autonomy* – Using an LLM as a controller to achieve a higher level of autonomous local action decisions or more automated command and control interactions to pursue automated attacks.
- *Novel Attack Types* -- The worst-possible security threat from GenAI would be large-scale discovery of entirely new attack classes. Although the security industry will use this scenario to instill fear, there is no evidence that this has greater likelihood than discovery by human threat actors.

GenAI is Being Used to Bypass Security Measures

GenAI models can be trained to mimic user behavior or generate inputs that can trick biometric security systems, CAPTCHAs, and other AI-based security solutions.

GenAI Used for LLM-enabled Threats

Large language models (LLMs) offer various ways for hackers to carry out their nefarious acts. Traditional phishing campaigns can be made more lethal by using an LLM to help clean up the language or remove obvious errors make them look authentic; improperly crafted messages with grammatical mistakes and spelling errors are commonly used to identify fake messages. The technology can also be used to make the content of the messages unique and more customized to issues relevant to the target.

Another use of an LLM is to create code for the attack. This could allow for making a realistic landing page, without having to know how to use a programming or scripting languages. For example, a hacker can take a screenshot of a website of a bank and the LLM will create the code for it.

What this means is that there will need to be new approaches for dealing with social engineering attacks.

Publicly available and open source LLMs potentially lack adequate security against prompt injection vulnerabilities and attacks. A threat actor can take control of the LLM and force it to produce malicious outputs because of the implicit confusion between the control and data planes in LLMs.

Besides prompt injection, there are other types of attacks on LLMs such as once a cybercriminal has access to a model's structure, they exploit existing vulnerabilities.

Using GenAI for Boosting Cybersecurity

Organizations with good cybersecurity monitoring tools produce massive amounts of security-relevant data daily, which can be almost incomprehensible to the human mind. However, GenAI and machine learning (ML) offer some of the best technologies for identifying patterns in these data stores. By analyzing enormous amounts of data and then finding patterns in the data to replicate in cybersecurity-centric decision making, GenAI can help organizations overcome some of the common challenges they face in detection and response. In the realm of GenAI, there are many categories of data analytics and approaches leading to new outcomes:

- *Machine learning* – helps learn the habits of the of the human subject, and once learned, it can be used to identify the human subject.
- *Natural language processing (NLP)* -- Interaction between computers and humans using a natural language model. A common application of this is spam identification in email.
- *Expert systems* -- These try to emulate the decision-making ability of a human expert to solve complex problems.
- *Vision systems* – These systems enable machines to identify objects and can be used to identify a human subject by the way they nod or shift their eyes during their interactions on a computer.
- *Speech* – While the most common use of these systems is to turn speech into text, as well as those that translate from language to language, in the GenAI applications the human subject can be identified by the type of words selected by the user and the cadence of their voice.

These areas often overlap with each other, and real-world solutions can make use of multiple approaches at once. GenAI systems can be used for an advanced multi-factor authentication (MFA) factor in biometrics-based identification by using the following concepts:

- *Perception* -- Understanding images, audio, voice, video and text and the content within them.
- *Reasoning* – Drawing conclusion from the existing data analyzed and predicting when new data does not conform to the conclusions from the existing data.
- *Planning* -- Inferring the required steps to reach a goal such as biometric identity of a person based on existing data.

- *Motion* – Using motion detection and extending it through GenAI to predict motion such as movement of the body of a person or head or the eyes based on previously collected data about such movements.
- *Typing cadence* -- How a user types has been shown to be unique from user to user, and can be used to identify the user.
- *Natural language processing* -- Understanding human language and extending it with GenAI to confirm identity of a human being by detecting subtle changes in speech patterns and choice of words and sentence construction used by a human being talking on the phone or in a video call by converting speech to text.

Note that all of these methods above can be used for continuous identification to achieve security throughout the user interaction session.

AI and GenAI Driven Threat Detection and Prevention

While AI and GenAI provide attackers with powerful tools, it can also serve as a formidable ally in defense. AI and GenAI are rapidly changing how security teams manage cyberthreats and enhance the speed and efficiency of their defensive algorithm deployment. AI and GenAI help them streamline the early phases of an incident investigation by sifting through large volumes of data such as log data and vulnerability scans data and spotting anomalies in the patterns. These advanced techniques provide security experts with a comprehensive overview of potential attack modes and endpoints, and also nip any attacks that may have started through continuous AI-driven monitoring tools and reduce false positives. Enhancing predictive analytics and improving threat detection, allows them to refine investigation methods and engage AI-driven protection mechanisms.

AI and GenAI driven cyberattacks are rapidly growing challenges and threats to society. They involve using advanced machine learning algorithms to identify vulnerabilities, predict patterns and exploit weaknesses. The efficiency and rapid data analysis advance a hackers' capability to gain a tactical advantage, leading to rapid intrusions or destruction.

AI and GenAI can also help organizations by transforming patch management by ensuring that they are using the latest most secure software and applications. Recent data breaches have shown a consistent pattern of misconfigurations and use of obsolete versions of software missing security patches, a situation that is readily used by cybercriminals for successful attacks.

AI and GenAI powered tools are helping firms detect and reverse software attacks. These include advanced solutions like AI-based hyper-automation and vulnerability protections. These tools go beyond traditional patch management methods and ensure protections of all endpoints and unauthorized access efforts. These AI-driven tools offer enhanced efficiency, security, and regulatory compliance in addressing evolving digital threats.

Predicting Cyberattacks and Building Defenses

While real time detection is critical in intercepting cyberattacks, these must be fed with predictive analytic data that they can use to identify the threat.

By analyzing post attack patterns and system vulnerabilities, GenAI can efficiently predict potential threats enabling proactive risk mitigation. This requires constant learning to improve prediction accuracy and is highly dependent on available datasets. For example, GenAI can analyze past attack patterns and vulnerabilities to predict potential future threats, allowing organizations to proactively implement security measures. GenAI's adaptability and real-time analysis empower predictive analytics by providing valuable insights into future scenarios that can enable better decision-making and risk mitigation strategies.

A critical step in preventing a breach is detection. GenAI based attacks are designed to avoid detection and *fly under the radar*. The following sub-sections discuss how GenAI can be used to detect GenAI driven attacks.

Predictive Analysis

By analyzing post attack patterns and system vulnerabilities, GenAI can efficiently predict potential threats enabling proactive risk mitigation. This requires constant learning to improve prediction accuracy and is highly dependent on available datasets. For example, GenAI can analyze past attack patterns and vulnerabilities to predict potential future threats, allowing organizations to proactively implement security measures. GenAI's adaptability and real-time analysis empower predictive analytics by providing valuable insights into future scenarios that can enable better decision-making and risk mitigation strategies.

Preventing Identity Attacks

Identity attacks have taken a very sophisticated turn with GenAI. So, it is natural that GenAI would also come to be the key factor for advanced phishing detection and biometric identity protection.

Phishing Detection and Prevention

GenAI can analyze email content and identify behavior to detect patterns associated with phishing attempts. It can alert users to not allow deceptive cyberattacks and prevent potential data breaches. This requires regular monitoring of emails. For example, if your organization monitors email traffic and detects phishing attempts, all such future attempts can be blocked.

Enhanced Biometrics Based Authentication

GenAI generates highly realistic biometric data to improve the resilience and accuracy of biometric authentication systems. It requires capturing the dynamic biometric behavioral aspects of users we discussed earlier with a high level of data training accuracy. For example, GenAI can generate synthetic facial recognition patterns that closely mimic human faces and facial expression. This synthetic data is then used to test and refine facial recognition systems to ensure they can accurately distinguish between real faces and spoof attempts such as photos or masks. By improving the resilience and accuracy of biometric authentication, GenAI empowers organizations to provide more secure identity verification that guards against unauthorized access in real-world applications like secure facility access or mobile device unlocking.

Anomaly Detection

GenAI's ability to analyze large datasets allows timely identification of irregular activities that indicate security threats. Timely detection of potential threats to data integrity and network security can be used to drive continuous monitoring and need for prompt follow up actions.

For example, if an organization monitors network traffic and GenAI observes a sudden spike in outbound data transfers from a user's account during non-standard working hours, it can swiftly recognize this anomaly as possible data exfiltration. GenAI then triggers an immediate alert, allowing security teams to investigate and mitigate the potential threat, thus preventing sensitive data breaches and ensuring the integrity of the network.

Adaptive Threat Detection

GenAI can be used to neutralize GenAI driven cyber threats that evolve rapidly, and be able to adapt to changing cyberattack tactics and strategies. GenAI gives your systems a proactive defense mechanism through real time recognition of evolving threats. To make this work you will need of large relevant threat datasets, constant updates for threat modes and modifications to adapt to new threats.

For example, GenAI can monitor network traffic and detect an unusual surge in data requests that is indicative of a potential distributed denial of service (DDoS) attack. GenAI can then take immediate action to mitigate the attack, such as diverting traffic away from the targeted server and alerting security teams.

GenAI-Driven Network Detection

It's likely a fallacy that attackers with newly acquired privileged credentials will immediately use them in new or unusual ways. With a GenAI-driven security approach, it's more critical to look for anomalous activity related to the attackers' ultimate goals and objectives, which is to access sensitive systems and data. By building a behavioral model over time, GenAI-driven XDR can map common access models and network traffic patterns to critical data stores and look for anomalies to those patterns and models. One key to this is developing historic interaction models of observed privilege and then comparing new ones against this.

For example, GenAI can monitor network traffic and detect an unusual surge in data requests that is indicative of a potential distributed denial of service (DDoS) attack. GenAI can then take immediate action to mitigate the attack, such as diverting traffic away from the targeted server and alerting security teams.

How GenAI Drives Zero Trust

Zero Trust security operates on the principle of "never trust, always verify," meaning no user or device is automatically trusted, regardless of their location or network position. This principle drives all uses of AI and GenAI for enhancing the Zero Trust model.

The following sections discuss the key aspects of using GenAI in a Zero Trust environment. These include:

- Automated Threat Detection

- Real-time Anomaly Detection
- Contextual Access Control
- Adaptive Security Policies
- Suspicious Activity Identification

Automated threat detection:

Threat detection in cybersecurity is the process of identifying and responding to potential security risks or malicious activities targeting an organization's digital assets. It involves monitoring network traffic, endpoints, and log data, using techniques like behavioral analysis and anomaly detection to detect and respond to threats.

In the context of Zero Trust security, automated threat detection leverages AI and machine learning to continuously monitor and analyze network traffic, user behavior, and device activities, identifying and responding to potential threats in real-time. Automated threat detection requires the following key functions:

- *Real-time Monitoring* – continuous monitoring of network traffic, user behavior, and device activities for suspicious patterns or anomalies.
- *AI and Machine Learning* -- AI algorithms and machine learning models are used to analyze data, identify potential threats, and trigger automated responses.
- *Threat Intelligence* -- feeds integration to identify known threats and vulnerabilities.
- *Endpoint security solutions* -- such as those from CrowdStrike, Sentinel One and Palo Alto Networks to perform real-time security and compliance checks.

GenAI algorithms based on LLMs can analyze vast amounts of data across the network to identify suspicious patterns and anomalies that might indicate a security breach, enabling faster threat detection and response compared to traditional methods.

GenAI based automated threat detection and threat prediction systems can detect and respond and adapt to manage threats faster than traditional security methods and reduce the risk by responding in real-time to risk of data breaches and security incidents. It can help the organization strengthen it's overall security posture and protect sensitive data.

Real-time Anomaly Detection

Any deviation from established patterns can indicate a security risk. These deviations in the observations from security monitoring software are called anomalies. Anomaly detection is the process of examining specific data points and detecting suspicious deviations from established patterns.

The three main classes of anomaly detection techniques are unsupervised, semi-supervised, and supervised. Essentially, the correct anomaly detection method depends on the available labels in the dataset. Popular supervised models used in anomaly detection include random forest, decision tree and K-Nearest Neighbors

(KNN). Isolation Forest and Local Outlier Factor are two examples of unsupervised ML models that can be used to detect deviations.

AI based anomaly detection is the process of identifying unusual patterns or outliers in datasets that do not conform to expected behavior, by using artificial intelligence and machine learning algorithms. AI assistance improves the anomaly detection by automating the process which is otherwise manual and time consuming. AI based anomaly detection involves training models on data to recognize normal behavior and then flagging deviations from these norms.

An example of anomaly detection is in the use of a credit card by a customer which uses algorithms to identify the deviations such as types of purchases, unusual spending, large purchases in a new location, and other unusual patterns in real-time, This alert for potentially fraudulent activity is then reviewed by the bank directly and can help trigger additional authentication for the protection of the customer.

Constant monitoring is a resource drain. The predictive mechanisms provided through GenAI can reduce this drain and can flag unusual behaviors or deviations from normal user patterns, allowing for immediate investigation and mitigation actions. This capability allows LLMs to assess whether a flagged product is genuinely anomalous or if it aligns with the vendor's usual product range. Additionally, LLMs can offer explanations for why a product is considered anomalous, enhancing the clarity and interpretability of the results

GenAI, particularly LLMs, is revolutionizing anomaly detection by providing a more nuanced and contextual understanding of data, enabling proactive identification of potential issues and offering explanations for detected anomalies.

Furthermore, GenAI is transforming anomaly detection by enabling businesses to detect subtle, complex patterns that traditional methods often overlook. By learning normal behavior patterns and flagging deviations with precision, it has proven value across sectors like finance, healthcare, manufacturing, and cybersecurity.

Contextual Access Control

User behavior is an important security measure. Contextual access control (CAC) is a security approach that dynamically assesses access requests based on multiple factors beyond just user identity, such as device (company managed device or personal device), location (on secure company premises or outside), time access is requested (normal working hours), and network conditions (trusted network vs. public network), and if the user has exhibited unexpected behavior. These factors are used to make informed decisions about granting or denying access.

CAC uses real-time data and analytics to evaluate the risk associated with each access request, rather than relying solely on static policies. These can be used specifically to allow or restrict access to sensitive data from specific devices or locations. This can also be used to protect against phishing and malware attacks. And it can automatically and dynamically enforce compliance with security policies.

As we have seen, GenAI can be very useful in automating analysis; in this case for user behavior, device posture, and network conditions to make real-time access control decisions, granting access only when all factors align with security policies. GenAI can enhance contextual access control by dynamically adapting access permissions in real-time based on real-time user access context related factors and intent, offering a more secure and personalized user experience.

Furthermore, GenAI can learn from new threats and adapt security policies dynamically, providing a more responsive security posture against evolving cyberattacks.

Suspicious activity identification:

Suspicious activity, especially in the case of financial transactions, refers to abnormal actions compared to the normal parameters of the transactions such as volume of funds, target location for funds transfers, types of transactions, and authorizing entities for the transactions. A Suspicious Activity Report (SAR) is a formal report submitted to a regulatory body. Fraud analysts are required to review the transactions and their related context such as previous alert history to determine if it may be fraudulent that required a more detailed investigation. This is time consuming scrupulous work that requires creating reports for each incident for delivery to regulators. Many fraudulent activities may slip through in this time-consuming process.

GenAI can analyze user interactions with applications and data to identify potentially malicious activity, even if it appears seemingly normal. By combining existing predictive AI workflows around suspicious activity monitoring with GenAI, the predictive insights from the LLMs can be built up as reports thereby streamlining the reporting process.

GenAI Challenges and Considerations for Zero Trust:

Zero Trust Security combines the principles, authentication safeguards and policies that can drive AI assisted security that operates on the principle of maintaining rigorous verification, never assuming trust, and confirming every access attempt and transaction.

Data quality:

AI models run on huge volumes of data of which an estimated 80% is unstructured, mostly screenshots, along with other content. That data can be useful for analysis it there is a clear knowledge and understanding of the type of business it applies to, what that data includes, and the relevance and accuracy of that data. The data can be a valuable resource for understanding the security challenges and the mitigations applied over time.

AI and GenAI are increasingly being used by bad actors so ensuring the quality of data for training AI and GenAI is critical. The effectiveness of GenAI heavily relies on the quality and completeness of training data.

False positives:

False positives, where AI incorrectly flags legitimate activity as malicious, are a significant concern with GenAI, particularly in applications like fraud detection and cybersecurity, potentially leading to unnecessary investigations and disruptions. a false positive occurs when a system incorrectly identifies a situation or event as positive (e.g., fraudulent activity, a security threat) when it is actually negative (e.g., legitimate transaction and not a threat). Too many false positives lead to extensive manual analysis thereby requiring careful tuning and validation to minimize unnecessary noise, which wastes resources and causes a reduced trust in the AI system.

GenAI models are only as good as the data they have been trained on. GenAI models can sometimes generate false alerts when the training data is inadequate to distinguish between legitimate activity and fraudulent activity. However, GenAI can be used to also mitigate the false positive issue by relearning on new more comprehensive data how to distinguish between legitimate and fraudulent activities.

Explainability:

Understanding how GenAI reaches its conclusions can be difficult, which can pose challenges in debugging and validating security decisions. It is essential for building trust in the system especially when the system is used for making critical decisions with major financial and legal impact. It allows the human developers to improve the AI and GenAI contribution. GenAI systems, especially deep learning systems are complex and can contain biases based on the learning data that can lead to unexpected outcomes if not understood by the developers. Explainability helps the security team understand the factors that influence the GenAI output so that they can program the systems better.

Examples of how GenAI can be used in Zero Trust

AI and more specifically, Gen AI, can play an important role in ensuring Zero Trust network security, specially, through user behavior analytics, network traffic analysis, application security monitoring, and email security.

User behavior analysis

Analyzing user login patterns, location, and device usage to identify potential compromised accounts are the very basics of understanding normal user behavior. However, to fully comprehend user behavior, a very large number of factors must be accounted for in real time and the user responses mapped. The resulting data is enormous and cannot really be analyzed effectively by human security teams in real-time and at a reasonable cost. This makes use of AI very important.

While even using AI it is possible to analyze very large volumes of data in real-time, it requires significant computing resources to achieve timely results. GenAI, with its predictive capability and content generation, can automate the data analysis and identify complex patterns and relationships in user data that would be impossible for humans to detect. Not only does this help in understanding user behavior in real-time but it can also help in predicting what the user behavior should be in a given situation and alerting on deviations from those expectations.

As we have seen, this capability of anomaly detection can be applied in many ways including cybersecurity at one end and marketing campaigns at another. GenAI can provide real-time insights in the user behavior for logging into a system and accessing and using data so that any deviation such as unexpected large scale data exfiltration can be flagged and the security team alerted. This can identify suspicious user behavior in real time and prevent security breaches.

Network traffic analysis

Anomaly detection can also play a major part in detecting malicious network traffic patterns that might indicate a targeted attack. By enabling real-time anomaly detection, predictive analytics and routine monitoring tasks, any deviations from normal expected network traffic patterns can be identified in real-time and mitigated. GenAI models can be trained on normal traffic patterns and potential threats experience in the past. By monitoring the network traffic in real-time, a GenAI model trained on normal traffic pattern can identify deviations in real-time and can also predict potential network threats by extrapolating on the different types of threats and the frequency of occurrence.

GenAI can also reconfigure the network automatically in real-time based on the deviations observed to prevent future threats from those deviations.

Application security monitoring

Logging and alerting have been the traditional methods for monitoring applications. Observability solutions such as Datadog, Splunk, Dynatrace, AppDynamics and others have been used to monitor, analyze and optimize application security. They allow businesses to collect, index, search and visualize massive amounts of machine generated data. The goal is to detect potential issues before they affect end-users. They can be used to visualize the state of infrastructure components. They can help identify suspicious activity within applications based on user interactions and data access.

Most of these tools have already incorporated AI capability to perform real time analysis of the data and provide alerts in real-time. More advanced capabilities are being developed using GenAI. GenAI's integration into observability is a significant advance in delivering actionable insights to users, and is poised to revolutionize the observability landscape. It can analyze vast datasets efficiently. If offers pertinent insights into the observability data and makes recommendations and can even automate changes to configurations to mitigate risks.

Email Security

The Zero Trust approach of "Never Trust, Always Verify" applies to emails where the model assumes that no one inside the network is automatically trusted and every attempt to access resources needs to be continuously verified. Zero Trust based e-mail security focuses on verifying every e-mail, regardless of the sender, before allowing it into an inbox. It assumes that no e-mail is automatically trustworthy, and every e-mail must go through strict authentication and authorization controls. So, the focus is on verifying the sender's identity and authorization to deliver the message. Zero Trust focuses on strong authentication mechanisms such as multifactor authentication (MFA) to verify the sender's identity. An additional approach used is to limit access to e-mail resources based on the principle of least privilege, ensuring that users have the necessary permissions. Examples of Zero Trust e-mail security solutions include DMARC (Domain-based Message Authentication, Reporting & Conformance), Mailprotector, and Microsoft Defender for Office 365

These solutions isolate suspicious email links and deferred attacks, gain visibility in and block or retract phishing and spear phishing attempts, isolate malicious web content through web apps, and identify malicious apps that have unnecessary permissions

GenAI a further enhances Zero Trust based e-mail security by enabling faster, more accurate thread detection, and more effective responses to emerging threats including sophisticated phishing and malware attacks. GenAI Can analyze vast data sets of emails, URLs, attachments and other data sources within emails to identify anomalies and patterns indicative of presidential threats. Furthermore, GenAI can interpret e-mail content and user behavior to understand the context of an e-mail and identify deceptive tactics. It can detect new emerging threats the traditional security systems may miss by learning from past threats and predicting future attacks so that proactive defense strategies can be implemented in real time. GenAI Enhances Zero Trust further through continuous analysis and protection.

Security Hardening of Networks and Systems

Security hardening of networks and systems is well-known, but security defenders have been increasingly challenged by the sophistication of the end-point attacks created through use of GenAI by cybercriminals. The following approaches are a starting point for use of GenAI to mitigate such attacks.

Automated Security Patch Generation

GenAI can help identify attack areas and vulnerabilities patterns from network endpoints, APIs, log data, and historical data over time and create and test patches dynamically for software vulnerabilities, effectively accelerating the security patching process. This approach also helps in testing effectiveness without risking production systems and applying constant updates and modifications. For example, if a critical software vulnerability is discovered in a widely used application, GenAI can swiftly analyze the vulnerability, create a customized patch, and test it in a controlled environment. After generating the patch, GenAI can simulate various scenarios and test the patch's effectiveness without risking production systems. Once tested, the GenAI system can automatically apply the patch.

Malware Generation and Analysis

GenAI provides a controlled environment for cyber security researchers to analyze and understand malware behavior. Analyzing malware behavior and it's use by training teams to respond to evolving threats ensures continuous security enhancement and malware protection. For example, cybersecurity experts can use GenAI to generate artificial malware samples based on known attack vectors and vulnerabilities. By analyzing these samples, they can uncover new insights into malware behavior, propagation techniques, and evasion tactics employed by cybercriminals.

XDR Based Network Hardening

XDR (Extended Detection and Response) expands on NDR (Network Detection and Response) and picks up where NDR leaves of. Organizations can use XDR driven by GenAI to detect malicious activity across multiple systems, and it can detect threats that other security solutions cannot. NDR is focused on monitoring network traffic and events to look for common signals of compromise that may include lateral movement, common exploitation scenarios, data exfiltration, command and control, and more.

XDR models bring a more integrated approach to threat detection and response by incorporating additional events and tools beyond NDR. XDR delivers visibility across more security-related events and information, including endpoint events and endpoint detection tools, network traffic detection, integrated event management through SIEM, and cloud data, while applying analytics and automation to address today's increasingly sophisticated threats. XDR combines these technologies to provide a single, unified view of an organization's security posture. It provides visibility into more assets and devices and can detect and respond to threats in real time.

Use Cases for GenAI-Driven Network Detection

It's likely a fallacy that attackers with newly acquired privileged credentials will immediately use them in new or unusual ways. With a GenAI-driven security approach, it's more critical to look for anomalous activity related to the attackers' ultimate goals and objectives, which is to access sensitive systems and data. By building a behavioral model over time, GenAI-driven XDR can map common access models and network traffic patterns to critical data stores and look for anomalies to those patterns and models. One key to this is developing historic interaction models of observed privilege and then comparing new ones against this.

Workforce training and governance

Workforce training at all levels has been absolutely critical for security posture management. GenAI can drive the security posture management, but it needs advanced workforce training to understand and use the new set of tools, technologies, and processes to effectively use GenAI.

Threat Simulation and Training

GenAI simulates various cyber threats and attacks scenarios to train professionals for real world threats for enhancing preparedness for rapid threat changes. By leveraging GenAI in threat simulation and training, organizations can better prepare their cybersecurity teams to effectively identify, respond to, and mitigate cyber threats.

New Emerging GenAI Challenges Faced by SOC Teams

Human error is known to be a top vulnerability, so SOC teams need to emphasize comprehensive GenAI based cyberattack methods training and cybersecurity awareness programs tailored for the roles of their workforce members. Training and upskilling SOC teams to effectively leverage GenAI technologies is important in navigating the complexities of modern cybersecurity. Integrating comprehensive training programs that familiarize cybersecurity professionals with the nuances of GenAI enables them to harness its capabilities and enhance their cybersecurity posture. GenAI will augment, not replace, SOC analysts in cybersecurity.

Data Masking and Privacy Preservation

GenAI has the remarkable ability to create synthetic data that closely resembles real data sets. This is particularly useful when working with sensitive information that needs to be protected. By generating data that mimics the real thing, organizations can avoid the risks of using actual data sets that may contain confidential or personally identifiable information. This synthetic data can be used to train security models and algorithms without compromising the privacy of individuals or exposing sensitive data.

Boosting AMTD Using GenAI

We discussed Automated Moving Target Defense (MTD) in the previous chapter. In this section, we will explore how GenAI can have a major impact on the effectiveness of AMTD.

As we saw in the previous chapter, AMTD is a natural evolution of the end-point protection with the capability to provide protection from AI-driven cyber-attacks. Current technologies for cybersecurity defense have been reactive but AI and especially GenAI present the opportunity to make them proactive. The goal is to make it more difficult for the attackers to sustain an exfiltration attack.

According to Gartner, combining AMTD solutions at different layers of the technology stack provide a defense-in-depth capability which can be augmented with GenAI in many significant ways including the following:

- Predict potential attack opportunities that cybercriminals may use and pre-plan and prepare AMTD instantaneous reconfiguration action plans.
- Add decoys at scale that mislead the attackers into expending time and resources.
- Dynamically determine using GenAI the best options for optimizing the timing for rotating targets based on dynamic cyberattack detection to prevent the attack becoming successful. The assets can include host servers, applications, even endpoints or even data stores.
- Using GenAI, select the best options for automated movement, reconfiguration, morphing the security posture.
- Confuse the cyber-attackers to disrupt the kill chain.

5 – Security Standards, Regulations, & Frameworks

Cybersecurity and data security regulations are standards set by regulatory bodies or governments, that guide organizations on protecting the confidentiality, integrity, and availability of data. These essentially aim at safeguarding the information assets including sensitive data stored and in use within the organization from destruction, tampering, unauthorized access, and other security risks.

Security laws are important for purposes that extend beyond just achieving regulatory compliance. These include:

- Ensuring the privacy and confidentiality of personal information of individuals whose data is being processed.
- Minimizing the risks of data breaches and cyber threats.
- Maintaining the reliability and accuracy of the data.
- Building a healthy business environment with improved customer confidence.
- Promoting commitment to cybersecurity.

Security standards and regulations are a structured set of protocols, policies, and technical and organizational measures designed to protect organization assets, including data, from unauthorized access, use, disclosure, alteration, or destruction.

Security Standards vs. Data Security Standards

There is a distinct difference between security (or cybersecurity) standards and data security standards. Cybersecurity standards include broad IT security standards that cover the entire infrastructure, networks, and systems. Data security standards are more specific, focusing more narrowly on protecting the data itself regardless of where it resides. They augment the broad IT standards with a clear focus on protecting data.

Examples of Cybersecurity Standards include the United States NIST cybersecurity regulations and standards, ISO 27001and CSA, and other standards which cover all aspects of the organization's security.

Data Security Standards: such as the General Data Protection Regulation (GDPR) in Europe and subsequent regulations derived from GDPR and enacted within the United States and other nations in almost all continents, enforce specific rules for data handling and processing, often with penalties for non-compliance. These regulations and standards are designed to ensure data confidentiality, integrity, and availability (the CIA triad). They protect sensitive data from cyber threats, prevent costly data breaches, and comply with legal obligations, ultimately safeguarding an organization's reputation, maintaining customer trust, and avoiding significant fines and legal consequences. Adherence to these standards also fosters a more resilient and efficient business environment by promoting better data management, enhancing cybersecurity, and providing a competitive advantage.

Note that the data security standards are incremental and complementary to the general cybersecurity standards and not a replacement. The general cybersecurity standards also cover many aspects of data security. This chapter focuses on cybersecurity (or security) standards and regulations. The next chapter will focus on data privacy and data privacy standards and regulations.

Security Compliance

Security compliance is the process of an organization ensuring its IT systems, data handling, and operations meet mandatory legal, regulatory, and industry-specific standards. More specifically, data security compliance is the process of following specific legal, regulatory, and industry standards for collecting, storing, managing, and protecting sensitive data to ensure its confidentiality, integrity, and availability. It involves implementing security measures to prevent unauthorized access and data breaches, thereby protecting customer, financial, and employee information

If an organization collects sensitive data, security compliance and data security compliance are not only important but may be mandatory for regulatory reasons. Compliance with the cybersecurity standards helps in the following ways:

- **Protecting Network and IT Assets**: Prevent malicious actors from accessing the organization's networks, servers and software assets to prevent unauthorized modifications or damage to your IT assets and potential ransomware attacks.
- **Protecting Sensitive Data**: use of robust security measures protects personal, financial, and proprietary information from unauthorized access, theft, and misuse.
- **Preventing Data Breaches**: implement the necessary tools and practices to reduce the risk of data breaches and cyberattacks.
- **Avoiding Penalties and Legal Action**: Non-compliance can lead to substantial fines, legal action, and even criminal penalties, making compliance a necessity to avoid costly consequences.
- **Building Customer Trust**: Demonstrating a commitment to data protection through compliance fosters trust and loyalty among customers, assuring them that their data is being handled responsibly.
- **Enhancing Reputation**: Companies that prioritize and adhere to data security regulations are seen as more trustworthy and reliable, enhancing their brand image and market position.
- **Improving Data Management**: Compliance requires organizations to improve their data governance and management practices, leading to better organization, accuracy, and security of data.

- **Ensuring Business Continuity**: By preventing data breaches and maintaining secure systems, compliance helps ensure that business operations are not disrupted by security incidents.
- **Gaining a Competitive Advantage**: Proactive compliance can differentiate a business in the marketplace, attracting customers and partners who value strong data security practices.

Security Compliance Frameworks are structured collections of policies, best practices, and controls that help organizations protect the organization's assets, business operations, sensitive data, manage cybersecurity risks, and meet regulatory requirements. These frameworks provide a systematic way to identify threats, implement security measures like encryption and access controls, and respond to incidents, ensuring adherence to legal obligations and industry standards. Compliance frameworks have been mandated by government regulators as well as by industry consortiums.

Security Standards, Regulations & Frameworks

Security standards and regulations that require compliance are formal guidelines, laws, and frameworks designed to protect sensitive information by ensuring its confidentiality, integrity, and availability. Standards like NIST, ISO 27001, and SOC 2 provide technical and organizational best practices and compliance certification for cybersecurity, while regulations like NIST (mandatory for US federal agencies and contractors), GDPR, HIPAA, and PCI-DSS are legal mandates that define data handling responsibilities and penalties for non-compliance. Together they form a comprehensive approach to demonstrable and measurable data security across your organization.

A cybersecurity framework is a structured set of standards, guidelines, procedures, and best practices designed to help organizations manage and reduce cybersecurity risks. These frameworks provide a structured and standardized approach and guidance, and a comprehensive roadmap for assessing, monitoring, mitigating potential threats, and meeting regulatory compliance. By establishing consistent processes and controls, they help organizations implement a proactive security strategy, manage regulatory requirements, mitigate risks, foster a security-minded culture, and facilitate communication among security professionals and stakeholders.

Most cybersecurity frameworks have been created and are driven by international consortiums and by federal governments. Others are driven by industry consortiums and by other professional organizations. The following lists the most common cybersecurity frameworks including international and national (United States) frameworks.

US National Frameworks

- **FISMA** (The Federal Information Security Management Act, 2002) sets requirements for federal information systems.
- **FedRAMP** (Federal Risk and Authorization Management Program): provides a standardized approach to security assessment, authorization, and continuous monitoring for cloud products and services.

- **Federal Information Processing Standard (FIPS 140-2)** is a standard developed by NIST which defines security requirements for cryptographic modules used to protect sensitive, unclassified information in IT systems.
- **NIST SP 800-53:** A comprehensive catalog of security and privacy controls for federal information systems.
- **NIST 800-171**: For protecting controlled unclassified information (CUI).
- **NIST CSF** (Cybersecurity Framework): A voluntary framework to manage and reduce cybersecurity risk. It provides standards, guidelines, and best practices.
- **NIST RMF** (Risk Management Framework): structured, risk-based approach which provides a comprehensive set of guidelines for managing and reducing cybersecurity risk.

International Frameworks

- **ISO 27001/27002**: international standard for information security management systems (ISMS) and a code of practice for information security controls.
- **ISO 42001**: A newer framework that may be used as a model for future frameworks, focusing on artificial intelligence management.
- **GDPR** (General Data Protection Regulation): has associated frameworks and strict requirements for handling personal data.

Control & Assessment Frameworks

- **CIS** Critical Security Controls: A prioritized set of actions to protect systems and data from known cyberattack vectors.
- **COBIT** (Control Objectives for Information and Related Technologies): A framework for IT management and governance.
- **SOC 1, SOC 2 and SOC 3**: An auditing standard for service organizations that handle customer data, focusing on security, availability, processing integrity, confidentiality, and privacy.
- **CSA CCM** (Cloud Security Alliance Cloud Controls Matrix): A framework for cloud security controls.
- **CMMC**: Established by the U.S. Department of Defense (DoD) to ensure that defense contractors and companies handling sensitive government information meet specific cybersecurity standards.

Industry-Specific Standards

- **NERC-CIP**: The North American Electric Reliability Corporation Critical Infrastructure Protection standard, focused on bulk electric systems security.

Other Notable Security Frameworks & Regulations

- **MITRE ATT&CK**: A knowledge base of adversary tactics and techniques based on real-world observations.
- **Zero Trust Architecture (ZTA)**: Not a framework but a security model based on explicit verification and least privilege access to minimize risk.

You are encouraged to review in-depth each of the cybersecurity and data security compliance frameworks listed above. Security compliance frameworks listed above all have some key characteristics in common to ensure compliance with the regulations and standards they are designed for as listed below:

- **Risk Management**: They help organizations identify, assess, and mitigate cybersecurity threats and vulnerabilities.
- **Regulatory Adherence**: Frameworks ensure compliance with local, national, and global laws and regulations that the framework is designed to comply with.
- **Data Protection**: They provide guidance and specific recommendations for implementing controls, such as data encryption, access controls, and incident response plans, to safeguard sensitive information.
- **Best Practices**: Frameworks incorporate industry best practices and recommendations to enhance an organization's security posture.
- **Trust and Reputation**: Adhering to a framework can build customer trust and demonstrate a commitment to data security.

Security Framework Components

A Security Framework typically has many components that drive certification bodies to register and document a formal assessment of an organization's compliance as spelled out in the framework and associated laws, regulations and standards. These components can include the following:

- **Risk Assessment and Management**: Processes for identifying, documenting potential risks and creating a roadmap to mitigate the risks.
- **Security Policies and Procedures**: Internal policies and standards derived from the national and international regulations and standards for data handling, access, and security management.
- **Technical Controls**: Specific security controls and measures like data encryption, access controls, data loss prevention, and sensitive data storage management.
- **Incident Response**: Plans and procedures for responding to data breaches and security incidents. These can involve immediate action to minimize damage from the breach, reporting to compliance governance agencies, and public handling of communications.
- **Audit Protocols**: Mechanisms for monitoring, reviewing, and attesting to security controls on a periodic basis.
- **Employee Training**: Security awareness programs to educate staff on their role in data protection.

US Security Standards

The US Federal government established the security practices for federal computer systems and requires federal agencies to conduct periodic assessments of the risk and magnitude of harm that could result from the unauthorized access, use, disclosure, disruption, modification, or destruction of information and information systems that support the operations and assets of the agency and address information security throughout the life cycle of each agency.

The standards used in the US include US standards as well as European and International Standards.

FISMA – Federal Information Security Modernization Act

FISMA was originally passed as the Federal Information Security Management Act in 2002 as part of the E-Government Act. Today, FISMA refers to the Federal Information Security Modernization Act of 2014, passed in response to the increasing volume of cyber-attacks on the federal government.

The Federal Information Security Modernization Act 2014 codifies the Department of Homeland Security's role in administering the implementation of information security policies for federal Executive Branch civilian agencies, overseeing agencies' compliance with those policies, and assisting OMB in developing those policies. It defines the framework of guidelines and security standards to protect government information and operations. FISMA requires all federal agencies to develop, document, and implement agency-wide information security programs.

FISMA requires implementing a comprehensive security program based on NIST 800-53r5 and NIST RMF. It requires implementation of risk assessments and security controls to address those risks. It further requires managing risks and implementation of monitoring systems for security threats and incidents.

Organizations must maintain an inventory of their assets and categorize their information systems and associated data based on risk and then implement the appropriate security controls defined by NIST standards, such as FIPS 199 and FIPS 200.

Continuous monitoring observability tools are required to be implemented along with tools for handling incident response. Vulnerability tools must also be implemented to protect their systems.

FIPS 140-2 -- Approve Cryptographic H/W and S/W Modules

This Federal Information Processing Standard (FIPS 140-2) specifies the security requirements that will be satisfied by a cryptographic module, providing four increasing, qualitative levels intended to cover a wide range of potential applications and environments. It consists of the following four levels:

- Level 1 is the lowest – Basic security requirements with production grade equipment and coatings and at least one tested encryption algorithm.

- Level 2 -- Raises the level to tamper evidence feature -- features that show tampering seals and should run on an operating system that has been approved by Common Criteria at EAL2.
- Level 3 – Requires strong enclosures and tamper resistant circuitry which includes attack detection such as tamper/detection response circuitry, and identity-based authentication.
- Level 4 – Highest level -- physical envelope of protection around modules, high level of detection and response useful for operation in physically unprotected areas. Used for cryptographic modules. Includes erasure of device in case of an attack.

Controlled Unclassified Information (CUI) level of information may be processed by cryptographic modules certified for FIPS 140-2 Level 1 but do not require the Top Secret, Secret, or SCI (Sensitive classified information) levels. Note that Federal classifications are Unclassified, Public Trust, Confidential, Secret and Top Secret at increasing levels of security.

Areas covered by FIPS 140-2 include:

- Cryptographic module specification and parts
- Roles
- Services
- Authentication

It provides for a finite state model, physical security, operational environment, cryptographic key management, prevention of electromagnetic interference, and attack mitigation.

Cryptographic modules for compliance with FIPS 140-2 can be provided by the private sector or the public sector for use by the US federal government. The module is provided along with a compliance certificate. The module vendors pay for cryptographic module certification. FIPS 140-2 Certification is provided through the Cryptographic Module Validation Program setup under NIST and Canadian Center for Cybersecurity compliance. FIPS compliance is also recognized around the world as one of the best ways to ensure cryptographic modules are secure. Note that FIPS 140-2 is not a regulatory framework for sensitive data.

FedRAMP

FedRAMP (Federal Risk and Authorization Management Program) is a federal government framework that provides a standardized, uniform set of security standards and processes that CSPs (cloud service providers) must comply with for the security assessment, authorization, and continuous monitoring of cloud products and services used by the U.S. federal government and that handle federal data. It is designed to protect sensitive information and streamline the adoption of secure cloud technologies across government agencies.

FedRAMP was created under a memorandum by the OMB (Office of Management and Budget). GSA (General Services Administration) established the FedRAMP Program Management Office (PMO). FedRAMP resides within the GSA.

FedRAMP consists of three primary entities that authorize services and determine certification:

- Joint Authorization Board (JAB) which includes the CIOs (Chief Information Officers) from the Department of Defense, Department of Homeland Security, and General Service Administration. JAB serves as the primary governance and decision -making body for FedRAMP.
- Program Management Office (PMO) assists and guides agencies through the FedRAMP Authorization process.
- 3PAOs (Third Party Assessment Organizations) play a critical role as independent assessors checking the cloud provider's security implementation and risk posture.

CIA, US Post Office, Department of Defense, Department of Homeland Security, and other federal agencies are required to use FedRAMP. Agencies can search the FedRAMP marketplace for Cloud Service Providers (CSPs) and cloud services that have already been certified and received a FedRAMP designation.

CSPs are required to comply with FedRAMP to do business with a federal agency and must go through a rigorous security assessment to demonstrate that their cloud solutions meet the stringent security standards set by FedRAMP. CSPs seeking authorization undergo assessments performed by accredited and independent Third-Party Assessment Organizations (3PAOs) which are accredited by the American Association for Laboratory Accreditation (A2LA) and is recognized by the FedRAMP Program Management Office (PMO). Based on the 3PAO's assessment and the CSP's security documentation (like the System Security Plan), either the partnering federal agency grants the Authority to Operate (ATO), or a Provisional ATO (P-ATO) may have been issued previously by the JAB (Joint Authorization Board).

After a successful assessment, a CSP can receive authorization to provide their cloud services to federal agencies. The framework also mandates continuous monitoring to ensure that cloud services maintain their security posture over time.

FedRAMP certification is required for CSPs only. However, if a non-CSP organization develops a cloud service that a federal agency will use, then that organization's cloud service needs to meet FedRAMP standards to obtain an Authority to Operate (ATO).

National Institute of Standards and Technology (NIST)

FISMA established the NIST Special Publications 800-53, 800-59, and 800-60. Additional security guidance documents have been developed in support of the project including NIST Special Publications 800-37, 800-39, 800-171, 800-53A and NIST Interagency Report 8011.

NIST maintains a number of standards that define the security requirements for on premises (data centers) and cloud environments. These standards are also required to be followed by all entities doing business with the federal government as well as all financial institutions that collect and manage employee and customer personal sensitive data. You may refer to https://www.nist.gov/ for a detailed description of all NIST standards.

The following is a list of the NIST information technology related standards.

- *NIST 500 -292* – NIST Cloud Computing Reference Architecture (RA) and Taxonomy.
- *NIST 500-294* - Cloud computing security reference architecture – includes conceptual models, reference architecture, and controls framework.
- *NIST 800-30* – Risk management guide for IT systems and data centers – it defines vulnerabilities/threats.
- *NIST 800-37* -- Is a guide for applying a Risk Management Framework (RMF). It defines automation of controls wherever possible, with a focus on continual improvement and near real time risk management and, limiting risk level at the process level and management level are part of the framework. Cost metrics and perceived threats are not a part of the framework.
- *NIST 800*-39 -- Offers a risk management framework that is general enough to be applicable to both the public and private sectors
- *NIST 800-53* – Security and Privacy Controls for Federal Information Systems and Organizations. Firms choose this because these standards are in public domain and available for free and have been widely accepted within US for use by all financial institutions and large corporations that have a business interest in supplying software to the US government or are regulated by the government consumer protection laws. There is no official international acceptance of NIST. However, NIST compliance is viewed as a very positive basis for security compliance.
- *NIST 800-57* – Provides cryptographic key management guidance. It consists of three parts – Part 1 – General practices, Part 2 organization planning, and Part 3 -- specific application guidance. Part 2 is the most important.
- *NIST 800-61* – Computer security Incident handling/response lifecycle. It provides practical guidance for building incident response capabilities and outlines a four-phase life cycle—Preparation; Detection & Analysis; Containment, Eradication, & Recovery; and Post-Incident Activity.
- *NIST 800-63* – Suite provides technical requirements and risk management assurance levels for federal agencies implementing digital identity services.
- *NIST 800-64* -- Guideline is to assist agencies in building security into their IT development processes in every phase of their SDLC.
- *NIST 800-92* -- Guide to Computer Security Log Management, it establishes guidelines and recommendations for securing and managing sensitive log data.
- *NIST 800-122* – Protecting the confidentiality of Personally Identifiable Information focusing on reducing risks of unauthorized disclosure.
- *NIST 800-145* - Working definition for cloud computing as a model for enabling convenient, on-demand network access to a shared pool of configurable computing resources.

- *NIST 800-160* Vol 1 – Systems Security Engineering: Considerations for multi-disciplinary approach in the Engineering of Trustworthy Secure Systems.
- *NIST 800-171* -- protecting Controlled Unclassified Information (CUI) in non-federal systems. It is mandatory for federal contractors (such as defense) and sub-contractors' IT systems and networks

NIST standards have very extensive coverage and need to be studied in-depth to ensure full compliance.

NIST Standards that define Controls

A wide range of security controls are required to ensure security of data. NIST controls are meant to enhance an organization's cybersecurity program, risk posture, information protection, and security standards. NIST 800-53 is mandatory for federal agencies, but any other organization can use the standard to improve their own security program. NIST defines over 1,000 security controls.

Six Principles of NIST

The six principles of NIST are: Identify, Protect, Detect, Respond, Recover. and Govern (added in NIST 2.0)

- ***Identify***. Make a list of all equipment, software, and data your organization uses. This should include all data center servers and end-user devices such as laptops, smartphones, tablets, and point-of-sale devices.
- ***Protect***. The organization should control who can log on to their extended network, and use their organization issued devices as well as BYOD devices. NIST also requires the organization to use appropriate security software to protect their data at rest as well as in transit. All of their security related software must be updated and kept current to ensure that all security patches have been applied. A complete set of policies and standards must be defined, and they should also specify how data is destroyed after use. All workforce members must be made aware of and trained to identify and manage risks.
- ***Detect.*** Monitor the organization's infrastructure on a continual basis to detect all access to their systems and software and prevent unauthorized use. Their security staff must actively monitor any alerts and alarms caused by unauthorized access attempts.
- ***Respond***. The organization should have formal plans for addressing all potential risk events or emergencies that may put their data assets at risk. This plan should prescribe how to keep the business up and running and how to recover from a disaster. Some events may require regulatory responses such as workforce, customers, law enforcement, and regulatory agency notifications. Every event or attack should be investigated and contained. The response plan along with policies and standards should be updated to reflect lessons to prevent future events.
- ***Recover.*** All equipment and software that could be impacted by similar potential future events should be updated. It is always very beneficial to inform the organization's workforce and customers about the events, how they were mitigated and what actions have been taken to prevent such attacks and event in the future.

- ***Govern***, Establishes the organization's cybersecurity risk management strategy, expectations, and policy. Unlike the original five functions which focus on technical implementation, the Govern function dictates how an organization will achieve those outcomes in alignment with its mission, business goals, and risk appetite.

NIST SP 800-53 r5 Control Families

NIST 800-53 r5 consists of 20 control families. The Table below describes the Security and Privacy Control families for NIST SP 800-53 r5. The source document for this is the NIST SP 800-53 Rev.5 Security and Privacy Controls for Information Systems and Organizations.

https://csrc.nist.gov/pubs/sp/800/53/r5/upd1/final .

It lists over 1000 controls (clauses).

ID	FAMILY	ID	FAMILY
AC	Access Control	PE	Physical and Environmental Protection
AT	Awareness and Training	PL	Planning
AU	Audit and Accountability	PM	Program Management
CA	Assessment, Authorization, and Monitoring	PS	Personnel Security
CM	Configuration Management	PT	PII Processing and Transparency
CP	Contingency Planning	RA	Risk Assessment
IA	Identification and Authentication	SA	System and Services Acquisition
IR	Incident Response	SC	System and Communications Protection
MA	Maintenance	SI	System and Information Integrity
MP	Media Protection	SR	Supply Chain Risk Management

Table 5-1 : NIST Families

While it may be useful to review the NIST standard to fully understand the full scope, from the data security perspective, the families of interest from the perspective of data security include AC, AT, AU, CA, CM, IA, IR, RA, and SI. Security teams will need to review the specific controls within each family to determine if it should be included in their compliance list.

Compliance with NIST SP 800-53 r5 is mandatory for U.S. federal agencies and contractors who handle federal information systems. NIST SP 800-53 r5 is also foundational to frameworks such as Nist RMF and NIST CSF, and the Cybersecurity Maturity Model Certification (CMMC) for DoD contractors.

The following table lists a representative selection of NIST controls most relevant for cybersecurity and data security on premises and in the public, private and hybrid cloud environments.

Family	Description
AC	• (AC-1) Policy and Procedures • (AC-2) Account Management • (AC-3) Access Enforcement • (AC-4) Information Flow Enforcement • (AC-5) Separation of Duties • (AC-6) Least Privilege

	• (AC-7) Unsuccessful Login Attempts • (AC-8) System Use Identification • (AC-9) Previous Login Notification, • AC-10) Concurrent Session Control • (AC-11) Device Lock • (AC-12) Session Termination • (AC-13) Supervision and Review – Access Control • (AC-14) Permitted Actions without Identification or Authentication • (AC-15) Automated Marking • (AC-16) Security and Privacy Attributes • (AC-17) Remote Access • (AC-18) Wireless Access • (AC-19) Access Control for Mobile Devices • (AC-20) Use of External Systems • (AC-21) Information Sharing • (AC-22) Publicly Accessible Content • (AC-23) Data Mining Protection • (AC-24) Access Control Decisions • (AC-25) Reference Monitor
AT	• (AT-1) Policy and Procedures • (AT-2) Literacy Training and Awareness • (AT-3) Role-based Training • (AT-4) Training Records • (AT-5) Contacts with Security Groups and Associations • (AT-6) Training Feedback
AU	• (AU-1) Policy and Procedures • (AU-2) Event logging • (AU-3) Content and Audit Records • (AU-4) Audit Log Storage Capacity • (AU-5) Response and Audit logging Features • (AU-6) Audit Record Review, Analysis and Reporting • (AU-7) Audit Record Reduction and Report Generation • (AU-8) Time Stamps • (AU-9) Protection of Audit Information • (AU-10) Non-repudiation • (AU-11) Audit Record Retention • (AU-12) Audit Record Generation • (AU-13) Monitoring and Information Disclosure • (AU-14) Session Audit • (AU-15) Alternate Audit Logging Capability • (AU-16) Cross-organizational Audit logging
CA	• (CA-1) Policy and Procedures • (CA-2) Control Assessments • (CA-3) information Exchange • (CA-4) Security Certification • (CA-5) Plan of Action and Milestones

	• (CA-6) Authorization • (CA-7) Continuous Monitoring • (CA-8) Penetration Testing • (CA-9) internal System Connections
CM	• (CM-1) Policy and Procedures • CM-2) Baseline Configuration • (CM-3) Configuration Change Control • (CM-4) Impact Analysis • (CM-5) Access Restrictions for Change • (CM-6) Configuration Setting • (CM-7) Least Functionality • (CM-8) System Component Inventory • (CM-9) Configuration Management Plan • (CM-10) Software usage Restrictions • (CM-11) User-installed Software • (CM-12) information Location • (CM-13) Data Action Mapping • (CM-14) Signed Components
IA	• (IA-1) Policy and Procedures • (IA-2) Identification and Authentication (Organizational Users) • (IA-3) Device identification and Authentication • (IA-4) Identifier Management • (IA-5) Authentication Management • (IA-6) Authentication Feedback • (IA-7) Cryptographic Module Authentication • (IA-8) Identification and Authentication (Non-organizational users) • (IA-9) Service Identification and Authentication • (IA-10) Adaptive Authentication • (IA-11) Re-authentication • (IA-12) Identity Procedure
IR	• (IR-1) Policy and Procedures • (IR-2) Incident Response Training • (IR-3) Incident Response Testing • (IR-4) incident Handling • (IR-5) incident Monitoring • (IR-6) Incident Reporting • (IR-7) Incident Response Assistance • (IR-8) incident Response Plan • (IR-9) Information Spillage Response • (IR-10) Integrated information Security Analysis Team
RA	• (RA-1) Policy and Procedures • (RA-2) Security Categorization • (RA-3) Risk Assessment • (RA-4) Risk Assessment Update • (RA-5) Vulnerability Monitoring Scanning • (RA-6) Technical Surveillance Countermeasures Survey

	• (RA-7) Risk Response • (RA-8) Risk Impact Assessments • (RA-9) Criticality Analysis • (RA-10) Threat Hunting
SI	• (SI-1) Policies and Procedures • (SI-2) Flaw remediation • (SI-3) Malicious Code Protection • (SI-4) System Monitoring • (SI-5) Security Alerts, Advisories, and Directives • (SI-6) Security Privacy Protection Verification • (SI-7) Software, Firmware and Information Integrity • (SI-8) Spam Protection • (SI-9) information Input Restrictions • (SI-10) Information Input Validation • (SI-11) Error Handling • (SI-12) Information Management and Retention • (SI-13) Predictable Failure Prevention • (SI-14) Non-persistence • (SI-15) Information Output Filtering • (SI-16) Memory Protection • (SI-17) Fail-safe Procedures • (SI-18) Personally Identifiable information Quality Operations • (SI-19) De-Identification • (SI-20) Tainting • (SI-21) Information Refresh • (SI-22) Information Diversity • (SI-23) Information Fragmentation

Table 5-2 : NIST Control applicable to Data Security

Given this vast number of clauses for the NIST standards, one way to address them is for organizations to create their own standards documents that cover the domains and list the clauses that need to be addressed by creating controls applicable to their business domain and their organization. NIST 800-53 is a Cybersecurity Framework

As a cybersecurity framework, NIST 800-53 is specifically a risk-based detailed and comprehensive catalog of security and privacy controls designed to protect information systems and manage cybersecurity risks for U.S. federal agencies and related contractors. While the term "framework" is often associated with the NIST CSF (Cybersecurity Framework), which provides a high-level, voluntary approach, NIST SP 800-53 offers a more comprehensive, mandatory (for federal systems) set of controls required by NIST RMF.

Here's a breakdown of why NIST 800-53 is considered a framework:

- A Structured System of Controls: It provides a catalog of specific security and privacy controls that organizations must implement to protect their information systems.

- Risk-Based Approach: The framework guides organizations in selecting and implementing controls based on the specific risks to their systems, ensuring a standardized approach to risk management.

Comprehensive and Detailed: Unlike the more voluntary NIST Cybersecurity Framework (CSF), NIST SP 800-53 offers a broad and detailed set of security and privacy controls for federal information systems

NIST Cybersecurity Framework (CSF)

NIST CSF is a voluntary framework to manage and reduce cybersecurity risk. It provides standards, guidelines, and best practices along with a comprehensive approach to cybersecurity, encompassing risk management, governance, and incident response. It is organized around six core functions: Identify, Protect, Detect, Respond, Recover, and Govern. These functions provide a high-level overview of the different aspects of cybersecurity management. It provides a taxonomy of cybersecurity outcomes, to be used by any organization. It includes specific guidance on managing supply chain risks and integrating privacy considerations.

Source: NIST CSF Documentation: https://www.nist.gov/cyberframework

Figure 5-1 : NIST Cybersecurity Framework (CSF)

Using this framework, requires assessing the current posture, identifying gaps, prioritizing and implementing improvements, communicating and collaborating across teams. This framework is used in the private sector to demonstrate security compliance for critical infrastructure by organizations doing business with the federal government.

- **Identify** – the organization's assets, data, risks, services and people.
- **Protect** -- secure these assets against adverse cybersecurity events.
- **Detect** – perform timely discovery of anomalies, compromises, and cybersecurity events.
- **Respond** -- contain and manage incidents, analyze the cause, mitigate and minimize further damage.
- **Recover** -- restore normal operations, and reduce incident impact

- **Govern** -- understand the context for cybersecurity, establish the cybersecurity strategy, identify the supply chain risk, define the roles and responsibilities, and authorities. Also establish policies, and the oversight of cybersecurity strategy.

NIST CSF Uses NIST SP 800-53 Controls

NIST 800-53 as described earlier is a comprehensive catalog of security and privacy controls that the CSF uses. NIST CSF is a methodology and NIST 800-53 provides the specific set of security and privacy controls that are selected, implemented, and monitored within the CSF process. An organization needs to choose the appropriate controls from the extensive NIST SP 800-53 catalog that are necessary for their specific systems and risk profile.

NIST RMF -- NIST 800-37 rev 2.0

NIST RMF (Risk Management Framework) is a structured, risk-based approach which provides a comprehensive set of guidelines for managing and reducing cybersecurity risks, including those related to IAM. NIST RMF is mandatory for federal agencies and organizations handling federal data. The NIST Special Publication 800-37 provides the official guidelines and methodology for applying the RMF as a systematic process for identifying, assessing, selecting, implementing, authorizing, and monitoring security controls to protect sensitive data and systems. The RMF is a seven-step process -- Prepare, Categorize, Select, Implement, Assess, Authorize, and Monitor -- that can be integrated into the system development lifecycle.

The NIST RMF Steps

NIST RMF helps ensure that, throughout the SDLC, information systems, organizations, and individuals are adequately protected, and that authorizing officials have the information needed to make credible, risk-based decisions regarding the operation or use of systems or the provision of common controls.

NIST RMF is organized into seven steps, including preparing, categorizing, selecting, implementing, assessing, authorizing, and monitoring.

- **Prepare** – establish security and privacy strategy and define roles. Establish risk management policies and risk appetite,
- **Categorize** – classify based on types of information and impact on CIA (Confidentiality, Integrity, Availability).
- **Select** – the appropriate NIST 800-53 r5 controls.
- **Implement** – design, develop and deploy the security privacy controls.
- **Assess** – determine if the controls are working and assess the effectiveness.
- **Authorize** – an authorized individual authorizes the decision to either operate based on the identified residual risk or remediate the implementation to conform with the risk appetite. The authorization boundary includes the people, processes, and information technologies (i.e., system elements) that are part of each system supporting the organization's missions and business functions.

- **Monitor** – continuously or periodically monitor and assess security status, and report on incidents or changes.

These are illustrated in the following diagram:

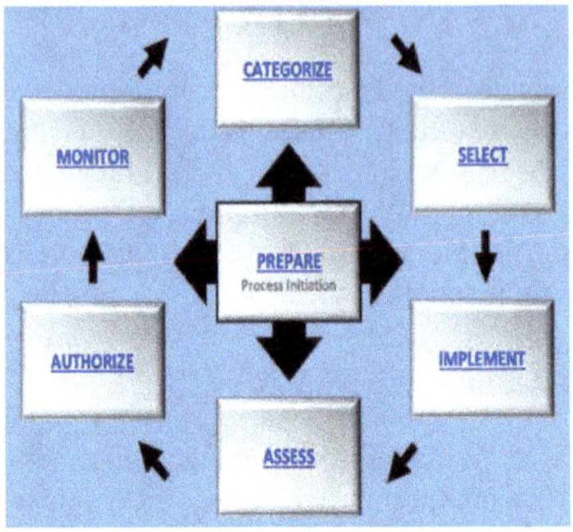

Source: NIST RMF on-line Documentation

Figure 5-4 : NIST Risk Management Framework (RMF)

NIST RMF Uses NIST SP 800-53 Controls

NIST 800-53 as described earlier is a comprehensive catalog of security and privacy controls that the RMF uses. NIST RMF is a methodology and NIST 800-53 provides the specific set of security and privacy controls that are selected, implemented, and monitored within the RMF process. An organization needs to choose the appropriate controls from the extensive NIST SP 800-53 catalog that are necessary for their specific systems and risk profile.

NIST RMF vs NIST CSF

The following is a quick high-level comparison between NIST RMF and NIST CSF.

Category	NIST RMF	NIST CSF
Purpose	Structured process for managing cybersecurity risk in US Federal agencies ad organizations handling federal data	Flexible framework for managing cybersecurity risk across public and private sector.
Structure	Rigid 7-step process	Flexible, 6 function model (including the new Govern function
Audience	US Federal agencies and contractors	Private sector, critical infrastructure
Adoption	Mandatory for US federal systems	Voluntary, widely adaptable

Table 5-3 : NIST RMF vs. NIST CSF

NIST 800-171 Rev 3

NIST 800-171 Rev 3 is a set of recommended security controls and requirements designed to protect Controlled Unclassified Information (CUI) in non-federal systems and organizations. It outlines a structured approach to cybersecurity by detailing specific controls across 14 families that define requirements to safeguard the confidentiality and privacy of CUI when it resides on non-federal systems.

Key Aspects of the NIST SP 800-171 Framework

NIST SP 800-171 provides a standardized framework for non-federal organizations that handle CUI as part of their business with the U.S. government. It is intended to help them safeguard sensitive data.

The 110 security requirements grouped into 14 families of this framework define the security requirements that address various aspects of information security, including access control, incident response, and system security. These requirements are a mix of technical controls such as encryption and access controls and non-technical controls such as training and awareness. These 14 families are:

1. Access Control
2. Awareness and Training
3. Audit and Accountability
4. Configuration Management
5. Identification and Authentication
6. Incident Response
7. Maintenance
8. Media Protection
9. Personnel Security
10. Physical Protection
11. Risk Assessment
12. Security Assessment and Monitoring
13. System and Communications Protection
14. System and Information Integrity

The requirements in NIST SP 800-171 are derived from NIST SP 800-53, a security framework for federal systems, but they are tailored to the specific needs of protecting CUI in non-federal environments.

The framework is periodically updated to reflect new cyber threats and technological changes, with the latest version being Revision 3, released in May 2024.

NIST SP 800-171 Certification

Organizations can achieve compliance through a process of self-assessment and documentation, which is then submitted to the Supplier Performance Risk System (SPRS) database. This involves identifying the CUI information, implementing selected and applicable security controls from the 110 outlined in NIST SP 800-171, and creating a System Security Plan (SSP). Based on this a Plan of Action and

Milestones (POAM) is developed. It can then be used for CMMC 3PaO certification

International Standards

This section describes the most common international standards actively used worldwide including the United States by all large organizations that are required to comply with these standards due to the nature of their business, size, or the type of data collected and managed by them.

ISO/IEC and ISO Standards Overview

ISO/IEC standards that apply to information technology include the following:

- *ISO/IEC 17788* — Documents provide an overview of cloud computing along with a set of terms and definitions.
- *ISO/IEC 17789* -- Specifies the cloud computing reference architecture including cloud roles, activities, functional components, diagrams, and their relationships.
- *ISO/IEC 20000* -- the international Service Management standard.
- *ISO 27001* – Dictates creation of an organizational information security management system (ISMS). Details what organizations can be *certified* for ISMS. This is preferred due to international acceptance, but it is not easy to implement. Furthermore, it does not favor cloud based, PC or open-source technologies. It has 35 control objectives, 114 controls across 14 domains including: InfoSec policies, organization of information security, HR security, asset management, access control, cryptographic, physical environment security, operations security, system acquisition, supplier relationship, information security incident management, information security business continuity management, and compliance.
- *ISO 27002* - Implementation guidance for ISO 27001 - electing, implementing, and managing information security controls mapped to an ISMS. An *audit* against it shows if the organization has adequate controls to meet ISO 27001. Note that SAS 70 (outdated) and SSAE 16 are audit standards for services providers and include some review of audit controls but not a cohesive program.
- *ISO/IEC 27008* – Provides guidance for auditors on ISMS.
- *ISO/IEC 27014* – IT – Provides guidance on principles for security techniques for governance of information security by which organizations can evaluate, direct, monitor, and communicate the information security related activities within the organization.
- *ISO/IEC 27017* – Information Technology – Code of Practice for Security techniques based on ISO/IEC 27002 for cloud services.
- *ISO 27018* – Privacy requirements for CSPs.
- *ISO/IEC 27034* – Offers guidance on information security to those specifying, designing, and programming or procuring, implementing, and using application systems. Defines concepts frameworks and processes. Defines Application Security Management Process (ASMP)

that assess security risks and lays out ANFs (Application Normative Frameworks). It also Lays out the ONF (Organization Normative Framework) for all components and applications defining business, regulatory, technical contexts, specifications, roles, processes, and Application Security Control (ASC) library. Multiple ANFs can be used with one ONF for each application.

- *ISO/IEC 27035* Preparation- Defines the steps: 1) Detection and Analysis, 2) Containment, Eradication, Recovery, 3) Postmortem, and 4) Preparation which handles communication, hardware, and documentation (lists, baselines, network diagrams). Detection Analysis covers alerts (end-point protection, network, host monitoring, SIEM). Eradication, Containment and Recovery takes systems off-line and cleans up compromised devices. Postmortem is a review to determine how to do better. For Cloud Preparation, it requires defining SLAs (Service Level Agreements), Governance with the CSP (Cloud Service Provider), how to get data specific to SaaS/PaaS, cloud junpkits (tools, software, and documentation needed for rapid incident response), collecting logs from clouds, and data server access. Note that for Detection, approaches used include logs from APIs (based on use of immutable servers), application stack maps, threat modeling, table-top exercise, monitoring cloud Management Plane.
- *ISO 27037:2012* – Evidence preservation.
- *ISO/IEC 27040* — provides security guidance for storage systems and ecosystems and information risks associated with the confidentiality, integrity and availability of information on various data storage technologies.
- *ISO/IEC 27050* – Electronic Discovery – Part 1 – Overview and Concepts
- *ISO/IEC 29100* – For PI (personal Information) Security -- Information technology – security techniques – privacy framework. Is applicable to natural persons and orgs involved in specifying, procuring, architecting, designing, developing, testing, maintaining, administering, and operating information and communications systems for PI.
- *ISO 31000:2018* – Risk Management - Principles and Guidelines, a framework for managing risk. PDCA (Plan, Do, Check, Act).
- *ISO 31010:2019* -- Risk management – Risk assessment techniques – provides guidance on the selection and application of techniques for assessing risk in a wide range of situations.
- *ISO/IEC 38500* – IT - Governance of IT for the organization – Provides a framework for effective governance of IT to assist those at the highest level of orgs to understand and fulfill their legal, regulatory and ethical obligations.

IEC 642443 is an international series of standards that address cybersecurity for operational technology in automation and control systems. It is mentioned here for awareness although it does not directly apply to data systems security for banking and financial institutions or large corporations.

ISO 270001 and ISO 270002 Standards

ISO 270001 and ISO 270002 are the most followed standards and are described in further detail here. They establish the requirements and procedures for creating an information security management system (ISMS). This serves both, as an operational controls regimen as well as an important audit and compliance guideline. The vocabulary and an overview of the ISO 270001 and ISO 270002 are provided in the ISO27000 standard.

A related standard, the ISO27701, is the international standard for privacy information management and its objective is to protect private information assets and to demonstrate compliance with privacy and data protection regulations.

Note that there are equivalent ISO/IEC standards to the ISO standards. ISO/IEC 27001 and ISO 27001 are similarly targeted at an ISMS. ISO and ISO/IEC are truly international standards but NIST 800-37 (Risk) and SOX (Financial) are US only, and GDPR is European.

Commonly known as ISO 27001, it is an international standard for Information Security Management Systems (ISMS) and a code of practice for information security controls. It requires organizations to conduct a comprehensive risk assessment, establish security policies and procedures, implement appropriate security controls. Annex A of the ISO 27001 documentation lists the controls.

ISO 27002 provides practical, detailed descriptions and guidance on implementing the information security controls selected from Annex A of ISO 27001. ISO 27002 is a controls implementation guidance but there is no certification for it.

An organization will need to implement the applicable controls from ISO 27001 Annex A, which documents how the controls are applied, and the rationale for the implementation of the control. Additionally, for each control that is excluded the organization should document the rationale for exclusion. Together these constitute the Statement of Applicability (SoA) which, in addition to the risk assessment, is a mandatory part of ISO 27001.

Annex A is a comprehensive list of 93 security controls, organized thematically (Organizational, Technological, Physical, People) as described below:

- Organizational controls: 37 controls related to how an organization manages information security.
- Technological controls: 34 controls focused on security in technology and systems, such as malware protection and data encryption.
- Physical controls: 14 controls addressing physical security, like securing physical and environmental areas.
- People controls: 8 controls covering the human element of security, including secure human resource management and personnel security.

Most of the security related controls are listed under Technical Controls.

The standard provides a framework for establishing, implementing, maintaining, and continually improving an ISMS. It allows organizations to be certified as compliant with international security standards, making it a strong choice for organizations seeking to demonstrate their commitment to security best practices.

Key Components of an ISMS:

The following lists the components and controls that an organization must implement for a comprehensive approach to safeguarding it's information assets.

1. *Policies and Procedures*: how the organization will handle information security matters, including access controls, data handling, and incident response.
2. *Controls*: specific measures implemented to protect information assets, such as firewalls, encryption, and access restrictions.
3. *Risk Management*: this involves identifying, assessing, managing risks to information security.
4. *Continuous Improvement*: ISMS is not a static system; it's designed to be continuously reviewed and improved to adapt to evolving threats and business needs.
5. *Enhanced Security*: ISMS provides a comprehensive approach to information security, reducing the risk of data breaches and other security incidents.
6. *Improved Compliance*: ISMS helps organizations meet regulatory requirements and contractual obligations related to information security.
7. *Reduced Costs*: proactively manage risks; avoid data breaches & compliance penalties.
8. *Increased Customer Trust*: demonstrates an org's commitment to data security
9. *Business Continuity*: maintain business operations in the event of a security incident.

ISO 27001 Certification

ISO 27001 compliance is voluntary. However, certification obtained by organizations from an accredited certification body demonstrates that an organization's Information ISMS meets the requirements of the ISO/IEC 27001 standard. This process typically involves the following three steps.

Implementing an ISMS

The requirements for establishing, implementing, maintaining and continually improving an ISMS were developed jointly by International Standards Organization (ISO) and International Electrotechnical Commission (IEC). These include:

- Determine which parts of the organization are covered by the ISMS, identify its assets such as data and infrastructure, processes, and stakeholders.
- Perform a thorough risk assessment to identify potential threats and vulnerabilities to information assets. Document the process and results. Assess the likelihood of an event and potential impact and create a prioritized list.
- Select from Annex A the applicable security controls based on your organization's business and the level of security required.

- Create and document information security policies, roles and responsibilities, and operational procedures.
- Establish security awareness training and deliver it to all personnel, ensuring they understand their roles and responsibilities and the importance of information security.

Conducting internal audits,

Once the ISMS has been established, the organization needs to monitor, measure, and review the effectiveness of the ISMS through internal audits and management reviews. Audits are performed in two stages.

- Stage 1 Audit: An initial audit to review the ISMS documentation and ensure it meets the standard's requirements.
- Stage 2 Audit: A comprehensive audit to verify that the ISMS has been implemented effectively and is operating as documented.

After certification, regular surveillance audits are conducted to ensure ongoing compliance and continuous improvement.

Undergoing a Certification Audit by an External Certification Body

Certification can be a complex process. The organization should invest in automation tools to streamline and expedite the certification process. Security teams should also engage mid- to senior-level managers who understand their departments best to ensure effective implementation. It is important to gain support from top-level executives to ensure organizational commitment of resources and authority to the certification process. Comprehensive documentation of policies, procedures, and controls is essential to demonstrate compliance and prove diligence.

ISO 27001 certifications are performed by independent, third-party Certification Bodies (CBs) that are licensed by an Accreditation Body (national or international authorities) to conduct the audits and assess compliance with the standard.

ISO 42001

ISO 42001 is a new international standard for an Artificial Intelligence Management System (AIMS), providing organizations with requirements for establishing, implementing, maintaining, and improving their approach to responsible AI development and use. It is a structured framework for governing AI, managing AI-related risks (such as bias, security threats, and privacy issues), and ensuring ethical considerations are addressed throughout the entire AI lifecycle.

Key highlights of this framework

- **Risk Management:** A core function of the standard is to provide methods for identifying, assessing, and mitigating risks associated with AI technologies.
- **AI Lifecycle Management:** The standard addresses the entire AI lifecycle, from planning and development to deployment and ongoing operations, ensuring risks are managed at every stage.
- **Ethical and Responsible AI:** Promotes responsible AI development and use, focusing on ethical considerations and societal impacts.

- **Integration with Other Standards:** The framework can be integrated with other ISO management systems, such as ISO 9001 (quality management) and ISO 27001 (information security), to create a comprehensive approach to managing different aspects of a business.

ENISA

ENISA (European Union Agency for Cybersecurity) does not spell out the types of assurance due to the large variety of providers and regulators. AS per ENISA, cloud risk assessment should provide means for customers to assess risks due to cloud migration, compare offerings from CSPs, reduce assurance burdens on CSPs but it does not reduce the risk of regulatory compliance.

ENISA provides regulatory bridges, threat landscapes, and practical guidelines for compliance, programmatic management as a defining trait of cloud computing even specifying through "WS API" which is specifically associated with the European Union Vulnerability Database (EUVD) service as a RESTful application programming interface provided ENISA.

ISO/IEC 27001 and ISO/IEC 27002 Controls

The ISO/IEC 27002 requires organizations to implement controls that meet its standards for an information security management system. A "control" in the ISO standard is defined as a measure that modifies or maintains risk. An information security policy, for example, can only maintain risk, whereas compliance with the information security policy can modify risk. Moreover, some controls describe the same generic measure in different risk contexts.

ISO 27002:2022 has 93 controls in the 2022 edition. These security controls are categorized into four control "themes."

- People (8 controls)
- Organizational (37 controls)
- Technological (34 controls)
- Physical (14 controls)

Furthermore, ISO 27001:2022 controls have five types of attributes so that they're easier to categorize. You can see the complete list of these 93 controls with their descriptions at the website:

https://www.iso27001security.com/html/27002.html

The 93 controls are each tagged with one or more values from each of these five 'attributes' so they can be grouped, selected, or filtered in other ways too:

- Control type: preventive, detective and corrective.
- Information security properties: confidentiality, integrity and availability.
- Cybersecurity concepts: identify, protect, detect, respond and recover.
- Operational capabilities: continuity, application security, governance, asset management, information security protection assurance, human resource security, physical security, system and network security, secure configuration, identity and access management, threat and vulnerability

management, continuity, supplier relationships security, legal and compliance, and information security event management.

- Security domains: governance and ecosystem, protection, defense and resilience.

The table that follows lists all 93 ISO controls.

#	ID	Name	Type
1	5.1	Policies for information security	Preventive
2	5.2	Information security roles and responsibilities	Preventive
3	5.3	Segregation of duties	Preventive
4	5.4	Management responsibilities	Preventive
5	5.5	Contact with authorities	Preventive
6	5.6	Contact with special interest groups	Preventive
7	5.7	Threat intelligence	Preventive
8	5.8	Information security in project management	Preventive
9	5.9	Inventory of information and other associated assets	Preventive
10	5.10	Acceptable use of information and other associated assets	Preventive
11	5.11	Return of assets	Preventive
12	5.12	Classification of information	Preventive
13	5.13	Labelling of information	Preventive
14	5.14	Information transfer	Preventive
15	5.15	Access control	Preventive
16	5.16	Identity management	Preventive
17	5.17	Authentication information	Preventive
18	5.18	Access rights	Preventive
19	5.19	Information security in supplier relationships	Preventive
20	5.20	Addressing information security within supplier agreements	Preventive
21	5.21	Managing information security in the ICT supply chain	Preventive
22	5.22	Monitoring, review and change management of supplier services	Preventive
23	5.23	Information security for use of cloud services	Preventive
24	5.24	Information security incident management planning and preparation	Corrective
25	5.25	Assessment and decision on information security events	Detective
26	5.26	Response to information security incidents	Corrective
27	5.27	Learning from information security incidents	Preventive
28	5.28	Collection of evidence	Corrective

29	5.29	Information security during disruption	Preventive
31	5.31	Legal, statutory, regulatory and contractual requirements	Preventive
32	5.32	Intellectual property rights	Preventive
33	5.33	Protection of records	Preventive
34	5.34	Privacy and protection of PII	Preventive
35	5.35	Independent review of information security	Preventive
36	5.36	Compliance with policies, rules and standards for information security	Preventive
37	5.37	Documented operating procedures	Preventive
38	6.1	Screening	Preventive
39	6.2	Terms and conditions of employment	Preventive
40	6.3	Information security awareness, education and training	Preventive
41	6.4	Disciplinary process	Preventive
42	6.5	Responsibilities after termination or change of employment	Preventive
43	6.6	Confidentiality or non-disclosure agreements	Preventive
44	6.7	Remote working	
45	6.8	Information security event reporting	Detective
46	7.1	Physical security perimeters	Preventive
47	7.2	Physical entry	Preventive
48	7.3	Securing offices, rooms and facilities	Preventive
49	7.4	Physical security monitoring	Preventive
50	7.5	Protecting against physical and environmental threats	Preventive
51	7.6	Working in secure areas	Preventive
52	7.7	Clear desk and clear screen	Preventive
53	7.8	Equipment siting and protection	Preventive
54	7.9	Security of assets off-premises	Preventive
55	7.10	Storage media	Preventive
56	7.11	Supporting utilities	Preventive
57	7.12	Cabling security	Preventive
58	7.13	Equipment maintenance	Preventive
59	7.14	Secure disposal or re-use of equipment	Preventive
60	8.1	User endpoint devices	Preventive
61	8.2	Privileged access rights	Preventive
62	8.3	Information access restriction	Preventive
63	8.4	Access to source code	Preventive
64	8.5	Secure authentication	Preventive
65	8.6	Capacity management	Preventive
66	8.7	Protection against malware	Preventive

67	8.8	Management of technical vulnerabilities	Preventive
68	8.9	Configuration management	Preventive
69	8.10	Information deletion	Preventive
71	8.12	Data leakage prevention	Preventive
72	8.13	Information backup	Corrective
73	8.14	Redundancy of information processing facilities	Preventive
74	8.15	Logging	Detective
75	8.16	Monitoring activities	Detective
76	8.17	Clock synchronization	Detective
77	8.18	Use of privileged utility programs	Preventive
78	8.19	Installation of software on operational systems	Preventive
79	8.20	Networks security	Preventive
80	8.21	Security of network services	Preventive
81	8.22	Segregation of networks	Preventive
82	8.23	Web filtering	Preventive
83	8.24	Use of cryptography	Preventive
84	8.25	Secure development life cycle	Preventive
85	8.26	Application security requirements	Preventive
86	8.27	Secure system architecture and engineering principles	Preventive
87	8.28	Secure coding	Preventive
88	8.29	Security testing in development and acceptance	Preventive
89	8.30	Outsourced development	Preventive
90	8.31	Separation of development, test and production environments	Preventive
91	8.32	Change management	Preventive
92	8.33	Test information	Preventive
93	8.34	Protection of information systems during audit testing	Preventive

Table 5-5 : ISO 27002:2022 Controls

Other US and International Standards and Frameworks

While NIST and ISO/IEC are the most widely used US and international standards, many other US and international standards and frameworks are also widely used, some of them mandatory for organizations providing services to the US government. This section describes some of the more prominent ones.

CIS Framework

The core concept of the CIS (Center for Internet Security) framework is the set of Critical Security Controls (CSCs), which are a prioritized set of best practices for cyber defense. CIS provides specific, practical safeguards grouped into categories like asset inventory, secure configurations, malware defenses, and vulnerability management. It provides actionable guidance consisting of specific and practical steps required to be implemented. It also focuses on prioritized recommendations which address the most prevalent and impactful cyber-attack vectors.

The CIS framework provides scalability in that it offers three categories of controls (Basic, Foundational, and Organizational), allowing organizations to implement them in stages based on their resources and risk. These levels are:

- IG1 (Basic Cyber Hygiene): Foundational controls for all orgs to prevent the common attacks. These are usually the first implementation of CIS.
- IG2 (Foundational): Builds on IG1, advanced technical controls for organizations with complex systems.
- IG3 (Organizational): most advanced safeguards for orgs with significant resources and expertise and a need for more stringent security.

Flexibility and Measurability: CIS controls are practical, measurable, and designed to work with other frameworks and governance schemes.

CIS Controls Categories

The CIS Controls as a collection of safeguards are organized into specific categories that cover key security aspects such as.

- **Asset Inventory:** keeping track of all hardware and software assets.
- **Secure Configuration:** ensuring enterprise assets and software are configured securely.
- **Malware Defenses:** implementing measures to detect and prevent malware.
- **Continuous Vulnerability Management:** regularly identifying and addressing vulnerabilities.
- **Incident Response Management:** develop plan and processes for handling security incidents.

CIS Framework Certification and Use

CIS provides a CIS Controls Accreditation program for organizations. It is a rigorous standard for services like CIS Controls implementation, auditing, and assessment services. Accreditation is granted by CREST (Council for Registered Ethical Security Testers). CREST certification is an international accreditation for technical information security companies and professionals, ensuring they meet rigorous legal, ethical, and technical standards, particularly for penetration testing, incident response, threat intelligence, and other cybersecurity services. For individuals, certifications include the GIAC's (Global Information Assurance Certification), GCCC (GIAC Critical Controls Certification) from GIAC, or training from organizations like the SANS Institute. These certifications validate skills in implementing the CIS Controls.

Certification and Use Process

The steps for certification and use of CIS include the following:

1. Assess Organization's Current State: Understand the organization's cybersecurity posture and resources.
2. Start with IG1: begin by implementing the basic cyber hygiene practices in Group 1.
3. Move to Higher Groups as Needed: As the organization's security maturity grows, the security team can adopt the more advanced controls in IG2 and IG3.
4. Using CIS Tools: The CIS Center for Internet Security offers tools like the CIS CSAT Pro help organizations assess their progress and manage their implementation.

COBIT

COBIT (Control Objectives for Information and Related Technologies) is a framework developed by ISACA (originally known as the Information Systems Audit and Control Association), a global professional organization which focuses on providing education, certifications, and resources in IT governance, cybersecurity, risk, and audit to professionals and the public. ISACA educates and also provides certification for IT audit, security, risk, and governance. The COBIT framework provides guidelines for managing IT governance, digital risk and cybersecurity thereby promoting digital trust. It works globally with governments, organizations and other institutions to shape digital policy and builds skilled public sector teams.

As a structured framework, COBIT offers a practical and structured approach for managing an organization's IT systems and data. Through its business focused approach, it aligns technical issues and control requirements and tools with business risk. The core aspects of COBIT include:

- Control objectives for effectively managing the IT processes.
- Management guidelines and tools for assigning roles and responsibilities to provide a uniform structure.
- Maturity models to assess capability and maturity of IT processes.
- Process descriptions to define inputs, outputs and key activities in a common language.

COBIT helps ensure strategic alignment between business objectives and IT strategy and strengthens risk management. By promoting transparency and accountability COBIT can help organizations in regulatory compliance such as SOX (Sarbanes -Oxley Act).

COBIT Certification

COBIT certifies individuals who complete the required training and pass the exams for the chosen certification level including:

1. COBIT 2019 Foundation – validates understanding of the COBIT Framework, its principles and managing IT.
2. COBIT 2019 Design and Implementation – for those designing a custom governance system for their organization.
3. COBIT 2019 Assessor – for experienced professionals who perform formal process assessments.

4. COBIT 2019 Bridge – test knowledge of changes from the previous COBIT 5 certification.

SOC (System and Organization Control)

An auditing standard for service organizations that handle customer data, focusing on security, availability, processing integrity, confidentiality, and privacy. SOC reports are third-party audits of a service organization's internal controls, specifically focusing on financial reporting (SOC 1) or security and other operational aspects (SOC 2). These reports provide assurance to customers that the organization's controls are designed and operating effectively, helping them manage risk and understand the security of their data. The three types of SOC reports are:

- **SOC 1:** Focuses on controls relevant to a user entity's internal control over financial reporting. It's often used by service organizations that process financial data or have a significant impact on a client's financial statements.
- **SOC 2:** Addresses a service provider organization's controls related to security, availability, processing integrity, confidentiality, and privacy. It's particularly relevant for organizations providing cloud services, SaaS companies, data centers and manage service providers.
    - **Type I and Type II:** SOC: reports can be Type I (covering a point in time) or Type II (much more detailed report covering a period of time and assessing the effectiveness of controls).
- **SOC 3:** is a publicly available, general-use report summarizing a service organization's security controls and compliance, focusing on security, availability, processing integrity, confidentiality, and privacy. It is less detailed than a SO 2 report

We will take a closer look at the SOC 2 report content and format.

SOC 2 Examination Steps

The following lists the key steps in a SOC2 examination process:

1. Scoping: – a professional auditor works with the security team at the organization for a better understanding of the overall environment.
2. Audit Planning: – the auditor walks the organization's security team through the SOC 2 examination process and provides an information request list IRL (In Real Life, a comprehensive, itemized list of information and evidence that security teams must collect to perform an investigation or complete an audit).
3. Testing and Review of Evidence -- the auditor begins reviewing the evidence and completes the required testing which is either performed remotely on site or a combination of both.
4. Closing Meeting and Draft Report -- the auditor can officially accept the evidence and begin preparing the draft report. When the organization receives the draft report, it will have the opportunity to provide comments and suggest updates; the draft report is returned with a signed copy of the management representative's letter that accompanies it. This is an important part of the independent nature of the auditor relationship.

5. The Final Report -- The SOC 2 examination comes to an end with the delivery of the final report. The auditor will address any comments the firm had submitted in the draft at which point the report is finalized and delivered to the firm electronically and also, if requested, as a hard copy. The following diagram is a snapshot of a very small part of an SOC 2 report. If you start implementing a SOC 2 report, you will need to familiarize yourself with all of the criteria sections.

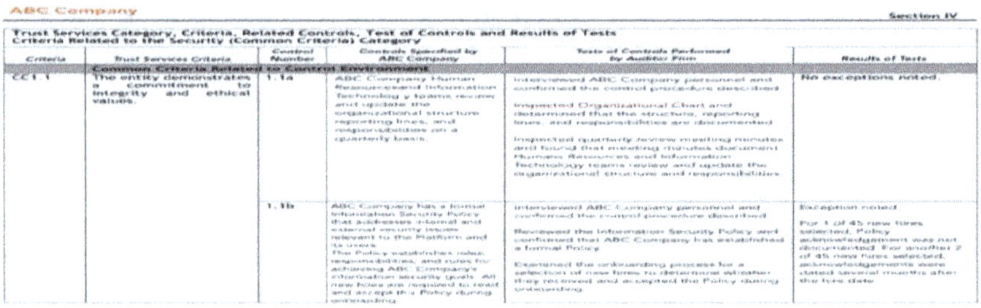

ABC Company — Section IV

Trust Services Category, Criteria, Related Controls, Test of Controls and Results of Tests
Criteria Related to the Security (Common Criteria) Category

Criteria	Trust Services Criteria	Control Number	Controls Specified by ABC Company	Tests of Controls Performed by Auditor Firm	Results of Tests
	Common Criteria Related to Control Environment				
CC1.1	The entity demonstrates a commitment to integrity and ethical values.	1.1a	[illegible]	[illegible]	No exceptions noted.
		1.1b	[illegible]	[illegible]	[illegible]

Figure 5-6 : SOC 2 Report Example

CSA CCM

CSA CCM (Cloud Security Alliance - Cloud Controls Matrix) is a cybersecurity framework for cloud security controls providing a detailed checklist of 197 control objectives structured into 17 domains. It offers standardized security, governance, and compliance best practices for cloud service providers (CSPs). The CCM is a free, publicly available resource that can be implemented using the CCM Machine Readable Version or guideline

- Comprehensive Coverage: Covers areas like application security, data security, identity management, and incident response.
- Audit Guidance: Provides a baseline for assessing cloud security posture, often paired with the Consensus Assessments Initiative Questionnaire (CAIQ).
- Standardization: Maps to industry regulations and standards, facilitating compliance and risk management.
- Alignment: Designed for cloud Service Providers (CSPs) and enterprise customers to align on security expectations.

For a detailed list of CSA CCM families and controls refer to the documentation at:

https://cloudsecurityalliance.org/research/cloud-controls-matrix#

CCM and NIST Domains Most Relevant to Cybersecurity

CSA CCM has a lot of similarity with the NIST families of controls as described in the following table. The numbers column shows the number of specific controls under this topic.

NIST	CSA

AC	25	Access Control	AIS	7	Application and Interface Security
AU	6	Audit and Accountability	BCR	11	Business Continuity Management and Ops Resilience
CA	9	Assessment, Authorization and Monitoring	GRC	8	Governance, Risk Management and Compliance
CM	14	Configuration Management	HRS	13	Human Resources Security
IA	12	Authentication and Authorization	IAM	16	Identity and Access Management
IR	10	Incident Response	TVM	10	Threat and Vulnerability Management
PT	8	Personally Identifiable Information Processing and Planning	UEM	14	Universal End-point Management
RA	10	Risk Assessment			No direct equivalent but spread across the rest.
SC	23	System and Communication Protection			No direct equivalent

Table 5-6. : Comparison of NIST and CSA CCM Control Families

CMMI

CMMI (Capability Maturity Model Integration) is a comprehensive framework of best practices for improving process maturity and performance. The CMMI began in 1987 as the Capability Maturity Model (CMM), a project at the Software Engineering Institute (SEI).

Quality Managed CMMI Level 4 (or CMMI4) is a specific high-maturity milestone within that framework in which organizations use statistical techniques to control and predict performance. CMMI emphasizes the use of data to understand and control processes, and it includes collecting data on process performance, analyzing it statistically, and using the results to manage projects and improve processes, predict process outcomes more accurately, and identify potential problems before they escalate.

CMMI4 Process Areas

Key aspects of the CMMI4 framework include:

22 Process Areas: The Continuous Representation models process capability within each of the 22 process areas individually. It allows the organization to tailor their improvement efforts.

Process Improvement Framework: CMMI is not a methodology itself, but rather a framework that organizations can use to improve their existing processes.

Maturity Levels: It defines five maturity levels (Initial, Managed, Defined, Quantitatively Managed, and Optimizing) that organizations can achieve as they enhance their processes.

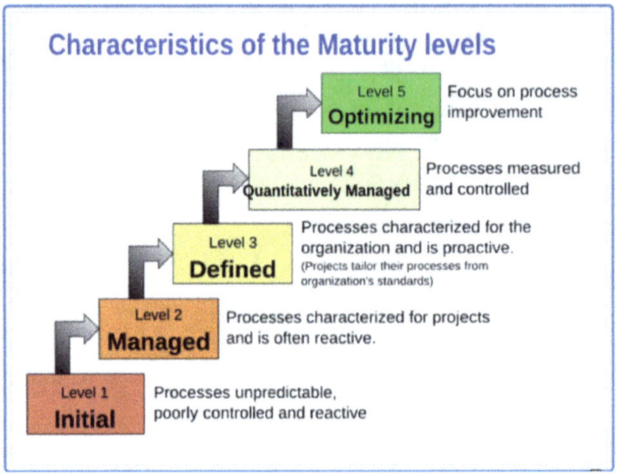

Figure 5-7 : Characteristics of CMMI Maturity Levels

Process Areas: CMMI identifies specific process areas (like project planning, requirements management, risk management) listed in the following table that organizations should focus on to improve performance.

ACRONYM	PROCESS AREA
CAR	Causal Analysis & Resolution
CM	Configuration Management
DAR	Decision Analysis & Resolution
IPM	Integrated Project Management
MA	Measurement & Analysis
OID	Organizational Innovation & Deployment
OPD	Organizational Process Definition
OPF	Organizational Process Focus
OPP	Organizational Process Performance
OT	Organizational Training
PI	Product Integration
PMC	Project Monitoring & Control
PP	Project Planning
PPQA	Process & Product Quality Assurance
QPM	Quantitative Project Management
RD	Requirements Definition
REQM	Requirements Management
RSKM	Risk Management

SAM	Supplier Agreement Management
TS	Technical Solution
VER	Verification
VAL	Validation

Table 5-7 : CMMI Process Areas List

CMMC (The Cybersecurity Maturity Model Certification)

CMMC is a framework established by the U.S. Department of Defense (DoD) to ensure that defense contractors and companies handling sensitive government information meet specific cybersecurity standards. It's designed to protect Controlled Unclassified Information (CUI) and Federal Contract Information (FCI) from cyber threats.

- **Purpose:** The CMMC is a program that requires all organizatioins working with the DoD to demonstrate that they are adequately protecting sensitive information.
- **Scope:** It applies to all organizations in the Defense Industrial Base (DIB) that handle CUI and FCI.
- **Compliance:** CMMC compliance is determined through a tiered system, where the level of certification required depends on the sensitivity of the information and the contractor's role within the supply chain.
- **Framework:** The CMMC framework is based on the NIST SP 800-171, which outlines cybersecurity best practices.
- **Assessment:** CMMC compliance is assessed through third-party assessment organizations (C3PAO) or, in some cases, self-assessment.
- **Requirements:** CMMC compliance requires implementing specific cybersecurity controls, such as multi-factor authentication, regular auditing, and training.

CMMC Levels

CMMC levels define the three tiers of CMMC 2.0 framework. These levels define the required cybersecurity practices and compliance based on the sensitivity of the data (Federal Contract Information (FCI) or Controlled Unclassified Information (CUI)) that an organization handles and its exposure to persistent threats. The levels are:

- **Level 1 (Foundational)**: This level focuses on basic cyber hygiene and is designed for organizations handling only FCI. It includes practices like password management and media protection.
- **Level 2 (Advanced)**: This level builds upon Level 1 and requires organizations to implement the 110 security controls specified in NIST 800-171. It's geared towards organizations handling CUI.
- **Level 3 (Expert)**: This is the most rigorous level, requiring compliance with NIST 800-171 and additional controls from NIST 800-

172. It's designed for organizations handling CUI and subject to advanced persistent threats.

The CMMC levels are cumulative. The specific CMMC level an organization needs to achieve depends on the type of information they handle contracts they are working on.

CMMC 2.0 Certification Steps

The following describes the key steps ion preparing for and achieving CMMC 2.0 certification.

1. Determine Target CMMC Level: The DoD will specify the target level for CUI and FCI
2. Assess Current Cybersecurity Maturity: Self-assessment
3. Develop and Implement a Plan to Address Gaps: policies, procedures, technologies
4. Choose a C3PAO: from Cyber-AB (Cybersecurity Accreditation Body) marketplace
5. Undergo CMMC Assessment: C3PAO will revies docs, conducts interviews,
6. Receive Certification: CMMC-AB will issue your organization a CMMC certification

Supporting Frameworks & Regulations

The following two frameworks can be seen as supporting frameworks and not really standards or frameworks on their own. They are included here due to their contribution to ensuring a secure cybersecurity posture.

MITRE ATT&CK Framework

The MITRE ATT&CK framework is a publicly available knowledge base of adversary tactics and techniques based on real-world observations. MITRE ATT&CK provides a library of known adversary tactics and the adversary's technical goals, techniques and how those goals are achieved, and procedures that describe the implementations of the techniques.

The MITRE Corporation is a federally, funded, non-profit research and development organization.

Teams

The MITRE ATT&CK data is used by designated security teams including Blue, Red, and Purple teams along with threat hunters and incident response teams.

- *Blue teams*: defensively focused, concentrate on securing a network and its associated data. Often inside the SOC (Security Operations Center), they track security incidents, manage technologies, administer security controls,

- *Red teams*: penetration teams, adopt an adversarial approach to test the blue team's defenses. Testing is episodic, and coverage delivered is vastly smaller than blue team's defenses.
- *Purple teams*: the functions of the red and blue teams are tightly coupled and execute in a coordinated fashion to provide immediate and continuous improvement to the overall security. Adopt a combined red/blue approach for thinking like an adversary and testing defensive technologies.

With MITRE ATT&CK as a foundation, an organization can direct their security teams to focus their security controls on the most probable methods of adversary attack. Continuous, automated testing allows teams to ensure that security controls are focused on what matters most and to verify that they are effective.

The security teams can use Cyber Threat Intelligence (CTI) to determine what the organization's adversaries do, and use that information to improve their security program's effectiveness against known threats and threat behaviors by taking a single group of threat actors and looking at its behaviors as they're structured in ATT&CK.

Understanding analytics is important so the security teams need to look at the data sources listed for each ATT&CK technique including process and command line monitoring and file and registry monitoring (Sysmon, Windows Event Logs, EDR, logs) and packet capture (network device/software).

SIEM – Incorporating Analytics: including Mitre's Cyber Analytic Repository (CAR), ThreatHunter Playbook (from ATT&CK techniques in log data), Detection Lab scripts to test analytics, BOTS (e.g. Splunk's Boss of the SOC dataset with red team attacks), BRAWL Public Game and ATT&CK Navigator to visualize data on the ATT&CK matrix, including analytic coverage.

Conducting Emulations and Advanced Analytics

Emulations help in understanding real-world cyberattacks by mimicking the tactics, techniques, and procedures. Advanced analytics refer to the creation and use of analytical techniques and tools, such as those in the MITRE Cyber Analytics Repository (CAR), to detect and respond to adversary behaviors documented within the MITRE ATT&CK framework. Depending on your situation you can perform these at one of the following levels.

1. Level 1: Limited resources – choose technique, choose test, execute test, analyze detections
2. Level 2: Moderate resources -- emulate a real adversary you care about to provide more value.
3. Level 3: Advanced resources -- adversary emulation plan draws on the greatest strength of combining red teaming with your own threat intelligence:

Make MITRE ATT&CK Operational

This is a complex process because it requires integrating the framework into every stage of the organization's security operations and strategy. The goal is to proactively counter adversary behavior based on real-world observations. The following steps are required to operationalize MITRE ATT&CK in your environment:

1. Assess and prioritize threats faced by the organization including adversary behaviors, threat actors and their tactics, and your own log data to identify risks.
2. Conduct gap analysis by comparing by the organization's current security capabilities with a prioritized list of MITRE ATT&CK defined techniques to analyze logging gaps and detection gaps.
3. Enhance detection and mitigation to ensure that the detection rules are able to catch the techniques identified as high priority gaps and the endpoint SIEM integrations are configured correctly.
4. Use attack simulations to validate the effectiveness of the organization's enhancements using the red and blue teaming approach. Perform attack and breach simulations.
5. Use the results to improve response, collaboration across teams and train the Security Operations Center (SOC) teams to use MITRE ATT&CK mappings. Also provides reports for various security teams and leadership.

Zero Trust Architecture (ZTA)

ZTA is not a framework, but an important security model based on explicit verification and least privilege access to minimize risk. It moves away from "trust but verify" model to "never trust, always verify". No user or device should be automatically trusted, regardless of whether they are inside or outside the network perimeter. It requires continuous verification and authentication for every access request, emphasizing strict access controls and least-privileged access. The following lists the key aspects of achieving ZTA.

- Least-Privileged Access: grant users only the minimum level of access needed to perform their tasks, limiting the potential damage from a compromised account or device.
- Continuous Monitoring and Dynamic Access Control: continuously monitor user activity and network traffic to detect and respond to threats in real-time, adapting security policies as needed. Continuously evaluate user and device behavior to determine if access should continue to be granted or revoked, even after a connection has been established.
- Assume Breach: assume that the network has already been breached and focus on protecting critical assets and data, rather than solely relying on perimeter security.
- Identity and Access Management (IAM): strong authentication methods like multi-factor authentication (MFA) and single sign-on (SSO) are crucial to verify user identities.
- Micro segmentation: divides the network into smaller, isolated segments to limit the impact of a breach and prevent lateral movement. This helps in reducing the attack surface to limit access.
- Prevent lateral movement uses strong authentication verification for every access request, regardless of whether it originates from inside or outside the network.

- Set up Security Groups: Security Groups act as a crucial component for granting access control and managing traffic based on device, application in a segmented network. Use least privilege access.
- Endpoint and Device Security: ensures that all devices accessing the network are secure and compliant with organizational policies.
- Data Protection: encrypts sensitive data and implements access controls to protect it from unauthorized access.

Integrating Zero Trust with Identity and Access Management (IAM) and security tools involves using IAM as the foundation for implementing Zero Trust principles, such as continuous authentication and least privilege access, supporting Zero Trust concepts like multi-factor authentication (MFA) and risk-based authentication. Furthermore, security tools like SIEM and UEBA can be integrated with IAM to enhance threat detection and response capabilities within a Zero Trust framework.

Architectural Frameworks

While not true cybersecurity frameworks, these architectural frameworks provide a methodology for integrating security deeply into the entire enterprise architecture lifecycle, enabling organizations to align security with business goals, manage risks, ensure compliance, and create more effective, cohesive strategies for protecting digital assets.

TOGAF 9 (created in 1995, TOGAF9 released in 2009)

Open Group Architecture Framework version 9 is a comprehensive structure and supporting tools for the entire architecture lifecycle consisting of planning through developing enterprise architectures.

The Following diagram describes the TOGAF 9 Capability Framework with a focus on the ADM.

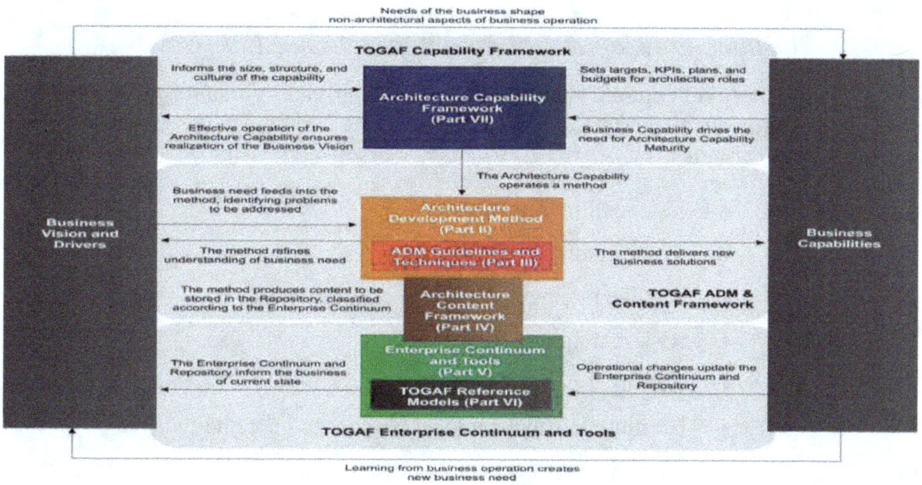

Source: DICT Solutions

Figure 5-8 : TOGAF 9 Capability Framework

The Architecture Development Method (ADM) is an iterative sequence of steps to develop an enterprise-wide architecture. It also defines the tools for enterprise architecture development methodology. The ADM Guidelines and techniques are deigned to support the application of the ADM.

The Architecture Content Framework is a detailed model of architectural work products including deliverables, artifacts within deliverables, and he architecture building blocks.

The Enterprise Continuum is a model for structuring a virtual repository and methods for classifying architecture and solution artifacts.

The TOGAF 9 requirements management and implementation consists of several phases as follows.

Phase A	Architecture Vision	Scope, stakeholders, architecture vision, approvals.
Phase B:	Business Architecture	To support an agreed architecture vision.
Phase C	Information Systems Architectures	Development of information systems
Phase D	Technology Architecture	For an architecture project.
Phase E	Opportunities and Solutions	Implementation projects, work packages
Phase F	Migration Planning	Implementation/Migration - move from baseline to target.
Phase G	Implementation and Governance	Architectural oversight to ensure alignment with the target architecture
Phase H	Architecture Change Management	Manage changes to the architecture in a structured manner

Table 5-8 : Phases of TOGAF9

Architecture Capability as an Operational Entity

The Architecture Capability Framework provides guidance on establishing an operational enterprise architecture practice which includes the following capabilities:

- Financial management
- Performance management
- Service management
- Risk management
- Resource management
- Communications and stakeholder management
- Quality management
- Supplier management
- Configuration management
- Environment management

The following diagram shows the business capabilities contributing to the architecture that provides the basis for business operations.

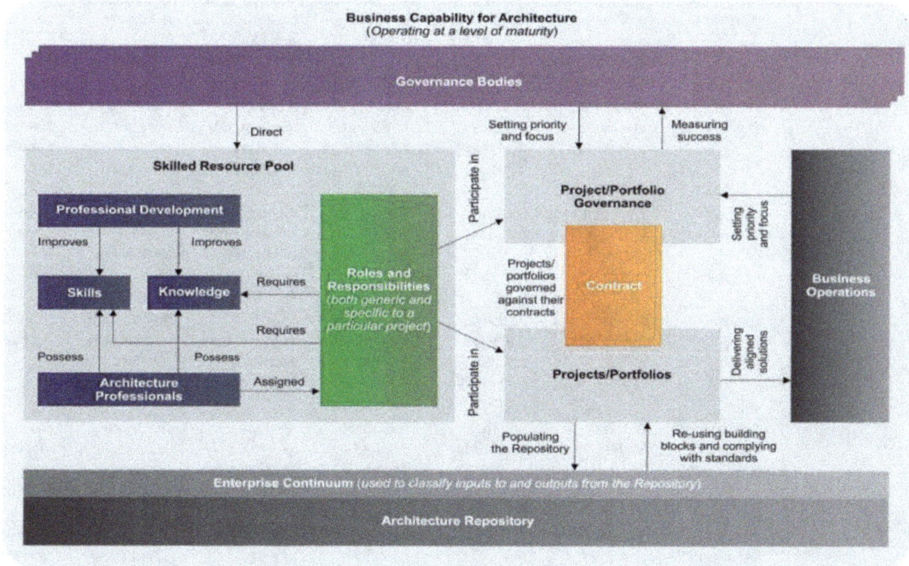

Source: DICT Solutions

Figure 5-9 : TOGAF 9 Business Capability for Architecture

SABSA

SABSA (Sherwood Applied Business Security Architecture) 1996 has been evolving since 1996. The most recent release is the TSI W105 – SABSA Enterprise Security Architecture Principles (2026) introduced the PAB (Principles, Advantages, and Benefits) framework to translate abstract concepts into business value. A whitepaper published in 2023 provided frameworks for assigning responsibility in security architecture along with recommendations for using security frameworks like NIST CSF.

The SABSA Security Architecture Layers include:

1. Contextual - Business
2. Conceptual - Architect's
3. Logical - Designer's
4. Physical - Builder's
5. Component - Trade Specialist's
6. Management - Managers'

It is a model and methodology for risk-driven enterprise information security architecture and service management, to support critical business processes. It is similar to the Zachman Framework.

The following table needs to be filled out as a detailed spreadsheet covering all aspects of the detail noted in the table for the SABSA framework.

SABSA Matrix	Assets (What)	Motivation (Why)	Process (How)	People (Who)	Location (Where)	Time (When)
Contextual (Business)	The business assets, goals, and objectives to be protected.	The business risk model.	The business process model.	The business organization and its relationships	The business geography	Business time dependency
Conceptual (Architect's)	A business attributes profile.	The security control objectives.	Security strategies and architectural layering	A security entity model and trust framework.	The security domain model.	Security-related lifecycles and deadlines.
Logical (Designer's)	The business information model.	Security policies.	The security services.	An entity schema and privilege profiles.	Security domain definitions and associations	Security processing cycles.
Physical (Builder's)	The business data model.	Security rules, practices, and procedures	The security mechanisms	Users, applications, and their interface	The platform and network infrastructure	Control structure execution.
Component (Trade Specialist's)	Detailed data structures.	Security standards.	Security products and tools.	Identities, functions, actions, and ACLs.	Processes, nodes, addresses, and protocols.	Security step timing and sequencing.
Management (Manager's)	Assurance of operational continuity.	Operational risk management.	Security service managemen t and support.	Application and user management and support.	The security of sites and platforms.	The security operations schedule.

Table 5-9 : SABSA Framework Spreadsheet

6 -- Data Security Standards & Regulations

These regulations and standards are designed to ensure data confidentiality, integrity, and availability (the CIA triad). They protect sensitive data from cyber threats, prevent costly data breaches, and comply with legal obligations, ultimately safeguarding an organization's reputation, maintaining customer trust, and avoiding significant fines and legal consequences

Examples of Sensitive Data

Exposure and exfiltration of sensitive data can have a significant financial damage, loss of reputation, business disruption and even legal consequences including fines and even jail terms. So, it is important to protect sensitive data. Sensitive data can consist of *direct identifiers* such as:

- Full name
- Social Security number (SSN)
- Driver's license number
- Passport information
- Biometric records (fingerprints, DNA)
- Mother's maiden name

Other forms of data about individuals, called *indirect identifiers* can also be used to uniquely identify an individual often when combined with multiple types of data often through extrapolation:

- Date of birth
- Mailing address
- Email address
- Financial information (bank account, credit card numbers)
- Medical records

The responsibility of a business collecting, storing and using sensitive data and to protect sensitive data is enforced by regulators and is mandated by national and state governments, multi-national consortiums, and industry consortiums. These are enforced through data security regulations and standards.

Given that most data security standards are directly derived from or patterned after GDPR, there are some common themes that run across all of them including the following:

- **Administrative Controls**: Policies, procedures, and training to guide employee actions and ensure data is handled responsibly.
- **Technical Controls**: Implemented to protect data, such as encryption and access controls (like two-factor authentication), and firewalls.
- **Physical Controls**: Measures to protect data, including limiting physical access to sensitive data storage locations.
- **Confidentiality**: Protecting data from unauthorized disclosure.
- **Integrity**: Ensuring data is accurate and has not been tampered with.
- **Availability**: Guaranteeing that data is accessible when needed by authorized users.
- **Data Subject Rights**: Granting individuals rights over their personal data, such as the right to access, correct, or delete their information.
- **Breach Notification**: Requirements for timely notification to regulatory authorities and affected individuals in the event of a data breach.

Common Themes That Drive Data Security Compliance

The common themes listed below drive all data security standards as the basis for data protection and the rights of the data subjects (who actually own the data) according to most standards. These themes include the following:

- **Lawful Basis**: There should be a lawful basis for collecting and processing personal data. These bases include contractual obligations, legal obligations, vital and legitimate business interests, public tasks, and cases where data subjects give their consent.
- **Data Subject Communication**: Individual data subjects should be transparently and clearly communicated to with details about the purpose of data collection, its use, the retention period, and final disposition.
- **Data Integrity**: The integrity, confidentiality, and accuracy of data must be maintained by the collecting and using organizations.
- **Limited Data Collection**: Any personal information which is unnecessary for the specified purpose must not be collected.
- **Data Subject Rights**: The data subjects have various rights including the right to access their personal data, the right to erasure of data, the right to rectification of incorrect data, the right to object to processing of data, and rights related to data portability.
- **Data Breach Management and Reporting**: In case of a data breach, it should be notified to the relevant supervisory authority as soon as the organization comes to know about it and within the time stipulated by the regulatory authority.
- **Data Transfers**: Any international data transfers must fulfill certain requirements like ‘adequacy decisions’, security management during transfers, data subjects’ rights compliance by receiving party, and other requirements as stipulated by the standard.

Data Security Compliance

Data security compliance is the process of following specific legal, regulatory, and industry standards for collecting, storing, managing, and protecting sensitive data to ensure its confidentiality, integrity, and availability. It involves implementing security measures to prevent unauthorized access and data breaches, thereby protecting customer, financial, and employee information

If your organization collects sensitive data, data security compliance is not only important but may be mandatory for regulatory reasons. Compliance helps in the following ways:

- Protecting Sensitive Data: Use of robust security measures to protect personal, financial, and proprietary information from unauthorized access, theft, and misuse.
- Preventing Data Breaches: Implementation of the necessary tools and practices to reduce the risk of data breaches and cyberattacks.
- Avoiding Penalties and Legal Action: Non-compliance can lead to substantial fines, legal action, and even criminal penalties, making compliance a necessity to avoid costly consequences.
- Building Customer Trust: Demonstrating a commitment to data protection through compliance fosters trust and loyalty among customers, assuring them that their data is being handled responsibly.
- Enhancing Reputation: Companies that prioritize and adhere to data security regulations are seen as more trustworthy and reliable, enhancing their brand image and market position.
- Improving Data Management: Compliance requires organizations to improve their data governance and management practices, leading to better organization, accuracy, and security of data.
- Ensuring Business Continuity: By preventing data breaches and maintaining secure systems, compliance helps ensure that business operations are not disrupted by security incidents.
- Gaining a Competitive Advantage: Proactive compliance can differentiate a business in the marketplace, attracting customers and partners who value strong data security practices.

Consequences of non-compliance?

Non-compliance with standards can result in business financial loss and loss of reputation, and can further result in regulatory authorities' enforced penalties that can be financial, civil and even potentially criminal.

Data Security Standards Around the World

Increasingly sophisticated attacks by malicious actors driven by ransomware, state actors sponsored by nations, malicious groups driven by financial gain, revenge for political and other reasons, and also driven even by the thrill of notoriety, has made cybersecurity and data security protections paramount for all organizations collecting and using sensitive data that, if compromised, can cause substantial harm to their business and reputation.

Businesses have often misused data collected about their customers and clients to drive their own profitability by reselling their data assets to unscrupulous companies for customer profiling for targeted selling. This resulted in the government sponsored regulations to promote the rights and privacy protections of data subjects.

Data security standards exist globally to protect personal and sensitive information from theft, misuse, and unauthorized access, driven by increasing reliance on digital data, escalating cyber threats, and the legal and reputational risks of data breaches.

Common data security standards and regulations enumerated in the following sections, include international laws and regulations, US Federal Government and State Government laws and regulations, and industry standards.

International Laws and Regulations

While many nations have enacted laws in the last ten or more years, the most common ones you may encounter are the ones listed below due to the size of the economy and populations of the nations that enacted them.

- GDPR (Europe's General Data Protection Regulation)
- DPDP Act (India's Digital Personal Data Protection Act (DPDP Act) of 2023)
- PIPEDA (Canada's Personal information Protection and Electronic Documents Act)
- PIPL (China's Personal Information Protection Law)
- LGPD (Brazil's General Data Protection Law)
- Federal Law No. 152-FZ (Russia's Personal Data Law)
- Privacy Act 1988 (Australia's Data Privacy Law)

This is just a representative list. You are encouraged to explore the laws in each country that your organization will have a business interest and customers in.

United States Federal Laws and Regulations

The notable United States Federal data privacy laws and regulations include:

- HIPPA (Health Information Portability and Accountability Act, 1996).
- GLBA (Graham Leach Bliley Act, 199).
- COPPA (Children's Online Privacy Protection Act, 2003).
- HITRUST (Health Information Trust Alliance) founded in 2007 along with the HITRUST Common Security Framework (CSF).
- PCI-DSS (Payment Card Industry – Data Security Standard, 2004).
- SOX (Sarbanes-Oxley Act, 2002).
- FTC (FTC Act of 1914) gave it the authority to prohibit "unfair or deceptive acts or practices" and it enforces FCRA – Fair Credit Reporting Act, COPPA, and GLBA.

United States Laws and Regulations by Individual States

United States does not have a common law like the GDPR that is applicable to all states uniformly. So, states have enacted their own laws. 20 states listed below have enacted comprehensive consumer data privacy laws. Many other states have legislative actions in progress to define and enact privacy laws in their own states.

1. California CPRA (California Privacy Rights Act 2018, amended and enhanced CCPA)
2. Colorado Privacy Act (CPA), 2021
3. Connecticut Data Privacy Act (CTDPA), 2023
4. Delaware Personal Data Privacy Act, 2025
5. Florida Digital Bill of Rights (FDBR), enacted as SB 262 in 2023
6. Indiana Consumer Data Protection Act, 2023 (effective in 2026)
7. Iowa Consumer Data Protection Act (ICDPA), 2025
8. Kentucky Consumer Data Act (KCDPA), 2024 (effective 2026)
9. Maryland Online Data Privacy Act (MODPA), 2024 (effective 2025)
10. Minnesota Consumer Data Privacy Act (MCDPA), 2025
11. Montana's Consumer Data Privacy Act, 2024
12. New Hampshire Privacy Act (NHPA), 2025
13. Nebraska Data Privacy Act (NDPA), 2025
14. New Jersey Data Privacy Act (NJDPA), 2025
15. Oregon Consumer Privacy Act (OCPA), 2025
16. Rhode Island Data Transparency and Privacy Protection Act (RI-DTPPA), 2024
17. Tennessee Information Protection Act. 2025
18. Texas Data Privacy and Security Act (TDPSA), 2024
19. Utah Consumer Privacy Act (UCPA), 2023
20. Virginia Consumer Data Protection Act (VCDPA), 2021

International Laws and Regulations In-Depth

While covering all of the international laws and regulations is outside the scope of this paper, I have covered GDPR in depth and compared with other international laws and regulations as a comparative table. (note that this table has been copied from my book "Enterprise Data Security Around the World").

GDPR (Europe's General Data Protection Regulation)

The core regulatory content of the EU Privacy Law is contained in the 99 articles of GDPR. GDPR does not prescribe security technologies, but each GDPR principle aligns with a set of candidate technologies for managing personal data risk. GDPR tests the dimensions: legal, procedural, and technical. Technology is the primary enabler for GDPR providing solutions, repeatability, and scalability.

Legal Dimension: The GDPR is a law. As proposed by the European Parliament, the GDPR will apply to all personal data, regardless of whether it is located inside the EU zone or transported outside the EU zone.

Procedural Dimension: Depending on business and data volume, compliance with the GDPR may require that new roles, responsibilities, accountabilities, and processes may have to be implemented.

Technical Dimension: The GDPR includes many data protection principles and requirements that must be enabled by technology, or that require technology to limit impact to internal operations. For example, technical professionals can support the GDPR program by using technology to make a process repeatable and scalable.

GDPR Compliance Requirements

Only the regulatory authorities can ultimately decide what is and what is not compliant. Secondly, determining what is required to address GDPR is a business decision based on risk and not initially a technical one.

GDPR Privacy Principles

The following describes the selected controls supporting the GDPR Privacy Principles.

- Consent Management
- Right to Access
- Ability to Erase Personal Data
- Data Portability
- Protection by Design and by Default
- Pseudonymization (Data Masking)
- Records of Processing Activities
- Continuous Compliance
- Breach Notification
- Data Privacy Impact Assessment (DPIA)
- International Data Transfers

The Core Principles of the GDPR Framework

The following describes the core principles of GDPR that every organization storing and using personal information about a data subject residing within an EU country or is an EU citizen residing in other nations must comply with:

- **Lawfulness, Fairness, and Transparency**: Data processing must be legal, fair, and transparent, with clear communication to individuals about data collection and use.
- **Purpose Limitation**: Data can only be collected for specific, legitimate purposes that are clearly defined to the individual at the time of collection.

- **Data Minimization**: Only the data absolutely necessary for the stated purpose should be collected and stored.
- **Accuracy**: Personal data must be accurate and kept up to date. See data subjects' rights on correcting data.
- **Storage Limitation**: Data should only be kept for as long as is necessary for the purpose for which it was collected.
- **Integrity and Confidentiality**: Data must be processed securely to prevent unauthorized access or loss.
- **Accountability**: Organizations are responsible for demonstrating compliance with the GDPR principles and for implementing appropriate measures, such as data protection by design and by default.

Data Subject Rights

The framework empowers individuals called data subjects with rights regarding how their personal data is being treated and managed by data controllers:

- **Right to be informed**: Individuals have the right to know how their data is being collected, stored and used.
- **Right of access**: Individuals can request access to their personal data.
- **Right to rectification**: Individuals can request that inaccurate data be corrected.
- **Right to erasure**: Individuals can request the deletion of their personal data.
- **Right to restrict processing**: Individuals can request that the processing of their data be limited.
- **Right to data portability**: Individuals can receive their data in a format that allows them to transfer it to another service.
- **Right to object**: Individuals can object to certain types of data processing.
- **Rights in relation to automated decision-making**: Individuals have rights concerning automated processes that could have legal or significant effects on them.

Lawful Basis for Data Processing

GDPR imposes on data controllers who collect personal information about individuals (data subjects) mandated obligations to legally process personal data; organizations must identify a lawful basis. These include consent from the data subject to fulfill a contracted or legal obligation for which the data subject is a party, or for a public task such as a government requirement, to protect the interest of the data subject, and for the legitimate interests of the data controller or a third party, provided these are not overridden by the individual's interests or fundamental rights

The 99 Articles of GDPR

The Following describes the 99 articles that form the basis for GDPR compliance. Note that Articles 15 – 23 are the data rights outlined in the privacy policy. These are the articles that organizations will be most concerned with for compliance.

General definitions and principles

- Articles 1 – 4 : General foundational provisions for the regulation:
- Articles 5 – 11 : Fundamental rules for processing personal data and the conditions under which data processing can be lawful.

Requirements for the Entities

The requirements for entities are embodied in the following articles

- Articles 12 – 23 : Rights of the data subject.
- Articles 24 – 43 : Data controllers and processors (definitions, responsibilities, related activities, etc.)
- Articles 44-50 : Transferring to third parties for international entities.

Other Regulatory Requirements

- Articles 51 - 59 -- Independent supervisory authorities.
- Articles 60 - 76 -- Cooperation and consistency between data protection authorities.
- Articles 77 - 84 – Rights of individuals for remedies, and for controllers their liability, and penalties.
- Articles 85 - 91 -- Provisions relating to specific processing situations.
- Articles 92 - 93 – Ensure democratic technical updates including inputs fro EU Parliament and member states.
- Articles 94 - 99 -- Final provisions for updates and changes to the GDPR and its enforcement.

GDPR Actionable Rights

The following describes the actionable rights of data subjects embodied in Articles 15-22 of GDPR that firms that are the data controllers must adhere to:

	Title	Description of the Right
15	Right of Access	The right to obtain confirmation from a data controller as to whether their personal data is being processed, and if so, access to this data and information about the purpose of processing.
16	Right to Rectification	The right to request that incorrect, inaccurate, or incomplete personal data be corrected and procedures for updating current personal information.
17	Right to Erasure	The right to request the deletion of personal data under certain circumstances, such as when the data is no longer necessary for its original purpose or when the data subject withdraws consent. This is the *Right to be forgotten.*

18	Right to Restriction on Processing	The right to request restriction of the processing of personal data in specific situations, for example, if the data subject contests the accuracy of the data.
20	Right to Data Portability	The right to receive the posed data in a machine-readable format and on-line access to download statements.
21	Right to Objection to Processing	The data subject right to object to the processing of their personal data in certain situations, particularly for direct marketing purposes or when based on legitimate interests.
22	Automated Individual Decision-making	Individuals have the right not to be subject to decisions based solely on automated processing (including profiling) that produce significant legal effects for them, unless certain exceptions apply.

Table 6-1 : GDPR Actionable Rights

GDPR Right to be Forgotten Implementation Requirements

For banks and other financial institutions obtaining and storing data subject records for business usage, one of the key challenges of GDPR will be how to implement the right to be forgotten. This not only requires institutions to manage and control the purpose and consent of processing records of the data subjects, but it also contains provisions specifically referencing other regulations that require the right to be forgotten.

The main regulatory drivers of personal data retention are in the codes of commercial law, yet there may be other exemptions which overrule the right to be forgotten, at least for a defined period. For example, for HR systems the compliance executives need to factor into employment contracts and their procedures around government record retention requirements.

For an organization's business the key focus will be the proliferation of PII data of the data subjects within their systems architectures. For example, the location of a withdrawal or a credit card transaction is used by their marketing division for marketing purposes. In parallel, it is crucial for a financial institution to keep this information for the length of the retention period to be able to improve the integrity of its balance sheet and processed transactions. Furthermore, this information may be needed for other purposes such as anti-money laundering, fraud detection, etc. As a result, processing of the personal data for the purpose of marketing is no longer allowed if the data subject has revoked consent and asked for data erasure; however, the data itself will not be immediately erased due to other obligations or longer retention periods.

This shows that GDPR requires institutions to have a much deeper understanding of the purpose for which personal data is being kept. To do this, each information item needs to be classified not only with a purpose, but also the source from which the financial institution or business has collected it. The data classes then need to be mapped to the applicable law and related retention phases. This drives the additional data columns in the database tables used for customer personal data.

Controls Responsibility for GDPR

GDPR defines specific rights and responsibilities by role of the individual or organization. The following describes who can delete or erase the information related to a data subject.

Data Deletion Control -- by Data Controller

- The Ability to systematically delete individual data subject information upon request.
- Implement a tracking mechanism for "deleted" records for government and regulatory requirements (typically 7 years).
- Implement Control mechanism for testing that the data has been properly anonymized or deleted and evaluate the impact on the data subject.
- Identify and document downstream impacts on other applications and partner systems.
- Ensure communications to data subjects.

Data Deletion – by Processor

- Ability to systematically delete all data of the data subject upon request by the data subject individual.
- All of the other controls as required for all data controllers.

Types of Storage That Need to be Processed for Erasure

- Iron Mountain or similar off-site climate controlled long-term secure storage.
- Backup tapes.
- All Systems of Record, Systems of Reference, and Systems of Engagement including all CSP (Cloud Service Provider) based storage.
- Data Warehouse databases.
- Log and application local storage.
- Email threads and communications.
- Phone records and IVR system data storage.

What Needs to be Deleted for Erasure Compliance

- Data Subject names, addresses, phone numbers, DoB, Gender, etc.
- Data subject's marital status.
- Data Subject email addresses.
- All forms of data subject's government issued identification.
- Bank records, account numbers, etc.
- Data subjects' employment data – employers, hire dates, termination dates, salary data, and Employee ID.

Data Erasure Process

Core activities for erasure include:

- Capture erasure request from data subject and confirm that the request has been received.

- Update "Consent" database to mark the record as "Erased".
- Compile list of relevant items; check retention period requirements for each item.
- Mark all relevant items "Erased" so they cannot be used in an application.
- Execute erasure or "wait" until expiration of retention period.
- Inform third parties and downstream applications and obtain confirmation.
- Test that erasure meets GDPR requirements.
- Inform data subject of the "erasure".

India Privacy Law

The Digital Personal Data Protection (DPDP) Act, 2023 was passed by both houses of the Indian Parliament and has received Presidential Assent. As specified in the Gazette of India it is "An Act to provide for the processing of digital personal data in a manner that recognizes both the right of individuals to protect their personal data and the need to process such personal data for lawful purposes and for matters connected therewith or incidental thereto."

Citizen Rights: The Act grants "data principals" (the equivalent of "data subjects" under the GDPR) four key rights against "data fiduciaries" including companies and government entities, including: (1) the right to confirm whether and how their data is being used; (2) the ability to correct misleading or false data; (3) data portability rights; and (4) a "right to be forgotten," or the authority to restrict companies from using data they previously shared. Unlike the GDPR, the DPDP *does not* require companies to delete such data completely.

Establishment of Regulatory Agency: The Act also calls for the establishment of a Data Protection Authority ("DPA"), now adopted by the Ministry of Information Technology, which would have the power to investigate, enjoin, and fine non-compliant entities. All data fiduciaries would be required to disclose data breaches to the DPA. The DPA would also have the authority to label certain entities as Significant Data Fiduciaries (SDFs) based on the volume and sensitivity of data they process, thus subjecting such entities to additional transparency, auditing, and reporting requirements. SDFs would be required to appoint a Data Protection Officer to oversee compliance with the law, comply with annual independent audits of their processing of personal data, and conduct impact assessments for new technologies or large-scale profiling or use of personal data. The DPA would also have the authority to mandate that other data fiduciaries be subject to these requirements, even if they are not categorized as SDFs. Finally, all data fiduciaries would be required to notify the DPA in the event of a data breach. Ther DPA would have the authority to mandate individual notification.

Data Fiduciary Obligations: All data fiduciaries would be required to implement "appropriate security safeguards," including de-identification, encryption, and tools to prevent misuse, unauthorized access, modification, disclosure, or destruction of personal data. The Act establishes temporal limitations on the processing and retention of personal data, prohibiting data fiduciaries from retaining personal data longer than "reasonably necessary" to satisfy its intended purpose or comply with legal obligation, and requires fiduciaries to undertake periodic review to ensure they are not unnecessarily retaining personal information.

China's PIPL

China's Personal Information Protection Law (PIPL) is a comprehensive privacy law that became effective in November 2021. Like EU's GDPR, it applies to personal information of natural persons in mainland China or Chinese citizens residing abroad, and imposes stringent rules for data processing, consent, cross-border data transfers, and provides individuals with rights to access, correct, and delete their data. PIPL mandates data handlers to implement a privacy program, appoint a Data Protection Officer, and conduct impact assessments, with significant penalties for non-compliance. Like GDPR, the key tenets of PIPL include:

- *Data Handling regulation*: sets the rules for the collection, storage, use, and transmission of personal information, requiring transparent and accountable processing activities.
- *Individual Rights*: the rights to know about, consent to access, and correct their personal information, as well as a right to request its deletion.
- *International Data Transfers*: conditions for transferring PI out of China. It may require informed consent from data subjects and downstream security.
- *Security Framework*: forms an overarching framework for data security and privacy.

Data collectors and Processors have specific responsibility that they must comply with:

- *Informed Consent*: must obtain voluntary, explicit, and informed consent before processing data subject PI.
- *Privacy Notices*: A clear and understandable privacy notice must be provided to individuals before their data is processed, outlining the purposes, methods, categories of data, and retention periods.
- *Security Measures*: must implement security measures to data subjects' PI from unauthorized access, leakage, or distortion.
- *Personal Information Protection Impact Assessments (PIPIAs)* are required before significant data processing activities.
- *Data Protection Officer (DPO)*: Organizations handling large volumes of data must appoint a DPO to manage privacy compliance.

Penalties for non-compliance can be severe. Minor violations can result in orders for correction, confiscation of illegal gains, and fines up to CNY 1 million for wrongdoers or CNY 10,000-100,000 for responsible individuals. Serious violations increase the penalties to closure of businesses and fines up to CNY 50 million or 5% of the previous year's turnover.

A Sampling of Other International Laws and Regulations

Country	**Law**	**Description**

Brazil	The Brazilian General Data Protection Act (in Portuguese, LGPD, Lei Geral de Proteção de Dados)	Similar to EU Privacy Laws, this Act applies if one of the following conditions is met: • The data processing takes place in Brazil. • The data processing is related to the offering or provision of goods or services in Brazil, or the processing of data of individuals in Brazil. • The personal data being processed was collected in Brazil
EFTA - European Free Trade Association (Switzerland, Norway, Iceland, Lichtenstein)	Individual Laws in each country based on the common source.	Similar to EU Privacy Laws Swiss law provides stringent privacy protections, particularly for banking information.
Canada	The Personal Information Protection and Electronic Documents Act (PIPEDA)	Like EU. Includes such specifics on filing complaints as how and with whom they are filed, and the remedies and enforcements available to the government for redress of such grievances. The EU acknowledges PIPEDA as satisfactorily addressing the principles of the Data Directive and the Privacy Regulation.
Russia	Federal Law No. 152-FZ on Personal Data, 2006, amended in 2020, 2021, and 2022.	Mandates storing Russian citizens' data in Russian databases, data breach notification obligations to Roskomnadzor(federal agency responsible for monitoring and censoring mass media) within strict timeframes, and the need for consent for data processing. It includes data subject rights, consent agreements, penalties.
Israel	Human Dignity and Liberty, 5752 -1992; the Protection of Privacy Law, 5741-1981	Like EU Privacy Laws it protects data collection, transfer, security, on-line privacy, breach notification, electronic marketing and enforcement.
Japan	The Act on the Protection of Personal Information ("APPI")	Like EU Privacy Laws. The Personal Information Protection Commission ("PPC"), a central agency acts as a supervisory governmental organization on issues of privacy protection.
Malaysia	Personal Data Protection Act 2010 (PDPA)	Defines sensitive personal data and protections for it, and requires users to register under the law. Administered by the Personal Data Protection Commissioner of

		the Ministry of Communications and Multimedia Malaysia.
Saudi Arabia	Kingdom of Saudi Arabia Personal Data Protection Law issued by Royal Decree No. (M/19) dated 9/2/1443H.	Similar to GDPR but international data transfers are stricter in some respects. Applies across all industry sectors. It has specific provisions for processing of health data, credit data and data for scientific research.
Singapore	Personal Data Protection Act (PDPA)	Similar to GDPR. Defines personal data as that which relates to any piece of information that could be used to identify an individual resident.
South Korea	The Personal Information Protection Act (PIPA)	Like EU Privacy Laws, it governs the collection, use, and processing of personal data
UAE (Abu Dhabi and Dubai)	Personal Data Protection Law, Federal Decree law No 45 of 2021	Has similar provisions as GDPR. Defines controls and provides for governance of personal data management.

Table 6-2 : International Data Privacy Laws and Regulations

United States Federal Laws and Regulations

The United States does not have one national law similar to the GDPR in Europe. The US has a collection of laws that serve the privacy requirements.

Laws in the United States of America

These include Administrative Law, Criminal Law, Civil Law and Case Law.

Criminal Law: Under Criminal Law, the state (US federal government or a state) is the plaintiff, and it can result in fines and incarceration. Generally, the issues of jurisdiction and subsequent prosecution are worked out in advance between law enforcement and court jurisdictional bodies.

Civil Law: Civil law is the body of law, statutes, and so on that deal with personal and community-based law such as marriage and divorce as opposed to criminal or military law. The parties involved in civil law matters are strictly private entities, including individuals, groups, and organizations. Typical examples are property boundaries, mineral rights, and marital and divorce cases. Civil cases are called lawsuits or litigation. Punitive measures for civil cases can include restitution of monetary damages or requirement to perform actions, but not imprisonment.

Case Law: Collection of "precedents" resulting from judgments in Federal or Civil Courts that are considered as prior interpretations of the Criminal or Civil Laws and fully applicable until overturned.

US Laws and Regulations Descriptions In-Depth

Although the US has no single national law, the following, in addition to the states enacted privacy laws, provide a range of other laws that an organization needs to take into consideration for their data privacy implementation.

The notable ones include:

Law	Description
GLBA (Graham Leach Bliley Act, 199))	GLBA (Gramm-Leach-Bliley Act) requires financial institutions and companies that offer consumer financial products and advice such as banks, brokerages and insurance companies to explain their information sharing practices to their customers and to safeguard sensitive data.
HIPPA (Health Information Portability and Accountability Act, 1996)	HIPAA (Health Insurance Portability and Accountability Act) is a federal law that requires creation of national standards to protect sensitive patient health information from being disclosed without the patients' consent or knowledge. It specifies the formats and content structuring for storage and transmission of patient identification and clinical data.
COPPA (Children's Online Privacy Protection Act, 2003)	COPPA (Children's on-line privacy protection). Administered by the FTC, COPP imposes certain requirements on operators of websites or online services directed to children under 13 years of age, and on operators of other websites or online services that have actual knowledge that they are collecting personal information online from a child under 13 years of age.
HITRUST (Health Information Trust Alliance founded in 2007, HITRUST Common Security Framework (CSF))	HITRUST is an organization that developed the HITRUST CSF®, a comprehensive, prescriptive, and certifiable security and privacy framework designed to help organizations of all sizes and industries manage the risk of handling sensitive data. It integrates various regulatory, legal, and industry-standard requirements, such as HIPAA, ISO, and PCI DSS, into a single, flexible framework.
PCI-DSS (Payment Card Industry – Data Security Standard, 2004)	PCI-DSS (Payment Card Industry Data Security Standard) is an industry consortium compliance agreement, not a law. It is designed to reduce payment card fraud by ensuring security controls around cardholder data. For example, organizations collecting and using credit information about consumers are not allowed to store in their databases the three-to-four-digit CSC or CVC (card security or verification code) printed on the back (usually in the signature area). It is used for validating that the cardholder is physically in possession of the credit card.
SOX (Sarbanes-Oxley Act, 2002)	SOX mandates that public companies establish and maintain internal controls for financial reporting and establishes accountability on executives for financial

	statement accuracy. It also includes protections for whistleblowers. SOX created the Public Company Accounting Oversight Board (PCAOB) to oversee auditors and established significant penalties for violations.
FTC (FTC Act of 1914 gave it the authority to prohibit "unfair or deceptive acts or practices" and it enforces FCRA – Fair Credit Reporting Act, COPPA, and GLBA)	Common Law Privacy Act – based on consent orders/decrees by the Federal trade Commission (FTC) and used by the FTC and the state AGs (Attorney Generals), it is used to prevent unfair and deceptive trade practices. It provides that consumers have the right to know about the personal information a business collects about them and how it is used and shared. It also embodies the right to delete personal information collected from them (with some exceptions). You will commonly find it used in the form of disclosures by banks, brokerages and other institutions that collect your information on how they store and how they share your personal data.

Table 6-3 : United States Nationwide Data Privacy Laws

Some of these laws are described in more detail in the following sections.

GLBA (Gramm-Leach-Bliley Act)

A U.S. federal law that requires financial institutions to safeguard consumers' nonpublic personal information (NPI) and protect its confidentiality. It mandates financial institutions to provide consumers with clear notices about their information privacy policies, explain how their data is shared, and offer them ways to "opt-out" of certain data sharing. The GLBA also prohibits obtaining consumer financial information under false pretenses. GLBA protects consumers data privacy and provides consumers control over how their financial data is shared.

The core components of GLBA are: 1) **The Privacy Rule** (financial institutions must inform consumers about their privacy policies and practices including how their data is used), 2) **The Safeguard Rule** (financial institutions must implement cybersecurity and data security controls to safeguard confidentiality of customer records) and 3) **The Pretexting Provisions** (prohibits acquisition of customer financial information through deceptive practices).

Implementation of GLBA requires financial institutions to establish a comprehensive information security program and appoint a qualified individual to oversee it, conduct risk assessments, identify vulnerabilities, and implement security controls such as, identity and access management, data encryption, secure software development practices, multi-factor authentication, and security training. They should also provide an opt-out option to consumers. Furthermore, all vendor agreements should require security controls to be implemented by the vendors.

An annual report must be presented to the organization's Board of Directors summarizing the status of the information security program, the results of the risk assessments, and any security violations.

Payment Card Industry Data Security Standard (PCI-DSS)

The PCI-DSS is an information security standard designed to reduce payment card fraud. Following the standard requires incremental security controls around cardholder data. The standard covers processing digital transactions and payments using credit or debit cards, storage of credit card data, transmission of cardholder information to another entity and controlling who has accessed protected cardholder data.

The following lists the key highlights of the PCI-DSS standard:

- An organization can never store Card Verification Code (CVC) number for any duration. It can only store consumer personal data, credit card number, address, email address, etc.
- It does not cover companies that offer credit card debt repayment counseling.
- It covers banks issuing credit cards, retailers accepting credit card payments, and businesses processing credit card payment on behalf of themselves of a retailer.
- A PCI-DSS violation can result in fines, suspension of credit card processing privileges, increased audit frequency. Jail time can be awarded only on a related crime. Fines can range for $5,000 to $10,000 per month.
- PCI-DSS defines merchant levels 1 through 4. These are based on the number of transactions over the course of a year but not on dollar value of transactions, location, or the combination of dollar value and number of actions:
    - > 6 million transactions/year
    - 1-6 M transactions/year
    - 20K – 1M transactions/year
    - <20K transactions/year
- The original standard has over 200 controls. It also has a mandatory breach reporting requirement for regulated sensitive data (PI).
- Tokenization or encryption are required for storing any credit card holder information.
- All merchants are required to: maintain a firewall to protect card data, avoid vendor supplied defaults, update antivirus software, maintain secure systems, restrict access on a need to know basis, assign unique ID to each person accessing cardholder data, restrict physical access to storage units, track and monitor all accesses to cardholder data, actively use test systems to monitor security posture, and maintain policies and governance of these policies.

PCI-DSS v4.0 Controls

CI-DSS (v4.0) consists of 12 core requirements organized into six control objectives, which further break down into over 300+ specific security controls.

The 12 Core Requirements are the foundational pillars, such as installing firewalls, changing vendor defaults, protecting stored data, and encrypting transmission. The 12 controls are grouped under six objectives with goals such as maintaining an information security policy and regularly monitoring and testing networks.

The 300+ PCI-DSS controls require organizations to build secure networks, protect cardholder data with encryption, maintain vulnerability management, enforce strict access controls, monitor networks, and maintain security policies. They include mandatory breach reporting requirements for regulated sensitive data (PI). Tokenization or encryption are required for storing any credit card holder information. All merchants are required to:

- Maintain a firewall to protect card data,
- Avoid vendor supplied defaults,
- Protect card data,
- Update antivirus software,
- Maintain secure systems,
- Restrict access to need-to-know basis,
- Assign unique ID to each person accessing cardholder data,
- Restrict physical access to storage units,
- Track and monitor all accesses to cardholder data,
- Actively use test systems to monitor security posture,
- Maintain policies and governance of these policies.

Organizations need to review the standard documentation for a more detailed understanding of the controls.

The PCI-DSS v4.0.1, released in June 2024 refines v4.0 by emphasizing stronger, continuous security including mandatory phishing-resistant MFA stricter card-skimming protections, and a "customized approach" for implementing security controls

PCI-DSS Certification

Organizations are assessed by Qualified Security Assessors (QSAs) who are qualified by the PCI Security Standards Council (PCI SSC), the governing body that owns and manages the PCI-DSS standard. After being assessed, the organization receives a Report on Compliance or Attestation of Compliance (AOC), which serves as a record of their compliance status.

To prepare for PCI-DSS certification, an organization must follow the following steps:

1. Understand the 12 core requirements and the 300+ controls and define internal standards and policies based on these.
2. Define and scope of the cardholder data environment (CDE), including data flows, connected systems, and third-party services being used to manage cardholder data.
3. Perform a risk assessment to identify vulnerabilities and risks to cardholder data.
4. Perform a gap analysis to identify gaps where systems are not compliant.

5. Implement security controls including network security, secure configurations and password management, protect stored cardholder data, install vulnerability management tools, and establish access control polices.
6. Establish policies and procedures for PCI-DSS compliance.
7. Conduct regular testing and monitoring with regular security testing, vulnerability scans, and penetration tests, and monitor the systems and address suspicious activity.
8. Manage continuous compliance by building an evidence repository, and maintain compliance as an ongoing process, and regularly review the security posture.

NERC-CIP

NERC-CIP (North American Electric Reliability Corporation - Critical Infrastructure Protection) Framework is a mandatory set of cybersecurity and physical security controls designed to protect the reliability and security of the North American Bulk Electric System (BES). These standards require electric utility owners and operators to implement security management controls, protect cyber assets, manage incidents, and monitor systems to prevent and respond to cyber threats and physical disruptions.

NERC CIP compliance is mandatory for entities that own or operate critical infrastructure within the Bulk Electric System. This includes electric utilities, power generation companies, and transmission operators.

The key aspects of NERC-CIP framework include the following:

- *Security Management Controls*: Establishing processes for access control, vulnerability management, security awareness training, and incident response.
- *System Security Management*: Implementing physical and electronic security controls for hardware, software, and communication systems within the Electronic Security Perimeter (ESP).
- *Incident Response and Recovery*: Developing plans and procedures for responding to and recovering from cybersecurity incidents.
- *Physical Security*: Protecting critical substations and other facilities from physical threats and unauthorized access.
- *Supply Chain Security*: Vetting and managing third-party vendors to prevent security risks from the supply chain.
- *Internal Network Security Monitoring*: Monitoring internal network communications to detect anomalous activity and improve incident response times.

NERC-CIP Certification

For certification, entities must demonstrate compliance with the NERC Critical Infrastructure Protection (CIP) standards through regular (annual) audits conducted by NERC or a Regional Entity, which verify the implementation of required security controls. For individuals, NERC offers the System Operator Certification Program, which requires passing an exam and completing continuing education.

The HIPAA Standard

HIPAA (The Health Insurance Portability and Accountability Act, 1996) protects sensitive Patient Health Information (PHI) and ensures privacy and gives patients control over their health information requiring healthcare organizations to implement management of data security in storage and in transit, and with patient rights management to access and correct their health records. It provides protection for sharing patient data with insurance providers and Health Information Exchanges.

The HIPAA Privacy Rule safeguards PHI, and the *Security Rule* protects a subset of information covered by the *Privacy Rule*. This subset includes all individually identifiable health information a covered entity that obtains and stores patient information creates, receives, maintains, or transmits in electronic form. This information is called *electronic protected health information,* or *e-PHI*. The Security Rule does not apply to PHI transmitted orally or in writing.

- HIPAA gives patients the right to access, to see, and get a copy of their health information. Organizations should send patient health information only to an entity they can you trust, whether individual or an organization.
- A patient's care provider is no longer responsible for the security of the patient's health information after it is sent to a third party.
- Organizations should send PHI as a password protected/encrypted attachment when possible.
- The Privacy Rule allows covered health care providers to communicate electronically

ANSI ASC X12 Standard

The ANSI ASC X12 Standard also called the EDI ASC X12, ANSI X12, ASC X12, or X12 Standard is a message formatting standard used for Electronic Data Interchange (EDI) documents. X12 HIPAA is a subset of the X12 standard that is used in the healthcare industry.

X12N Standard	Description
EDI 270	Eligibility, Coverage or Benefit Inquiry
EDI 271	Eligibility, Coverage or Benefit Information
EDI 275	Patient Information
EDI 276	Healthcare Claim Status Request
EDI 277	Healthcare Claim Status Notification
EDI 278	Healthcare Services Review
EDI 820	Payment Order/Remittance Advice
EDI 824	Application Advice correct and resubmit that transaction.
EDI 834	Benefit Enrollment and Maintenance -).
EDI 835	Healthcare Claim Payment/Advice
EDI 837-P	Healthcare Claim: Professional

EDI 837-D	Healthcare Claim: Dental
EDI 837-I	Healthcare Claim: Institutional
EDI 997	Functional Acknowledgment for Healthcare Insurance
EDI 999	Implementation Acknowledgment for Healthcare Insurance
EDI TA1	Interchange Acknowledgment

Table 6-4 : Sampling of ANSI X12N Standards Used for HIPAA Compliance

HITRUST (Health Information Trust Alliance)

HITRUST is a security standards organization and certifying body. HITRUST Core standard, the HITRUST CSF (Common Security Framework), is a voluntary industry agnostic security framework and organization that provides information risk management and compliance assessments and certifications.

HITRUST CSF

HITRUST developed the HITRUST CSF, a comprehensive, prescriptive, and certifiable security and privacy framework designed to help organizations of all sizes and industries manage the risk of handling sensitive data. HITRUST CSF is a risk-based approach that maps to over 50 authoritative security standards and regulatory requirements, including HIPAA, GDPR, NIST and ISO 27001, and others. It integrates many regulatory, legal, and industry-standard requirements, such as HIPAA, ISO, and PCI DSS, into a single, flexible framework. Organizations can achieve HITRUST certification by implementing the framework's controls and by undergoing rigorous assessment, which demonstrates a commitment to strong security and privacy protections.

Although originally focused on the healthcare industry's Protected Health Information (PHI), the HITRUST CSF is now an industry-agnostic framework that incorporates requirements from various regulations and standards like HIPAA, GDPR, NIST and ISO 27001. Although not federally mandated HITRUST certification has become an industry required certification. HITRUST helps organizations manage information risk, comply with regulations, and demonstrate their commitment to security.

HITRUST provides scalability through a suite of assessments and certifications based on its framework, including different levels of assurance. The assurance levels e1 (entry level for startups or low-risk organization), i1 (certifiable threat adaptive cybersecurity assessment for moderate risk organizations), and r2 (risk-based 2-year assured certification for maximum protection), which are designed to meet different organizational needs and risk profiles.

HITRUST certification requires ongoing validation to demonstrates a commitment to continuous improvement in information security practices. HITRUST also offers AI security and AI risk management assurance products to address the unique security challenges introduced by AI technology.

HITRUST CSF Security Controls

The HITRUST CSF (Common Security Framework) organizes security and privacy controls into 19 domains, which cover aspects of information protection, risk management, and regulatory compliance. The following describes these 19 domains.

1. *Information Protection Program*: maintaining a comprehensive cybersecurity and data security program.
2. *Endpoint Protection*: safeguards network-connected devices (endpoints) including laptops, desktops, mobile phones, and servers from cyber threats.
3. *Portable Media Security*: covers the security of data stored on removable media like USB drives.
4. *Mobile Device Security*: securing mobile devices used for accessing orgs data and systems.
5. *Wireless Protection*: secure wireless network and devises and prevent unauthorized access, and protect data transmitted over wireless connections such as WiFi.
6. *Configuration Management*: ensures systems and software are configured securely.
7. *Vulnerability Management*: identification, assessment, remediation of security vulnerabilities.
8. *Network Protection*: focuses on securing the organization's network infrastructure.
9. *Transmission Protection*: addresses the security of data transmitted over networks.
10. *Password Management*: covers the creation, storage, and management of strong passwords.
11. *Access Control*: ensures only authorized individuals have access to sensitive data and systems.
12. *Audit Logging & Monitoring*: logging and monitoring system activity for security purposes.
13. *Education, Training & Awareness*: security training and awareness programs for employees.
14. *Third-Party Security*: security of data and systems managed by third-party vendors.
15. *Incident Management*: covers the processes for responding to and managing security incidents.
16. *Business Continuity & Disaster Recovery*: business operations can continue running on disaster
17. *Risk Management*: identification, assessment, and mitigation of information security risks.
18. *Physical & Environmental Security*: covers the physical security of facilities and equipment.
19. *Data Protection & Privacy*: protecting sensitive data, ensuring compliance with privacy regulation.

HITRUST provides a risk-based method for assessing and managing security challenges, allowing for customized and scaled implementations of security controls to meet specific organizational needs, and is scalable for organizations of different sizes.

Certification: Organizations use the HITRUST CSF to implement and assess the appropriate administrative, technical, and physical controls. A certified HITRUST assessor audits the implementation of these controls, performing tests and collecting data to validate the organization's security posture. Upon successful completion of the audit, the organization earns HITRUST certification

Sarbanes-Oxley Act of 2002 (SOX)

SOX is a U.S. law mandating strict internal controls to ensure the accuracy and security of financial data for publicly traded companies. SOX compliance requires robust cybersecurity practices to protect sensitive financial information from unauthorized access, manipulation, and breaches, thereby safeguarding investor trust and preventing corporate fraud. SOX was passed in response to major corporate accounting scandals in the early 2000s, such as those involving Enron and WorldCom, which eroded public confidence in financial markets.

The primary goal is to improve the accuracy and reliability of corporate financial reporting and to protect the public and investors from fraudulent practices. It applies to all publicly traded companies in the U.S. and foreign companies doing business in the U.S.

SOX compliance requires organizations to implement 1) *Data Integrity* controls to ensure that financial data is accurate, reliable, and free from errors or tampering, 2) *Data Security* and cybersecurity measures that are essential to protect financial data from unauthorized access, breaches, and cyberattacks, 3) *Internal Controls* to establish, maintain, and document strong internal control frameworks, which include IT and data security protocols, 4) *Audit Requirements* for annual audits of their financial statements and internal controls to ensure compliance with SOX, 5) *Executive Accountability* tracking through signatures on annual reports con comply with the requirements of the law to holds corporate executives responsible for the accuracy of financial disclosures and the effectiveness of internal controls.

Technical aspects of SOX compliance

These include Access Control for limiting and monitoring who can access sensitive financial data, change management to ensure that changes to systems and financial data are properly controlled and documented, and Data Management for proper classification, storage, and handling of sensitive financial information. It also requires Regular Continuous Monitoring of networks, monitoring network, database, and user activity for suspicious behavior and a documented process for Data Backup and Recovery of financial data.

United States State Laws and Regulations Details

In the absence of a federal data privacy law, states within the United States have enacted their own laws. The following describes the 20 state laws currently in force.

California CPRA (California Privacy Rights Act 2018

CPRA is the amended and enhanced version of the original CCPA. It was the first state law in the United States followed by Vermont and Colorado. CPRA was patterned after GDPR but with some key differences.

CPRA Differences from GDPR

They differ significantly in their scope, requirements, and enforcement. GDPR applies to personal data of individuals in the EU, while CPRA focuses on California residents' data. GDPR emphasizes "privacy by default" and requires explicit consent for data processing, whereas CPRA provides consumers with the right to opt-out of the sale of their personal information. Key highlights of CPRA include:

- Applies to for-profit businesses that : 1) have a gross annual revenue exceeding $25 million; or 2) buy, sell, or share the personal information of 100,000 or more California residents or households; or 3) derive 50% or more of their annual revenue from selling consumers' personal information.
- Covers personal information of California residents, including data relating to their household.
- Focuses on Consumer rights. Including right to opt-out of the sale of PI, with requirements for businesses to provide a "Do Not Sell My Personal Information" link on their website.
- Does not specifically regulate automation or profiling, though the CPRA will expand on this.
- Excludes some health information, such as data collected for clinical trials.

Consumer rights:

- *Right to Know*: Consumers can request what a business has collected about them, used, and shared with third parties.
- *Right to Delete*: Consumers can request that businesses delete their personal data.
- *Right to Correct*: Consumers can request that businesses correct inaccurate PI.
- *Right to Opt-Out of Sale/Sharing*: Consumers can opt-out of the sale or sharing of their PI
- *Right to Limit Use/Disclosure of Sensitive Information*: Consumers can limit businesses use.
- *Right to Non-Discrimination*: prohibits businesses from treating customers or employees differently.
- *Businesses cannot discriminate* against consumers for exercising their CCPA rights.

VCDPA (Virginia Consumer Data Protection Act)

VCDPA lacks explicit legal basis requirements for processing personal data that GDPR has, instead focuses on purpose limitations and consumer rights. VCDPA does not require the appointment of data protection officers or the implementation of privacy-by-design principles, unlike GDPR.

- Applies to businesses that conduct business in Virginia or target Virginia residents with products or services. It has exemptions for non-profits, government agencies, and some other entities.
- Does not explicitly require a legal basis for processing. Instead, it focuses on purpose limitations, restricting how data can be used without explicit permission.
- adopts the principle of data minimization.
- Adopts the controller/processor distinction as well, mirroring GDPR's framework.
- Streamlines obligations and enforcement mechanisms, making it more business-friendly

As in the case of GDPR, VCDPA has the similar following consumer rights requirements:

- ***Access***: Consumers can request access to their personal data held by a business.
- ***Correction***: Consumers can request corrections to inaccurate personal data.
- ***Deletion***: Consumers can request the deletion of their personal data.
- ***Portability***: Consumers can request a copy of their personal data in a portable format.
- ***Opt-out***: Consumers can opt-out personal data for targeted advertising, sale, or profiling.
- ***Non-discrimination***: Businesses cannot discriminate against consumers exercising their rights.
- ***Vendor Contracts***: Businesses must have contracts with vendors for processing personal data.
- ***Privacy Notices***: Businesses must provide clear and concise privacy notices to consumers.

While enumerating all 20 state laws is not in scope for this book, the table below compares the key highlights of the laws enacted in 20 states in the United States.

#	Law	Description and Highlights
1.	California CPRA (California Privacy Rights Act 2018, amended and enhanced CCPA)	Establishes privacy rights and business requirements for collecting and selling Californians' personal information.
2.	Colorado Privacy Act (CPA), 2021	Five key rights for Colorado consumers include the 1) Right to access 2) Right to correction, 3)

		Right to delete, 4) Right to data portability, 5) Right to opt out.
3.	Connecticut Data Privacy Act (CTDPA), 2023	Includes stronger data protections for children but a similar framework as its predecessors such as CPRA.
4.	Delaware Personal Data Privacy Act, 2025	This Act has stronger privacy rights for consumers, such as heightening protections for children's data, broadening definitions of sensitive data, and being able to opt out of the processing of personal data for targeted advertising purposes.
5.	Florida Digital Bill of Rights (FDBR), enacted as SB 262 in 2023	Tackles issues related to tech platforms, like addressing alleged censorship of conservative viewpoints. The law requires search engines, such as Google, to disclose if they prioritize results based on political ideology and prohibits government-mandated content moderation on social media.
6.	Indiana Consumer Data Protection Act, 2023 (effective in 2026)	Regulates businesses that process the personal data of at least 100,000 Indiana residents, or ones that handle the information of at least 25,000 state consumers but derive more than 50% of their revenue from selling data
7.	Iowa Consumer Data Protection Act (ICDPA), 2025	Weaker data protections, does not grant consumers the right to delete or correct data collected by third parties.
8.	Kentucky Consumer Data Act (KCDPA), 2024 (effective 2026)	Applies to entities that conduct business in the state or target residents and manage the personal data of at least 100,000 consumers per year. That threshold drops to 25,000 consumers if a business derives more than half its gross revenue from selling personal data. Businesses will have the opportunity to remedy violations within 30 days without penalty. Exemptions under the law include government entities, federally regulated financial institutions, and nonprofits.
9.	Maryland Online Data Privacy Act (MODPA), 2024 (effective 2025)	Imposes more stringent privacy standards on businesses than similar laws in other states. Consumer

		advocates say language requiring a company to minimize the data it holds from the outset marks a departure from industry-supported measures elsewhere
10.	Minnesota Consumer Data Privacy Act (MCDPA), 2025	It diverges from other states by allowing consumers to question automated decisions made about them via profiling. Profiling occurs when a company uses personal data to evaluate or predict an individual's health, interests, economic status, or other characteristics
11.	Montana's Consumer Data Privacy Act, 2024	This Act limits the collection of personal data to only "adequate, relevant, and reasonably necessary" information. Residents have the right to opt-out or decline the sale of their personal data
12.	New Hampshire Privacy Act (NHPA), 2025	Consumers have the right to know what data a company collects and opt out of certain uses, such as targeted advertising.
13.	Nebraska Data Privacy Act (NDPA), 2025	The law excludes federally defined small businesses and includes numerous exemptions, such as for federally regulated financial institutions. Residents have the right to request that companies correct or delete their data. They can opt out of having their personal data sold or used for targeted advertising or profiling
14.	New Jersey Data Privacy Act (NJDPA), 2025	Provides New Jersey residents with comprehensive privacy protections against how companies collect and use their personal information
15.	Oregon Consumer Privacy Act (OCPA), 2025	One of the strongest data privacy laws passed to date, includes provisions on biometric data, sensitive and personal data, and children's data protections, and it doesn't have the same exemptions found in other state privacy laws.
16.	Rhode Island Data Transparency and Privacy Protection Act (RI-DTPPA), 2024	Drew criticism from consumer advocates who argued it doesn't meaningfully limit how companies collect or use personal information. Consumers will have the right to confirm what data a company

		collects, correct it, receive a copy, and opt out of certain uses. Companies must also secure consent before processing sensitive data.
17.	Tennessee Information Protection Act. 2025	Backed with bipartisan support, the Tennessee Information Protection Act enables consumers to confirm that a business has collected their personal data, obtain a copy of the information, and request that inaccuracies be corrected.
18.	Texas Data Privacy and Security Act (TDPSA), 2024	Comprehensive privacy law, giving residents more control over their personal data. Effective July 1, 2024, the Texas Data Privacy and Security Act (TDPSA) applies to large companies that do business in Texas or sell, collect, or process personal data. Small businesses are mostly exempt.
19.	Utah Consumer Privacy Act (UCPA), 2023	Takes a business-friendly approach to consumer protection but still It mandates that businesses with over $25M revenue, 100,000 consumers (or 25,000 and 50%+ revenue from sales), allow access, deletion, and opt-outs of data sales/targeted.
20.	Virginia Consumer Data Protection Act (VCDPA), 2021	Gives Virginians the right to access their data and request that their personal information be deleted by businesses. It also requires companies to conduct data protection assessments to process personal data for targeted advertising and sales purposes.

Table 6-5 : United States Privacy Laws by Specific States

Data Subject Access Request (DSAR)

Individuals, known as data subjects, have a right to obtain a copy of their personal data collected and held by an organization. Under data privacy laws like the GDPR and CCPA as well as many state laws in the US, individuals have the right to know what data is collected, how it's used, and with whom it's shared. Companies must verify the requester's identity and respond to these requests within a specific timeframe, typically one month. A DSAR, or Data Subject Access Request, is an individual's formal request to a company for a copy of the personal data the company holds about them.

A DSAR is a right granted by data privacy regulations such as the GDPR (General Data Protection Regulation) and CCPA (California Consumer Privacy Act) and a number of other laws based on or derived from these. These regulations require the organizations to respond to a DSAR within a set period, often weeks or a month, though extensions are possible for complex requests. Proper handling of DSARs is crucial for legal compliance and to maintain trust with individuals

A DSAR ensures that the individual can request and receive a copy of all personal data an organization has collected on them., verify it's accuracy and request corrections or even have the data deleted. Individuals also have a right to know what the organization is using their data for and get the details on how the data is processed, stored, and with whom it is shared.

Data Security Compliance

Data security compliance is a critical aspect of data governance that involves adhering to the security-centric rules and regulations set forth by supervisory and regulatory bodies, including federal agencies. These rules and regulations cover a broad spectrum of data security, including technical and organizational security measures, data security tools and solutions, and data breach prevention techniques and strategies.

The following describes key aspects of managing data for security compliance:

Data Discovery: identify and map out all sensitive and regulated data within the organization and document where it resides. These should also include AI datasets which may contain sensitive information used for training if any. Security teams should deploy tools for automatic data classification, especially for PII and financial data, and implement continuous visibility solutions like DSPM (Data Security Posture Management) to track operational data flows.

Catalog and Manage Data: The security team should establish a data catalog for data discovered in the previous step to provide an organized inventory with a searchable index of datasets. Metadata management approaches should be used to track data origin, usage and governance rules. Tagging sensitive data is important for regulatory reporting. Also ensure that the data catalog is updated automatically when datasets change.

Track Data Lineage and AI Traceability: The security team should track data movement through the system and in storage for auditing and compliance evidence. All AI models should be fully traceable.

Data Security, Encryption and Access Controls: Data at rest and in transit should be secured through strong encryption and all AI training data should be similarly protected. Role based access control (RBAC) and least privilege principles should be applied to ensure only authorized personnel can access any data, models or outputs. MFA (multi-factor authentication must be used for sensitive data access.

Data Minimization and Anonymization: While collecting and storing only the minimal amount of data necessary, anonymization and pseudonymization should be used to mask or hide or remove sensitive PII data.

Data Security Standards Compliance Tools

Many tools are in use for ensuring compliance with data security standards and ensuring privacy of the data collected by an organization.

Data Mapping Tools

Data mapping is the process of translating and aligning data fields between different systems. Data mapping is crucial for data privacy because it creates a map of all personal data, showing what's collected, where it lives, who uses it, and why. It helps in enabling compliance with data privacy laws like GDPR and CCPA. It also helps in standardizing data privacy fields such as "CustID" or "Customer ID" mapping for seamless data integration, migration, and analysis and for rapid responses to data subject access requests.

Data mapping tools with ETL (Extract, Transform, Load) capabilities and using visual interfaces ensure data quality using AI, supporting regulatory compliance, and unified customer views through automation to reduce manual effort.

These tools connect disparate data sources (databases, apps, files) for unified views and convert data types, formats, and structures (e.g., dates, addresses) to a common standard. They automate mapping using visual interfaces, reducing manual coding and errors, often with pre-built connectors and provide a bird's-eye view of data flow, crucial for privacy requests from data subjects and for regulatory audits.

Data Governance for regulatory compliance supports data quality, lineage, and compliance by tracking data movement and ensuring consistency.

Common Techniques provided by Data Mapping tools for supporting these functions include rules based (e.g. map only if value is > 0) conditional mapping, use of tables to find corresponding clause supporting lookup mapping, or a field values-based mapping.

Examples of Tools commonly used for Data Mapping include:

- Talent open Studio Open-source with rich connectors.
- Pentaho data Integration (Kettle): Visual data exploration and ETL.
- Boomi AtomSphere: Cloud-based integration platform.
- Map Force: Maps between various formats (XML, JSON, DBs, files).
- Alation/Osano: Focus on data intelligence, governance, and privacy.

Compliance Automation Tools

Data privacy compliance means an organization must follows laws, standards, and policies for handling personal data responsibly, ensuring that it has been collected with consent from the data subject, used transparently, stored securely, and that the organization respects individuals' rights (like access or deletion). Typically data privacy compliance implies adhering to regulations like HIPAA, GDPR. CCPA or their derivatives to avoid penalties and build trust. Data privacy compliance requires setting up and rigorously enforcing technical safeguards (cybersecurity, encryption) and organizational measures (staff training, consent management) to protect data and individuals' privacy rights.

Automating compliance makes data privacy compliance a lot easier by automating and using technologies like AI to automatically manage, monitor, and enforce adherence to industry regulations (like HIPAA, GDPR). Enforcement of internal policies, replacing slow, error-prone manual tasks with streamlined, continuous processes for tasks like evidence collection, reporting, and risk assessment are important components fo automation. It centralizes compliance activities and ensures consistent adherence by handling repetitive tasks and providing real-time alerts for potential violations, leading to increased efficiency and lower risk.

Compliance automation tools are software platforms that use technology, often AI and machine learning, to streamline managing regulatory requirements by automating evidence collection, control monitoring, risk assessment, and reporting, reducing manual effort for frameworks like SOC 2, ISO 27001, HIPAA and GDPR.

The following are some examples of commonly used automation tools:

- AuditBoard: Enterprise platform for risk, audit, and compliance workflows.
- Sprinto: Focuses on automating security controls for SMBs (SOC 2, ISO 27001).
- Vanta: Trust management platform with support for numerous frameworks.
- OneTrust: Specializes in data privacy and governance (GDPR, CCPA).
- LogicGate: Flexible GRC platform for unique organizational needs.

Privacy Impact Assessment Platforms

Privacy Impact Assessment (PIA) platforms are software tools that help organizations automate, manage, and streamline the process of analyzing how new or existing systems, projects, or technologies handle personal data, ensuring compliance with privacy laws (like GDPR or HIPAA), identifying risks, documenting data flows, and implementing mitigation controls before deployment, making privacy a proactive part of development.

PIAs provide automated workflows to guide users through steps like data mapping, risk identification, and control implementation, often with customizable templates. They include built-in templates and frameworks for leading privacy regulations such as GDPR and help track and document what information is collected, where it is stored, and how it moves across systems. Furthermore, they analyze potential privacy risks, bias, and compliance gaps, and suggest mitigation strategies.

An important PIA feature is its user interface in the form of a centralized dashboard that provides real-time monitoring and a unified view of assessment progress. In addition to the dashboard, PIAs allow creating reports and documentation for compliance and public disclosure.

PIAs are used by both government agencies as well as businesses. Government agencies (like DHS, GSA) use them to meet legal mandates.

Businesses in regulated industries (like healthcare, finance) also use them to ensure regulatory compliance. Organizations are also focusing more on developing new AI systems or processing sensitive data.

Consent Management Solutions

Consent is an important principle within data privacy regulatory standards. Consent is defined as the data subject's freely given, specific, informed, and unambiguous agreement to the collection, storage and processing of their personal data, signified by a clear affirmative action. It must be a genuine choice, presented in plain language, and the individual has the right to withdraw consent at any time.

For example, the key requirement for valid GDPR consent is that it is freely given and the data subject must have a genuine choice without coercion or pressure. It must also be specific and for a particular purpose, not a broad or vague agreement. Furthermore, for the consent to be informed, the data subject must know the identity of the data controller and the purpose(s) for which their data will be processed. Consent must be provided as a clear affirmative action such as a written statement, an electronic statement, or ticking a box (not pre-ticked) so that it is unambiguous. It is also a requirement of GDPR that the consent is revocable, that is the data subject can withdraw their consent as easily as they gave it, and this must be respected. An organization must maintain a documented methodology to track how and when consent was given and how it was revoked.

7 – Data Loss Prevention

Data is what drives the business and profits of every organization. As an organization's data footprint expands across on-premises, colocation service providers and various cloud service providers, along with SaaS applications, the organization's risk of a data breach and exposure also increases. Hackers and cybercriminals are seeking to exploit security vulnerabilities to access sensitive data that is spread across multiple data centers and data stores. The hackers and cybercriminals may be state actors with political motives, individuals extracting revenge or looking for financial gain though ransom activities. Ransoms to release locks on data can run into huge payouts from organizations.

Data security is an important subset of cybersecurity. Cyberattacks may have originated due to ransom demands or by state actors looking for political or national disruptions. But one of the primary reasons for cyberattacks is exfiltration of corporate data: employee IDs and password, sensitive customer personal information data and financial records of an organization. These can be sold by bad actors on the dark web to ready buyers who can monetize this data

Data Classifications

Data is classified as follows to apply appropriate security controls, ensuring sensitive (personally identifiable information (PI or PII) , restricted/highly confidential) data gets stronger protection like encryption and strict access rules, while public data needs minimal security. Even confidential data is sometimes called sensitive data, but it does not have the same security considerations as PII or credentials data.

- Public data consists of data distributed as datasheets, on websites, and mass emails and can be redistributed within or outside the organization. Some of this data such as annual reports and press releases may be protected by copyrights which require third parties to obtain written permission or license to redistribute.
- Internal data is for the organization's internal use and not for public release (e.g., employee handbooks, sales strategies, etc.)
- Confidential information (such as, financial records, vendor contracts, employee salaries) is data that if released to the public could harm the business. It is the most common type of data created and shared within the organization and is the default classification if one has not been explicitly defined.

- Restricted, Highly Confidential data is controlled access data that includes sensitive information that requires access limitations and is available to a limited number of employees, and authorized non-employees (temporary worker, contractor, consultant, or vendor), with a legitimate business purpose, and must be protected at all times. Data must be encrypted at rest and in transit.

The table breaks down further the restricted data into Highly Confidential, Authentication Credentials and Authentication Identifiers.

Classification	Description	Reason for Protection
Highly Confidential	Customer identity, Non-public information personally identifiable information (PII) government identification, driver license, passport, biometrics, or other government issued ID	Regulatory, Legal
Authentication Credentials	Username, password, credit cards, and mobile phone number.	Regulatory, Legal, reputation
Authentication Identifiers	DOB, mother's maiden name, phone # on account, parties to an account, etc,	Regulatory, legal, customer data
Confidential	Customer information, sales records, financial records, email, addresses, bank balances, etc.	Regulatory, Legal
Proprietary	Company's org charts, design documents, telephone directories, department reports, financial reports, emails, communications, etc.	Company's crown jewels
Private	Company's private data such as customer lists, customer account details other than PII.	Competitive critical information
Public	Published data visible to all – marketing literature, websites, etc.	No protection required.

Table 7-1 : Data Classification Types

Note: Authentication credentials and identifiers are also considered Highly Confidential.

Sensitive Data: Sensitive data is any data that if breached would cause damage to the mission of the organization. All of the classes of data listed in the table above except Private data are considered sensitive data that needs to be protected. Note that the Highly Confidential and Authentication data needs special care and protections for the cases of data at rest, data in transit and data in use. A data breach is any event in which an unauthorized entity is able to view or access sensitive data

Data Loss Prevention

Data loss prevention (DLP) includes all tools, technologies, and initiatives for preventing loss of data due to unauthorized access and exposure of confidential and highly confidential data (collectively sensitive data) that should be accessible only to authorized users with proper permissions, privileges, and justification to access the data. DLP technologies use data classification labels and tags, content inspection techniques, and contextual analysis to identify sensitive data and determine protection actions. They also provide centralized policy management that drive these actions. DLP solutions can be described as Enterprise DLP, Integrated DLP and Cloud-Native DLP.

Enterprise DLP

Financial institutions, and corporate and government organizations that hold PI (personal information) are required by international regulations and standards to ensure protection of their data assets. Enterprise DLP solutions satisfy the needs for regulatory compliance, internal policy and standards compliance, and overall proprietary and sensitive data protection. They provide centralized policy management and reporting, and implement controls and alerts across endpoints, networks, email, and cloud. They implement advanced content inspection and remediation.

Integrated DLP

These solutions include natively integrated services such as secure email or web gateway and endpoint. They also provide some level of policy management and reporting.

Cloud-Native DLP

These solutions address the cloud-native use cases such as, data security for SaaS applications and public cloud based applications. These solutions are customized for cloud environments.

Data Breach Protection

Data breach protection applies to protecting a set of personal data that is narrower than that protected in the more general privacy protections. The primary issue that businesses are contending with is that the law's requirements could threaten established business models throughout the digital sector. For instance, companies that generate revenue from targeted advertising over internet platforms — such as Facebook, Twitter, and Google — must, as the California law is currently written, allow California residents to delete their data or bring it with them to alternative service providers. This restriction could extend to internet service providers such as AT&T and Verizon, which collect broadband activity data (web browsing data) and could attempt to use it to generate behavioral profiles for marketing purposes.

Risk Management

For a business, risk management is a very important consideration to ensure proper security controls to prevent data exposure. It is even more important when breach of sensitive data or exposure of employee or customer personal information can result in significant penalties and loss of reputation. Risk assessment is the responsibility of every organization.

Risk appetite is the extent of risk in financial loss and the loss of reputation terms that an organization is willing to accept in the pursuit of its business, financial and strategic perspectives. Risk appetite reflects the risk management posture of the Board of Directors that drives the security controls and the security culture of the organization.

Risk management is qualitative and quantitative. Use qualitative assessments with new, untrained, or insufficient data. The documentation for risk assessments should include: the information security program details including policies, standards, procedures, guidelines and baselines; technical information including network diagrams, application documents, BCDR plan, incident response, etc.

The following describes the key considerations for risk management:

- Risk should always be considered from a business perspective often balanced by opportunity and not be compromised for profit, performance, or costs. In the case of cloud-based environments, risk is a shared responsibility with the CSP, but the organization cannot abdicate its own responsibility of ensuring proper identity and access management controls.
- Extending the network perimeter to the public clouds enhances opportunities for collaboration mostly by giving external partners and customers limited access to the data owner's data in the cloud. While this is risky, the comparable risk on legacy on-premises data is even higher in sending data out to partners or inviting partners into the protected corporate data centers.
- Some on-premises risks cannot be transferred to the cloud service provider such as liability for data exposure. The business or organization is ultimately responsible for liability from any data exposure. Some risks can be mitigated even in the cloud, but these must be clearly understood and negotiated when the CSP contract is established.
- While on premises data centers may experience resource exhaustion, it is conceivable that in the cloud also, a business continuity and disaster recovery threat can emerge and risk assessment must be performed for a contingency such as, all clients of the CSP demand extra resources at the same time or if the data centers experience a catastrophic failure.

Data Life Cycle

Any data created for an information system can undergo six phases during the course of its existence. These can best be remembered by the acronym CSU-SAD where the alphabets of the acronym are:

C S U – S A D – Create Store Use -- Share Archive Destroy

Data security applies to the full cycle of data through the six phases listed below. It must be protected during every phase of this cycle.

Phase	On-Premises Management	Public Cloud Management
Create	Data is created by a user when that person executes an application and enters information. The data must be classified at the time of creation and sensitive data (such as PI information) should be encrypted, masked or tokenized immediately before storing that data. The user may be a data subject or some other user acting as agent on behalf of user agent (such as a banker or stockbroker).	Data will most often be created by users accessing the cloud remotely. Depending on the use case, the data might be created locally, by users at their remote workstation, and then uploaded to the cloud, or in the cloud datacenter via remote manipulation of the data residing there. When data is created remotely, the data created by the user should be encrypted before uploading to the cloud unless the transport mechanism is based on TLS 1.3 protocol at the transport layer. It must be protected against obvious vulnerabilities, including man-in-the-middle attacks and insider threat at the cloud data center.
Store	Store is usually meant to refer to near-term storage. The activity in the Store phase occurs almost concurrently with the Create phase— that is, Store will happen as data is created. Sensitive data should be encrypted when stored (data at Rest) for mitigating exposure to threats within the datacenter	Storing data in the cloud requires special consideration, especially, if it includes sensitive data. Data is stored in logical pools spread across physical storage that spans multiple servers (sometimes in multiple locations), and the physical environment is typically owned and managed by a hosting cloud service provider company. Advantages of cloud storage include usability, sharing data and accessibility, disaster recovery and cost-efficient scalability. Data Security is an additional concern for data stored in the cloud, especially sensitive data.
Use	Data in use is transferred to an application and converted back to ciphertext if transmitted in encrypted form. It is more vulnerable than data at rest because, by definition, it must be accessible to those who need it. The more people and devices that have access to the data, the greater the risk that it will end up in the wrong hands at some point. Securing data in use requires user authentication and controlling access as tightly as possible	Operations in the cloud environment will necessitate remote access, so those connections will all have to be secured, usually with an encrypted tunnel. Best practices include: • Not storing sensitive information • Encrypting data; explore using Cloud Services to encrypt data • Using strong passwords for cloud access, specially, if sensitive data is stored. • Separate encryption key storage from data storage.
Share	Sharing data with downstream applications is a common practice, which leaves a lot of questions to be answered depending on if the data is	Data moved into the cloud is typically used for sharing with other applications and needs special protections because the data owner has no control on the receiver of the data.

	shared among applications on-premises, to the cloud or to third parties. Key issues include data lineage, data owner rights and ability to define usage, and ensuring that entities receiving the data will honor security requirements.	Key approaches to protecting this data such as encryption and Digital Rights Management (DRM) become even more important for the cloud.
Archive	Data archiving is the process of moving data that is no longer actively used, but may be important to be retained long-term for future reference or regulatory reasons, to a separate storage device for long-term retention.	Cloud archiving is often completely in a public cloud. Some key points to consider: • Does the archive include sensitive data and is it safe in the archive? • Is there a backup for the archive in case the cloud instance has a disaster? • Are all cloud data security rules applied to the archive?
Destroy	Sensitive data should be kept only as long as it is needed. Any data should also be destroyed when it is not needed to minimize the risk of disclosure and to reclaim storage space. Typical methods include: • Wiping and remote wiping (this requires multiple passes at replacing real data with fake data and reformatting multiple times). • Degaussing to remove all magnetic field. • Physical shredding of the hard disk or optical device.	The public cloud does not offer the option of degaussing or destroying the storage media by any other means. So, for data that is no longer needed and needs to be destroyed, an effective approach is crypto-shredding -- the process of encrypting the data once and then encrypting the encrypted data a second time with a different key, and then deleting both keys.

Table 7-2 : The CSU-SAD Data Life cycle

Data Security Posture Management

Best practices include continuously assessing the organization's data and security posture, automatically remediating issues with data policies, and maintaining compliance with industry regulations ensuring that data is known, protected, and governed depending on jurisdiction and data type.

- Use tools including AI based tools to discover data across the organization's infrastructure, including cloud, SaaS, and on-premises environments.

- Monitor changes and detect data drift from what is expected through continuous scanning and data mapping,
- Discover unknown data and identify whether it is sensitive or exposed to privacy or data security risks.

With data scattered across multiple clouds and data stores, security teams need continuous visibility into where their sensitive data resides, who has access, and which data is at risk. Data security tools need to provide automated data discovery and integrating data intelligence with on-premises data centers and other cloud risks. They should deliver DSPM telemetry without requiring additional tools and integrations. The tools should cover the areas such as on-premises or cloud misconfigurations, vulnerabilities, and other potential threats.

Protect Data at Rest, Data in Motion, Data in Use

Effective data protection requires knowing where your PI, PII or sensitive data is at all times. Organizations need to keep track of the data collected and used by their organization at all times. *Data Discovery Tools* can make the job of locating and tracking movement of data easier.

Data needs to be protected in three states: *at rest*, *in use*, and *in motion*. Each state presents unique security challenges. These challenges need to be addressed for all three states of the data. The table shows the data protections at rest, in-motion and in use for on-premises and cloud environments.

State	Protections	On-Premises	Cloud
Data at Rest	Encrypting Hard Drives or SSDs to protect data stored on them is the best way to ensure the security of data at rest. Also, storing individual data elements in separate locations decreases the likelihood of attackers gaining enough information to commit fraud or other crimes.	On-premises data is primarily protected by conventional perimeter-based defenses such as firewalls, passwords and anti-virus programs.	Encryption is the only real way to protect data at rest in the cloud because the cloud customer has no way to directly access or protect the hardware media.
Data in Motion	Data is at its most vulnerable when it is in motion. A growing volume of sensitive data is being transmitted digitally, forcing many organizations to replace couriers, faxes, and conventional mail service with faster options such as email. Policy filters that automatically detect sensitive information in	Data in motion from on-premises to the cloud must use secure transit paths and all data must have TLS 1.3 encryption at the transport layer. The same rule applies to data being transmitted from the public cloud to your or your partner's on-premises locations.	Data transmission within the public clouds is encrypted by default by the cloud service provider Data transmission from one cloud to another if managed by your

	email and attached files can automate the encryption process to further ensure security (and regulatory compliance Anyone with the right tools can intercept an email as it moves along this path.	It is also important for the encryption service the organization uses to cover mobile email applications.	organization needs to follow the same general rules as data transmitted from on-premises to the public cloud standard email service.
Data in Use	Data in use is more vulnerable than data at rest because, by definition, it must be accessible to those who need it. The more users and devices that have access to the data, the greater the risk that it will end up in the wrong hands at some point. The keys to securing data in use are to control access as tightly as possible	Organizations also need to be able to track and report relevant information so they can detect suspicious activity, diagnose potential threats, and proactively improve security. For example, an account being disabled due to a certain number of failed login attempts could be a warning sign.	Data in use in public clouds needs to follow the same rules as the on-premises data in use in terms of least privilege and role-based permissions for accessing and using the data, and reporting suspicious activity.

Table 7-3 : States of Data

Data Risk Assessment

Your organization needs to always assess risk from a workflow perspective.

1. Do employees access corporate systems from their personal devices or use company-issued devices to work from home?
2. What happens when employees take their devices on business trips? How is data transferred between devices or communicated to other stakeholders?
3. What your customers or business partners do with any sensitive files you send them?

Information will end up spreading across multiple devices and networks with varying degrees of security and risk. The following need to be addressed:

- What types of sensitive data does the organization store, use, or transmit?
- Who has access to this data and where, when, and why are they using it?
- How is data stored when it is not in use?
- How is access to databases controlled?
- What mechanisms are used to transport data?

- What are the pertinent laws, regulations, and standards?

Data Protection Best Practices

There are several data protection management practices. Some of the most commonly used include:

- *Data loss prevention (DLP)*: this consists of a set of tools and processes used to secure data from theft, loss, misuse, deletion, or other illegal or inappropriate forms of contact, or modification, or exfiltration.
- *Firewalls*: Typically, software tools used for monitoring and filtering the network traffic to ensure data is transferred or accessed only by authorized users. Firewalls can block access by unauthorized entities.
- *Encryption*: Altering the content of data based on an algorithm that can be reversed only with the right encryption password or key. Encryption protects data even if it gets stolen, since the data would be unreadable without the key required to decrypt the data.
- *Data erasure*: Deleting data that is no longer needed or relevant. Although no longer needed, the data may contain PI, PII or sensitive data which, if exposed, can harm the organization. This is also a requirement of the GDPR.
- *Data resiliency*: Building resiliency systems within the software and hardware of an organization's system to ensure the security in case of natural disasters or power outages. Disaster Recovery in case of a catastrophic data center failure or a ransomware attack is of paramount importance for your organization.
- *Data backups*: A plan to securely back up data on a daily and weekly basis is essential to address loss of data in case of failure or breach of the data centers. Such backup plans may include a separate physical disk or cloud.

Who is responsible for Protecting Data

The responsibility matrix in the following table illustrates the legal responsibility with respect to data exposure, notifications to the organization's customers affected by the breach, costs associated with remediation, and penalties if imposed by regulatory agencies. While this matrix describes some aspects of legal responsibility, the organization as the data owner (and more particularly, executives such as eh CEO, COO and CISO of the organization that created and or acquired the data) always have responsibility and legal liability in the case of a data breach or exposure even though the exposure may have been the result of negligence by a private cloud hosting provider or a public cloud service provider or the organization's own workforce member.

Data Processor	Organization Responsible	Legal Responsibility
The business	The IT Staff managing the entire physical network and software infrastructure	The organization has the responsibility for the security of ALL data assets. In addition, the

on-premises IT	within the organization. The organization must have defined policies and standards based on ISO, NIST, GDPR and other regulatory jurisdictions tailored according to the organization's risk profile.	organization has the responsibility for notifying the data subjects within the time period (number of days) of the occurrence of the disclosure based on the legal requirements of the governing jurisdictions.
Hosting Service Provider (HSP)	This is a shared responsibility structure because the hosting service provider has the network, storage and access control responsibilities.	However, The legal responsibility for the PII data rests always the organization and not the HSP. The terms of the contract drive the responsibility for the HSP to ensure that they maintain a secure environment for the PII data.
Cloud Service Provider (CSP)	The deployment model (IaaS, PaaS, SaaS) determines the shared responsibility structure. The organization has more responsibility for data security under the IaaS model than it does under the PaaS model and the least responsibility under the SaaS model.	However, the ultimate legal responsibility for the PI or PII data rests always with the organization and not the CSP. The CSP typically has a menu for security operations. The terms of the contract drive the responsibility for the CSP to ensure that they maintain a secure environment for the PII data. However, your organization may not have much leverage on the CSP.
Business Partners	Business partners who may use the PII data of your organization must not retain it or ensure that the data is maintained at the same level of security as your organization. Your organization must contractually bind the business partner to ensure data privacy and security	Despite the contract, the legal and notification responsibility for the PII data rests with the organization always, and not the business partner. The terms of the contract drive the responsibility for the business partner to ensure that they maintain a secure environment for the PII data and the damages sharing they are responsible for in case of a breach

Table 7-4 : Data Management Roles and Responsibilities

Ensuring data Confidentiality

To protect important data from loss or inappropriate disclosure, the organization needs to follow these approaches and best practices for effective ways to ensure the confidentiality of sensitive data in the organization:

- Restrict access to data strictly on a need to know and need-to-use basis.
- Implement a confidentiality policy that is actively socialized and rigorously applied and managed.

- Implement a data retention policy to remove unused or unneeded confidential data to avoid inadvertent exposure. Delete sensitive data no longer needed. Storage of unused or unneeded sensitive data increases chances of inadvertent exposure.
- Take physical security measures to protect all data in data centers and access controls for all confidential data on-premises and in the cloud environments.
- Develop and implement a cybersecurity program and assign a team for the governance of the program.
- Protect all confidential and sensitive data through binding non-disclosure agreements.
- Protect data at rest. Encrypt sensitive data at rest. Enable full disk encryption on all devices.
- Restrict confidential data to the office. Workforce members (employees and contractors) should not be allowed to carry confidential or sensitive data on their mobile devices

Types of Data Architecture

In the modern IT architecture, it is important to understand how the organization's businesses collect, use, and dispose of data. From a storage perspective, three types of data architecture stand out:

- *Application Data* – Data stored within a data store managed by the application; this is typically used only by that application.
- *Data Warehouses* – A compilation of data from several related applications such as customer data, order entry data, billing and payment data, and so on. This compiled data allows correlation and advanced reporting using artificial intelligence (AI) techniques. It acts as the single version of truth for all applications and can be stored for the duration of the required data retention period.
- *Data Lakes and Lakehouses* – These can be thought of as low-cost high-volume storage with high-performance analytics of all current and historical data, usually captured from the data warehouse(s) and retained for long periods of time in lower cost storage

Endpoint DLP solutions

Endpoint DLP is typically a software agent that looks for out-of-policy data use on endpoints such as laptops and mobile devices. Some endpoint DLP agents may also provide the ability to perform data discovery and classification. Additionally, as mobile devices proliferate, mobile security and mobile device management (MDM) vendors will add DLP functionality. Expect to see many endpoint DLP offerings include device control capabilities for controlling data leakage to USB drives and CD/DVD burners. Device control technology has traditionally been a standalone product or has been embedded in antivirus software and endpoint security suites. However, as DLP moves from a product to a function that vendors embed into all manner of products, endpoint device control solutions should be considered as part of DLP.

Look for all endpoint DLP software to offer device control solutions that engage with their DLP inspection engines to proactively prevent data leakage via removable devices

Web DLP

Web DLP looks for data leaks via web channels (HTTP and HTTPS protocols). To do this, it must inspect encrypted HTTPS traffic. This requires vendors to build some type of decryption engine into their web DLP solutions. Inspecting SSL/TLS can be problematic from both a technological and privacy perspective. It's generally accepted that security professionals tell users when they inspect their SSL encrypted traffic.

Gateway DLP

Gateway DLP solutions were the DLP products that vendors first introduced into the market almost a decade ago. While these solutions were able to provide some data loss uplift for their users, they often promised more than they could deliver. As new threats evolved and cybercriminals discovered new data loss channels, these ubiquitous, all-in-one solutions were not able to meet customers' expectations. From a security professional's perspective, the best solution would be a single appliance to deploy at the egress point — such as a primary Internet connection — and stop all unauthorized data from leaving the organization's boundaries. While this is the endgame of most DLP initiatives, it has not proven a successful model given the multiplicity of extrusion channels that can potentially leak data

Network DLP tools

Recently, Forrester defined a new network security space known as network analysis and visibility (NAV). This includes such tools as flow data analysis, metadata analysis, and packet capture analysis. NAV gives security professionals situational awareness in their internal and external network.

Currently NAV is focused on visibility — who is doing what and when. However, because NAV tools look at all data moving across inspected network segments, vendors extend these tools to improve data discovery and provide DLP functionality. By using NAV with DLP functionality, security professionals can enable DLP directly on their network and look for data leakage before it reaches other extrusion channels.

Email DLP

Email DLP is the most mature of the DLP channels. Typically, vendors build DLP control into modern antimalware email gateways. Email DLP got its first big break when healthcare organizations found they needed to encrypt emails containing electronic PHI (ePHI). This led to email encryption engines with lexicons that identified prohibited terms or data strings and automatically encrypted those emails. Today, compliance mandates usually require security professionals to encrypt emails containing sensitive or toxic data.

Cloud DLP

Cloud DLP protects sensitive data (like PII, financial info, IP) within cloud environments (SaaS, IaaS, PaaS, storage, and apps) from accidental leaks, theft, or misuse by automatically detecting, classifying, and enforcing policies to control its sharing, movement, storage, and preventing exfiltration. This helps in ensuring compliance and reducing risk. It works by classifying data, scanning cloud services such as storage, databases, and applications to find and label sensitive data, by identifying critical information using pattern matching and machine learning, and taking action like blocking, encrypting, or redacting data before it leaves controlled boundaries.

DLP then applies rules to control data movement, preventing unauthorized sharing or access to data, specially to prevent exfiltration of sensitive data and blocks risky actions. Sensitive data must always be encrypted in transit and at rest.

User and Entity Behavior Analytics (UEBA)

UEBA uses machine learning, algorithms, and data analytics to detect anomalous behavior by users, devices, and applications within a network. By establishing a baseline of normal activity, UEBA identifies threats—such as compromised accounts, insider threats, or malware—that traditional, signature-based security tools might miss. It uses machine learning technologies to identify anomalies, deviations from the established baseline such as users trying to access files that they have never accessed before or are unauthorized to access and transferring large amounts of data not typical of their usual patterns. These detected anomalies are assigned risk scores to prioritize the critical high-risk threats. Modern UEBA tools track user as well as non-human behavior by monitoring devices like routers and servers.

Common Tools used for UEBA

- UEBA Tools - Exabeam, Rapid7 InsightIDR, Microsoft Sentinel, Splunk UBA, Cyberhaven
- Anomaly Detection – Machine Learning – Azure Anomaly Detection, Google AI Platform, Splunk
- SIEM - Splunk, IBM QRadar, LogRhythm, Microsoft Sentinel, and Exabeam
- Network DLP – sensitive data exfiltration prevention Forcepoint, Symantec, McAfee Total Prot
- DLP -- Microsoft Purview, Google Cloud, Netskope, and Forcepoint, Palo Alto Networks

8 -- Application Security

Application Security (or AppSec) is the practice of securing software applications from vulnerabilities throughout their lifecycle, from development to deployment and beyond. It focuses on identifying, mitigating, and preventing security risks that attackers could exploit to gain unauthorized access or cause harm. It protects applications from threats like SQL injection, XSS (Cross-site Scripting), buffer overflows and data breaches by fixing vulnerabilities before they can be exploited, using methods like secure coding, penetration testing, WAFs (Web Application Firewalls) and RASPs (Runtime Application Self-Protection technologies).

The key aspects of AppSec protection include the following:

- **Vulnerability identification**: Using software tools for detecting potential weaknesses in code, configurations, and application functionality. It uses cybersecurity tools for scanning applications for issues like missing patches, misconfigurations, or weak passwords to allow for timely remediation and strengthen overall cybersecurity posture
- **Threat modeling**: Understanding potential threats and risks associated with the application. A proactive approach is used such as thinking like an attacker to find vulnerabilities, assess risks, and prioritize security measures before an attack occurs.
- **Secure coding practices**: Understanding requirements and implementing secure coding standards and best practices to prevent vulnerabilities. This requires integrating security practices throughout the development lifecycle, from the initial design to deployment, to proactively eliminate common flaws such as SQL injection and XSS (Cross-site Scripting). Adopting rigorous DevSecOps procedures is crucial.
- **Testing and analysis**: Utilizing manual and automated testing methods to identify and fix vulnerabilities. Several well-known tools such as Qualys and Veracode, among others, are in common use for this.
- **Security controls and mitigation:** Implementing security measures to protect against identified vulnerabilities and using safeguards (controls) to reduce the negative impact and exposure of a security risk but not necessarily eliminate it completely. This is achieved by implementing measures like firewalls, access controls, and employee training to counter threats like data breaches or unauthorized access, ensuring critical systems remain resilient and data is secured. It involves applying technical (MFA, encryption), administrative (policies,

training), and physical (locks, cameras) controls to lower risk to an acceptable level.

- **Shift left**: Integrating security into the development process early on, where tasks, responsibilities, or checks are moved to an earlier stage in the process to proactively find and fix issues. For example, in software testing, it means redesigning the DevSecOps pipeline to perform checks earlier in the development cycle rather than after coding is complete. The goal is to improve efficiency, reduce costs, and enhance quality by addressing problems at their source.

Applications are frequent targets of cyberattacks, and AppSec helps prevent data breaches, unauthorized access, and other security incidents. AppSec ensures the confidentiality, integrity, and availability of application data, which is crucial for meeting regulatory requirements and protecting sensitive information.

Security vulnerabilities can disrupt business operations, and AppSec helps maintain service availability and minimize downtime. A secure application experience builds trust with users (especially customers) and strengthens the organization's reputation.

Many tools and techniques are in use for AppSec. The following describes the types and functions of the leading AppSec tools:

- **Static Application Security Testing (SAST):** Analyzes application code for vulnerabilities without running the application.
- **Dynamic Application Security Testing (DAST):** Tests the application while it's running to identify vulnerabilities.
- **Penetration Testing**: Simulating real-world attacks to assess the application's security.
- **Application Firewalls**: Protecting applications from unauthorized access and malicious traffic.
- **Code Analysis tools**: Identifying coding errors and vulnerabilities.

In essence, AppSec is a proactive approach to cybersecurity that helps organizations protect their applications from threats and vulnerabilities, ensuring the confidentiality, integrity, and availability of data and services.

Static Application Security Testing (SAST)

SAST is an application testing approach that analyzes an application's source code, bytecode, or binaries without running the program to find security vulnerabilities early in the Software Development Lifecycle (SDLC). It acts like a "white-box" inspection, scanning for insecure coding patterns, logic flaws that affect cybersecurity, and preventing weaknesses such as SQL injection or XSS attacks, before the code is deployed. This helps developers fix the insecure code before it is deployed thereby preventing costly breaches.

The three main functions of SAST include:

- Code Analysis using tools that parse the code to build an understanding of its structure (Abstract Syntax Tree),
- Understanding the Data & Control Flow to map how data moves and how the program can execute (control flow) to help find insecure paths.

- Rule Matching to compare code patterns against databases of known vulnerabilities such as OWASP top 10.

Dynamic Application Security Testing (DAST)

DAST is a "black-box" security testing method that finds vulnerabilities in running applications by simulating real-world attacks from the outside, much like a malicious hacker would, without needing access to the source code. It sends malicious inputs like SQL injection or XSS to a live application and analyzes the responses to identify security flaws, such as misconfigurations, authentication gaps, and runtime issues. DAST is essential for finding issues that static code analysis (SAST) might miss and is often integrated into CI/CD pipelines for continuous security checks.

DAST tools like Qualys Web Application Scanning (WAS) probe the application's front-end by sending crafted requests (e.g., bad data, unusual verbs) and monitors the application's behavior and responses to detect vulnerabilities like injection flaws, broken authentication, or server misconfigurations. To simulate real world attacks, DAST tools use a black-box approach and test the application in its runtime environment, mimicking an external attacker who doesn't know the internal code. It catches issues missed by source code analysis, offering a more complete security picture and detects vulnerabilities such as SQL injection, XSS, authentication and authorization flaws, server configuration errors, and even business logic flaws that only manifest when the application is running.

Interactive Application Security Testing (IAST)

IAST is a more recent approach to finding software vulnerabilities by monitoring an application from the inside as it runs, combining elements of Static (SAST) and Dynamic (DAST) testing for greater accuracy and speed, pinpointing exact vulnerable code lines during testing within development pipelines. It uses sensors within the app to observe data flow and code execution in real-time, identifying issues like misconfigurations, SQL injection or XSS before production, making security a collaborative effort for development and security teams.

In the IAST approach, sensors (code or runtime-based) are placed inside the running application, and they provide real-time monitoring as testers or automated tools interact with the app; the sensors watch data flow and code execution. IAST can pinpoint vulnerabilities in the exact line of code and data path causing a vulnerability (e.g., sensitive data in a log).

IAST works within CI/CD pipelines, alongside automated testing (tools such as Selenium, JUnit) for continuous security.

By combining SAST and DAST through monitoring execution inside the box and offering detailed insights that SAST and DAST miss, it provides high accuracy by reducing false positives by understanding actual data flow and provides developers with the precise locations of flaws. It is comprehensive in that it finds flaws spanning code, frameworks, and third-party libraries.

Code Analysis Tools

Code analysis tools automatically scan source code for errors, vulnerabilities, and quality issues, helping developers write better, more secure code faster. Popular code analysis tool include SonarQube, Snyk, ESLint, Checkmarx, and Veracode. They integrate into DevSecOps for early detection (shift-left), catching issues like SQL injection, XSS, broken authentication, API attacks, etc., and supporting languages from Java (Checkstyle, SpotBugs) to JavaScript (ESLint) and Python (Pylint).

These code analysis tools are designed to catch coding errors that allow SQL injections, XSS, and hard-coded secrets, and allow insecure API usage and buffer overflows. They can also assess the code quality such as code duplications, maintainability and structural complexity of the code such as linearly independent paths. Some tools can also check compliance with standards such as OWASP and coding conventions best practices.

These tools are typically integrated into the CI/CD pipelines such as Jenkins, GitLab, GitHub Actions which can provide feedback and help catch issues and coding errors early in keeping with the shift-left principle.

Sampling of AppSec Tools

The following lists a sampling of the tools by type.

Static Analysis (SAST)

Analyze code without running it in keeping with the Shift-Left security principle. Examples of tools include:

- SonarQube: Popular, open-source, multi-language quality & security platform.
- Snyk: Real-time security scanning for code, dependencies, containers.
- ESLint: Finds/fixes problems in JavaScript/TypeScript.
- Checkmarx/Veracode/Fortify: Enterprise-focused security testing.
- Pylint/SpotBugs: Python/Java-specific, finds bugs/style issues.

Dynamic Analysis (DAST)

These tools test applications while running the application. Examples include:

- OWASP ZAP/Burp Suite: Web application security testing.

AI-Powered/Developer-Focused

These tools use the power of AI to review code and apply custom rules for analysis and correction.

- Aikido Security/Ox Security: AI for code review, custom rules.
- Semgrep: Lightweight, customizable security rules.

Veracode

Veracode is a cloud-based application security platform that helps organizations develop and run secure software. It offers a suite of tools and services to identify and fix vulnerabilities throughout the software development lifecycle (SDLC), from code to cloud. Veracode integrates with development workflows to help teams build security into their applications from the start. Provides SAST, DAST, Software Composition Analysis (SCA), Infrastructure-as-Code (IaC), and Penetration Testing. Continuous Software Security Platform: Enables organizations to define and manage security policies, gain visibility into their application portfolio, and track progress.

Qualys

Qualys is a cloud-based cybersecurity and compliance platform that helps organizations identify, assess, and manage vulnerabilities and security risks across their IT environments. It offers a range of tools and solutions for vulnerability management, cloud security, web application security, and more. Qualys's platform is designed to streamline security operations, reduce costs, and improve overall security posture. Qualys provides comprehensive vulnerability management solutions, including discovery, assessment, prioritization, and remediation of vulnerabilities. It provides cloud security, web application security, continuous monitoring, asset management, and compliance. Qualys utilizes a cloud-based platform and lightweight agents to continuously collect data about an organization's IT assets and applications.

Qualys offers code analysis capabilities, primarily through its Software Composition Analysis (SCA) for open-source libraries in containers, and also supports Infrastructure as Code (IaC) security, helping find vulnerabilities in deployed code and configurations, though it's more focused on runtime/deployed security than deep static source code review like dedicated SAST tools (e.g., CodeQL). Qualys integrates these into its broader security platform for risk management, finding supply chain issues and configuration flaws

Checkmarx

Checkmarx is a comprehensive platform for securing software development from coding to cloud deployment. It provides tools and services for identifying and remediating vulnerabilities throughout the software development lifecycle (SDLC). Checkmarx' platform integrates with various development workflows and tools, enabling teams to shift security left and build secure applications more efficiently. Checkmarx' SAST solution scans source code to identify vulnerabilities before the application is compiled and deployed. It provides SAST, SCA (software composition analysis), API Security, and integrations with CI/CD pipelines. It is a cloud-native platform. Checkmarx can identify and help remediate sensitive information like API keys and passwords inadvertently stored in code. And, it provides a comprehensive set of tools and services to help organizations build and maintain secure applications throughout their entire lifecycle.

Sonarcube

SonarQube is a platform used for continuous inspection of code quality, helping developers detect and fix issues like bugs, vulnerabilities, and code smells (surface-level indicators in source code that suggest deeper design problems or technical debt). It automates code reviews, provides detailed reports, and integrates with CI/CD pipelines and IDEs, ensuring higher code quality. SonarQube analyzes code for bugs, duplications, security vulnerabilities, and code smells. SonarQube integrates with various CI/CD pipelines, IDEs, and version control systems like GitHub, GitLab, and Bitbucket, streamlining the development process. It provides detailed reports and dashboards to visualize code quality metrics, making it easy to track progress and address issues. SonarQube supports over 20 programming languages, including Java, Python, JavaScript, C#, and more. It is open source.

Penetration Testing

Penetration testing (pen testing) is a simulated cyberattack against a computer system, network, or application to find exploitable security weaknesses before real attackers do, helping organizations proactively secure assets, meet compliance, and test security controls by mimicking threats like malware or social engineering. Testers use real attack tools to uncover vulnerabilities (like SQL injection, weak Wi-Fi, or insecure configurations) and assess the potential impact, improving defenses against ransomware and data breaches.

When testers find vulnerabilities, they try to exploit them to see how deep an attacker could get. Pen testing is typically comprehensive and can cover internal/external networks, web apps, wireless systems, cloud, personnel, and physical access.

The primary goal of pen testing is to identify and pinpoint vulnerabilities in code, infrastructure, or processes, and test defenses to determine how well existing security tools such as firewalls, IDS/IPS, etc. are working in preventing attacks. They also help in ensuring that standards compliance requirements are being met through the defenses.

There are essentially three types of pen testing:

- **Black Box**: simulates an external hacker attack by giving ethical testers no prior knowledge (credentials, internal network maps, source code) of the target system, forcing them to find vulnerabilities from an outsider's view using reconnaissance, scanning, and exploitation just like a real attacker
- **White Box**: is a transparent security assessment where ethical hackers have full knowledge (source code, architecture, credentials) of a system to find deep vulnerabilities, mimicking an insider threat, and thoroughly checking internal logic, code flaws, and misconfigurations often missed in other tests.
- **Grey Box**: security assessment that gives testers **partial knowledge** of a system, blending elements of black-box (no knowledge) and white-box (full knowledge) testing, often by providing standard user login credentials. It simulates a common real-world scenario, like an attacker with stolen credentials or a malicious insider, allowing testers to identify risks such as privilege escalation and excessive permissions.

Pen testing provides an assessment on your security posture, showing what an attacker could do and helps you strengthen your defenses effectively.

Web Application Firewalls (WAFS)

A Web Application Firewall (WAF) is a security tool that protects web applications by filtering, monitoring, and blocking malicious HTTP/S traffic between the internet and the application, acting as a shield against common attacks like SQL injection, XSS, and bots. It operates at the application layer (Layer 7) for deep inspection, unlike traditional firewalls. It sits in front of web apps, scrutinizing requests and enforcing security policies (rules) to prevent attacks that exploit application vulnerabilities, providing customized defense for e-commerce, banking, and any online service.

WAFs analyze HTTP requests (GET, POST, etc.) for malicious patterns, hidden data, and unusual behavior and performs policy enforcement by using rules (blocklists, allowlists, custom rules) to decide whether to allow, block, or log traffic.

WAFs operate at Layer 7 and inspect the content of requests. They act as a reverse proxy sitting between users and servers and inspect traffic before it reaches the application so that it can mitigate web exploits such as common threats such as SQL Injection, Cross-Site Scripting (XSS), and file inclusion. It can also identify and block malicious bots that can disrupt services or steal data. Security policies provided by WAFs can be customized to set appropriate rules based on the needs of the application. By logging and monitoring the content, WAFs provides insights into traffic and attacks for investigation. These insights are used for mitigating DDoS attacks by absorb large attack volumes.

WAFs Deployment

WAF deployment can be customized according to infrastructure need and latency requirements. These deployments can be of the types:

- **Network-based**: Physical appliances offering high performance and low latency to inspect and filter web traffic for applications on local servers.
- **Host-based**: Software running on the web server to protect a specific application by inspecting traffic at the operating system level, offering deep customization and cost-efficiency but consuming local server resources and adding management complexity compared to cloud or network WAFs.
- **Cloud-based**: Delivered as a managed service (e.g., AWS WAF, Cloudflare) that protects web applications by filtering, monitoring, and blocking malicious HTTP traffic before it reaches the organization's servers, guarding against threats like SQL injection, XSS, and bots. It can act as a virtual appliance.
- **Hybrid**: Combined on-premises and cloud-based security for unified protection, allowing organizations to secure both legacy apps and modern cloud-native applications with consistent policies, centralized management, and scalable defense against threats like bots, injection attacks, and API vulnerabilities across any environment (on-prem, multi-cloud, edge).

WAF vs. Traditional Network Firewall

These two types of firewalls have different goals and implementations.

WAF protects applications, understands HTTP, focuses on Layer 7 threats (e.g., SQLi, XSS) while Network Firewall protects the network perimeter, and uses simple rules (IP, port), focuses on Layers 3/4.

In essence, a WAF adds a crucial security layer, protecting the actual web application from sophisticated, application-layer attacks that other defenses might miss, working as part of a broader security strategy.

Threat Modeling Frameworks and Tools

Threat modeling frameworks provide structured methods to identify, communicate, and mitigate security risks in systems. Examples include PASTA, LINDDUN, and other effective tools.

STRIDE

STRIDE (Spoofing, Tampering, Repudiation, Information Disclosure, Denial of Service, Elevation of Privilege), a Microsoft's framework, is a most widely used threat modeling framework. It's popular for its simplicity and effectiveness in identifying security threats in software systems through six threat categories: Spoofing, Tampering, Repudiation, Information disclosure, Denial of service, and Elevation of privilege. It involves understanding the system's architecture, identifying potential vulnerabilities, and then assessing the risk associated with those vulnerabilities. By proactively identifying and addressing threats, organizations can improve their security posture and reduce the likelihood of successful attacks.

The STRIDE framework requires clearly defining the scope and objectives in terms of the security CIA triad: confidentiality, integrity, availability, along with identifying the key stakeholders and assembling a multidisciplinary team. The following describes the key aspects of using the STRIDE methodology.

- *Decompose the System*: create a visual representation such as a data flow diagram (DFD), to understand how data flows and where trust boundaries exist.
- *Identify trust boundaries*: where data flows between different security domains.
- *Identify Threats*: to systematically identify potential threat agents and potential attack vectors.
- *Assess and Mitigate Threats*: Analyze the likelihood and impact of each identified threat and determine appropriate countermeasures and mitigation strategies.
- *Document the findings*: and proposed mitigations.
- *Validate and Review*: Validate the effectiveness of the implemented mitigations.

The Threat intelligence tools need to be able to effectively use the available threat intelligence in the system and verify the threats using established sources of threat intelligence, such as Mitre Corp.'s ATT&CK and Common Attack Pattern

Enumerations and Classifications repositories of threat actor data and techniques. These need to be embedded in the tool.

It is important to create a comprehensive operational threat dashboard that displays a highly detailed and interactive view of the system's activities and tracks all the threat information available. Furthermore, this is augmented with a mitigation and countermeasures dashboard which displays mitigation and countermeasure recommendations, for example, security modifications, code changes or other actions. This capability should interact dynamically with the threat dashboard.

The system engine embedded with various rules and its adherence to various standards and regulations as required, can determine if the system can map security actions with the appropriate compliance requirements.

Common Threat Modeling Tools:

The following lists the common Threat Modeling tools in use:

- Microsoft Threat Modeling Tool: open source software built on the STRIDE methodology.
- OWASP Threat Dragon The open source, cross-platform Threat Dragon threat modeling tool was developed in 2016 by OWASP.
- Splunk Enterprise Security and Splunk Security Essentials uses a broad range of tools and resources, including AI and machine learning, to provide a risk-based assessment of an org's technology architecture. Splunk gathers performance data from across an org, analyzes it from multiple perspectives, and identifies and visualizes potential threats and vulnerabilities. Splunk Security Essentials is mapped to the Kill Chain and Mitre ATT&CK frameworks.
- ThreatModeler is an automated threat modeling tool for DevOps. It has three editions: Community, Appsec and Cloud.
- SD Elements: A tool that uses surveys to gather system information, identify threats, and provide actionable security countermeasures.
- PyTM: A Python-based open-source tool for developers wanting to integrate threat modeling into code-based workflows.
- CAIRIS: An open-source, platform-agnostic tool that supports comprehensive threat modeling and integrates with development lifecycles.

Container Security

Containerization is a virtualization method that bundles an application's required files, dependencies, and configurations in standard, isolated software packages bundling applications and dependencies, secured throughout their lifecycle (build, deploy, runtime). It uses tools and practices to protect against threats like vulnerabilities, malware, and misconfigurations, addressing unique risks from shared kernels and complex orchestration (e.g., Kubernetes). Containers offer application isolation and portability but need specialized security to manage new attack surfaces, focusing on image security, runtime monitoring, network protection, and secure orchestration. They are portable and their consistency allows them to run reliably across different environments (cloud, on-prem, desktop). They are typically lightweight because they share the host OS kernel, making them faster and less resource-intensive than Virtual Machines (VMs).

Cybersecurity Applied to Containers

Container security protects these lightweight units and the infrastructure from development to production by ensuring isolation such that if one container is breached, it's contained (sandbox-like), preventing lateral movement.

Since containers share the host kernel, vulnerabilities there or in the container itself can be exploited. Furthermore, containers present an expanded attack surface that includes container registries, runtimes (like Docker), and orchestrators (like Kubernetes) which add complexity and new entry points for attackers.

Key Areas of Container Security

Container security spans several security considerations including:

- **Image Security**: The container code images may be compromised so scanning images for vulnerabilities is important before deployment.
- **Runtime Security**: While running containers, they must be monitored for malicious behavior and enforcing policies.
- **Orchestration Security**: It is the practice of hardening and protecting automated container management systems (like Kubernetes) and the applications running within them, focusing on securing the platform itself (control plane, nodes) and enforcing policies for workloads, networks, secrets, and images, to prevent breaches.
- **Network & Infrastructure Security**: Protecting the host OS and network segmentation between containers.
- **Secrets Management**: Secrets used for containers include sensitive data (passwords, API keys, certificates) that applications need and must be managed securely to prevent exposure. Dedicated secret management tools such as Kubernetes Secrets and Docker Secrets are used to encrypt them at rest and in transit, mount them dynamically (not bake into images), restrict access (least privilege), and rotate them regularly, stopping hardcoded credentials that become part of the image layer

In summary, container security is the combination of the practices, strategies, and tools dedicated to protecting applications and their infrastructure throughout their lifecycle, from development to deployment.

Kubernetes has become the industry-standard, open-source platform for automating the deployment, scaling, and management of containerized applications. The following section is a deep dive in the use of Kubernetes.

Kubernetes (k8s) and Containers

Kubernetes, also known as k8s, is an open-source system for automating deployment, scaling, and management of containerized applications. It groups containers that make up an application into logical units for easy management and discovery.

Kubernetes is popular for on-premises use because it allows organizations to leverage the benefits of cloud-native infrastructure—such as automation, scalability, and efficiency—while maintaining control over their data, infrastructure, and costs. Infrastructure Control and Customization: on-premises k8s provides full control over the entire environment, from hardware selection to network and storage configurations. This is crucial for workloads that require specialized hardware, such as high-performance GPUs for machine learning, which may not be available or optimally configured in public cloud offerings.

k8s provides a consistent, standardized API across environments (on-premises, private cloud, public cloud). This cloud-agnostic nature allows organizations to easily move workloads between different environments, preventing reliance on a single cloud provider's proprietary service. k8s brings cloud-native capabilities (like self-healing, automated deployment, and resource optimization) to a private data center, allowing an enterprise to operate with the efficiency and agility typically associated with public cloud infrastructure.

A Kubernetes cluster consists of a set of worker machines, called nodes, that run containerized applications. Every cluster has at least one worker node. The worker node(s) host the Pods that are the components of the application workload. The control plane manages the worker nodes and the pods in the cluster. In production environments, the control plane usually runs across multiple computers, and a cluster usually runs multiple nodes, providing fault-tolerance and high availability.

Control Plane Components

The control plane's components make global decisions about the cluster (for example, scheduling), as well as detecting and responding to cluster events (for example, starting up a new pod when a deployment's replicas field is unsatisfied).

Control plane components can be run on any machine in the cluster. However, for simplicity, setup scripts typically start all control plane components on the same machine, and do not run user containers on this machine.

It is important to learn more about the following for a comprehensive understanding of Kubernetes:

- *Nodes* and their communication with the control plane.
- Kubernetes *controllers*.
- *kube-scheduler* which is the default scheduler for Kubernetes.
- *etcd*'s official documentation.
- Running multiple container runtimes in Kubernetes.
- Integrating with cloud providers using *cloud-controller-manager*.
- *kubectl* commands.

These are described in detail in the following:

kube-apiserver

The API server is a component of the k8s control plane that exposes the Kubernetes API. The API server is the front end for the k8s control plane.

The main implementation of a Kubernetes API server is kube-apiserver. kube-apiserver is designed to scale horizontally—that is, it scales by deploying more instances. Several instances of kube-apiserver can be run concurrently and k8s balances traffic between those instances.

etcd

Consistent and highly available key value store used as k8s' backing store for all cluster data. If your organization's k8s cluster uses etcd as its backing store, the security team needs to make sure you have a backup plan for the data.

kube-scheduler

Control plane component that watches for newly created pods with no assigned node and selects a node for them to run on. Factors taken into account for scheduling decisions include individual and collective resource requirements, hardware/software/policy constraints, affinity and anti-affinity specifications, data locality, inter-workload interference, and deadlines.

cloud-controller-manager

A k8s control plane is a component that embeds cloud-specific control logic. The cloud controller manager an organization link their cluster into their cloud provider's API and separates out the components that interact with that cloud platform from components that only interact with their cluster. The cloud-controller-manager only runs controllers that are specific to the organization's cloud provider. If the organization is running k8s on their own premises, or in a learning environment inside their workforce member's own PC, the cluster does not have a cloud controller manager.

As with the kube-controller-manager, the cloud-controller-manager combines several logically independent control loops into a single binary that is being run as a single process. It can be scaled horizontally (run more than one copy) to improve performance or to help tolerate failures.

The following controllers can have cloud provider dependencies:

- *Node controller*: Responsible for noticing and responding when nodes go down.
- *Job controller*: Watches for Job objects that represent one-off tasks, then creates pods to run those tasks to completion.
- *EndpointSlice controller*: Populates EndpointSlice objects (to provide a link between Services and Pods).
- *ServiceAccount controller*: Create default service accounts for new namespaces.

The above is not an exhaustive list.

Node Components

Node components run on every node, maintaining running pods and providing the Kubernetes runtime environment.

kubelet

An agent that runs on each node in the cluster. It makes sure that containers are running in a *Pod.* The *kubelet* takes a set of PodSpecs that are provided through various mechanisms and ensures that the containers described in those PodSpecs are running and healthy. The kubelet doesn't manage containers which were not created by k8s.

kube-proxy

kube-proxy is a network proxy that runs on each node an organization's cluster, implementing part of the Kubernetes Service concept. kube-proxy maintains network rules on nodes. These network rules allow network communication to the pods being run from the organization's network sessions inside or outside of their cluster. kube-proxy uses the operating system packet filtering layer if there is one and it's available. Otherwise, kube-proxy forwards the traffic itself.

Container runtime

The container runtime is a fundamental component that empowers k8s to run containers effectively. It is responsible for managing the execution and lifecycle of containers within the Kubernetes environment.

K8s supports container runtimes such as *containerd*, CRI-O, and any other implementation of the Kubernetes CRI (Container Runtime Interface).

Addons

Addons use k8s resources (DaemonSet, Deployment, etc.) to implement cluster features. Because these are providing cluster-level features, namespaced resources for addons belong within the *kube-system* namespace.

Selected addons are described in the following section for an extended list of available addons; consult Kubernetes detailed documentation.

DNS

While the other addons are not strictly required, all k8s clusters should have cluster DNS, as many implementations rely on it. Cluster DNS is a DNS server, in addition to the other DNS server(s) in the organization's environment, which serves DNS records for k8s services, containers started by k8s automatically include this DNS server in their DNS searches.

Web UI (Dashboard)

Dashboard is a general purpose, web-based UI for k8ss clusters. It allows users to manage and troubleshoot applications running in the cluster, as well as the cluster itself.

Container Resource Monitoring

Container Resource Monitoring records generic time-series metrics about containers in a central database and provides a UI for browsing that data.

Cluster-level Logging

A cluster-level logging mechanism is responsible for saving container logs to a central log store with search/browsing interface.

Network Plugins

Network plugins are software components that implement the container network interface (CNI) specification. They are responsible for allocating IP addresses to pods and enabling them to communicate with each other within the cluster.

Kubernetes Service Mesh Deployments

A **K8s service mesh** is a dedicated infrastructure layer for managing, observing, and securing the complex service-to-service communication (often called "east-west" traffic) within a Kubernetes cluster. It abstracts networking concerns away from application code, allowing developers to focus on business logic.

The *control plane* acts as the "brain" of the mesh, managing and configuring the data plane proxies. It provides an API for defining traffic rules, security policies, and observability configurations, and aggregates the telemetry data collected by the proxies

The *data plane* consists of lightweight proxies deployed as *sidecars* along each application container in a pod. These proxies manage all inbound and outbound traffic enforcing policies and collecting telemetry data.

Integrating Core Services

K8s service mesh integrates core services and provides advanced control over traffic flow, enabling sophisticated deployment strategies like canary releases, A/B testing, and blue-green deployments. It also handles load balancing, retries, timeouts, and circuit breakers to improve reliability. Additionally, it enforces consistent security policies across the cluster, including automated mutual TLS (mTLS) encryption for all service-to-service communication. This helps establish a "zero-trust" security model without requiring changes to application code. Furthermore, it collects logs and metrics.

k8s Observability Best Practices

Using k8s as a critical component of the infrastructure requires ensuring that best practices are adopted in the design and implementation. The following describes the key best practices that make k8s robust and secure.

Securing k8S components

Container security requires securing each component used within the cluster. Securing k8s components is of utmost importance to keep the cluster running in an uncompromised manner. The components that need to be secured include the network itself, the API servers, and the cluster components including the pods, volumes, etcd, kubelets, controllers, etc.

Network Security

While initially the security team may not implement network policies and just allow all the services to talk to each other, as the organization grows, their number of services can also grow exponentially. Not having proper networking policies will create chaos. Adding policies such as which services can access what resources, or other needed services will help the security team maintain control over their infrastructure. To achieve network security, the security team should apply network policies, monitor traffic, and leverage service meshes like Istio or Linkerd.

API Server Security

After etcd, the most critical Kubernetes component is the API server. If access to the organization's API server is exposed to an attacker by mistake, it can be a security disaster, because an attacker will be able to make changes to all the resources the organization has in their cluster. Securing the API server is achieved via third-party authentication for all access requests to the API server.

Admission Controller Security

Admission controllers keep an eye on whatever is getting deployed on an organization's kubernetes clusters. They can intercept every configuration that is applied on a cluster, as well as modify or verify them. So, its security is achieved through validating admission policies for every admission requests.

etcd Security

etcd security is achieved by implementing TLS for encrypted communication (client-to-server, peer-to-peer), enforcing mutual authentication with client certificates, using network firewalls for isolation, enabling encryption at rest for sensitive data, and configuring role-based access control (RBAC) with strong authentication. Key steps include generating and distributing certificates and configuring etcd flags

Kubelet Secuirty

Security is achieved by managing access to the kubelet by disabling anonymous access, always verifying the authorization mode: e.g. never run authorization in AlwaysAllow mode and shut down the read-only port to make sure that a kubelet in one node cannot access or make changes in other nodes. This can be enabled via a setting in the admission controller's configuration while starting the kubelet process so that anonymous access can be blocked.

Component Hardening

The following lists some component hardening approaches that can be used:

- Lock down etcd, kubelets, and the API server with TLS and RBAC.
- **Validate admission policy:** examples include enforcing guardrails like banning privilege escalation, and blocking untrusted registries.
- **Pod and workload protections:** Use NodeRestriction to prevent privilege escalation, and disable risky volume mounts.
- **Secrets and credentials management:** Secrets should be stored securely with tools like Vault and follow least-privilege access practices.

Kubernetes credentials and data security

After the protecting the container workload, the security team needs to protect their data and security credentials. The security team needs to protect these areas using the approaches listed below:

- Use secret managers -- Kubernetes by default doesn't encrypt secrets, so anything your organization stores in k8s secrets can be viewed by anyone who has access to view them. In such cases, tools like Vault become really important to run the organization's workload.
- Process whitelisting -- As the name suggests, this means the security team only allow certain processes to run in their k8s nodes instead of allowing just anything to run. This can be a very tricky task, as every time a team has to deploy a new application, they have to get it whitelisted.
- A service account should be used, not the cloud provider credentials If your organization's workload wants to connect to a cloud provider, the security team should always use a service account to provide the permission required to do so, following the least privilege model. Also, they should make sure not to use cloud credentials in the k8s configuration.

mTLS for Service-to-Service Traffic

mTLS (Mutual Transport Layer Security) is an enhanced security protocol that requires both the client and server in a network connection to authenticate each other using digital certificates, unlike standard TLS which only authenticates the server. This two-way verification ensures both parties are who they claim to be, establishing a stronger, encrypted connection, crucial for securing internal APIs, microservices, and Zero Trust environments by verifying device and workload identities

The Kubernetes API

The **Kubernetes API** is the front end of the k8s control plane, serving as the central interface through which users, external components, and internal cluster processes interact with the cluster. It is a *RESTful programmatic interface* that uses standard HTTP verbs (GET, POST, PUT, PATCH, DELETE) to query and manipulate the state of k8s objects.

Everything within k8s—such as pods, services, deployments, and nodes is represented as an *API object.* These objects have a kind -- apiVersion, and metadata, which includes name and namespace, which define their schema and properties.

APIs are organized into *API Groups and Versions* to manage the large number of resources and ensure backward compatibility as the platform evolves. These logical groups such as, /api/v1 for core resources like pods, or /apis/apps/v1 for high-level application management like deployments) and given versions (alpha, beta, or stable/GA) identify the APIs.

Standard operations on resources are referred to as *verbs*, which include get, create, update, patch, delete, list, and watch (for real-time updates).

The API server provides a number of very important services:

- **Centralized Control**: All operations in the cluster, from deploying applications to monitoring health, funnel through the API server, ensuring consistency and coordination across all components.

- **State Management:** Users declare the desired state of their applications and the cluster via the API (e.g., "run five instances of this pod"). The API server persists this desired state in etcd, the cluster's key-value store. Kubernetes controllers continuously work to match the actual state to the desired state.
- **Authentication and Authorization**: Every request is authenticated (verifying the sender's identity) and authorized (checking permissions via Role-Based Access Control, or RBAC) before being processed, ensuring secure access.
- **Extensibility**: The API can be extended with Custom Resource Definitions (CRDs), allowing developers to define new resource types and behaviors without modifying the core Kubernetes code.

While the API is a set of HTTP endpoints, most users do not interact with it directly using curl commands. Instead, they typically use one of these approaches:

- **kubectl** : The official command-line tool which translates user commands into API requests.
- **Client Libraries**: Programmatic access is available through official client libraries for languages like Go, Python, Java, and JavaScript, which simplify interaction for custom applications and automation.
- **Kubernetes Operators**: A method of packaging, deploying, and managing apps that uses the API to automate the entire lifecycle of the software it manages.

The Kubernetes API's design around a consistent, resource-based API is fundamental to its ability to manage complex, containerized applications in a scalable and flexible way. You can explore the full Kubernetes API Reference in the official documentation.

Helm Package Manager Software

The Helm package manager for Kubernetes, simplifies the deployment, management, and upgrades complex applications by packaging them into reusable templates called "charts," which bundle all necessary configuration (YAML files) for a Kubernetes application. It automates tasks, reduces manual work, and provides consistency for deploying applications and third-party software like databases or monitoring tools across different environments (dev, staging, production).

API Security

Application Programming Interfaces (APIs) pose extended security risks due to an increase in the attack surface that can result in parameter attacks, identity attacks, MITM attacks, viruses and injections.

Furthermore, APIs must be protected from various other threats, including unauthorized access, data breaches, and misuse. The best practicers for achieving API security include the following:

- Always use a secure Gateway to channel requests where they can be evaluated and controlled.

- Use a central OAUTH 2.0 Server to authenticate before issuing tokens,
- While JWT tokens can be used externally also, for robust security use them internally only, and always keep tokens secure.
- Data Protection: safeguard sensitive data using encryption and secure coding practices. Always use data encryption for data in transit (TLS 1.3) and at rest to protect sensitive data exchanged via the API.
- Always check for excessive data exposure because APIs returning more data than necessary, risk exposing sensitive data.
- Prevent Injection Attacks from malicious code injected into API requests to manipulate data or compromise systems through robust input validation, sanitization, and the use of parameterized queries or prepared statements, input validation, prepared statements, least privilege, audits.
- Denial-of-Service (DoS) Attacks: DDoS attacks overwhelm APIs with traffic to disrupt service availability. So, protect critical assets, how users connect to network, use CSP DDoS protectors, and secure the edge network.
- Security Misconfigurations: Prevent vulnerabilities arising from improper API configurations or lack of adherence to security best practices.
- Monitoring and Logging: Continuous monitoring of API traffic and activity to detect suspicious patterns, anomalies, and potential security incidents, enabling timely response and mitigation.
- API Lifecycle Security: API security should be integrated throughout the entire API development lifecycle (design, development, deployment, and ongoing management); proactively address vulnerabilities.
- Always use token exchange in service-to-service calls, to reduce credentials exposure. Instead of sending passwords with every request, tokens are issued after initial authentication, reducing the risk of credentials being stolen. Using tokens also reduces blast radius because tokens time-bound and scoped (e.g., for a specific API or action), so if stolen, their impact is limited to a short period and specific functions. Furthermore, tokens provide stateless scalability because servers have no need to store session state for every user, allowing easier scaling for high traffic, as tokens carry necessary identity and permission data.
- Use token scopes (e.g., for a specific API or action) for Coarse-grained verification at API Gateway.
- Use claims for Fine-grained access. Token claims are key-value pairs within a security token (like a JWT) that provide information (assertions) about the token's subject (user, application, etc.) and its context, used for authentication, authorization, and passing data between services, covering details like user ID, roles, permissions, issuer, and expiration. They function as the contract or API between the identity provider and the client application, allowing the client to verify the user's identity and access rights without further lookups.
- Use Zero Trust to achieve API Security. Zero Trust works with API security by treating every API request as untrusted by default,

regardless of its origin (internal or external), and enforcing strict, continuous verification and granular access controls before granting access to resources. This shifts security from perimeter-based defense to a proactive, identity-centric approach.

- Always Audit. Auditing achieves API security by systematically finding and fixing vulnerabilities through in-depth reviews, testing, and monitoring, focusing on strong authentication, authorization, data handling, and logging, ensuring APIs meet security standards (like OWASP API Security Top 10) and regulatory compliance (GDPR, HIPAA) before attackers exploit them, thus preventing data breaches and protecting reputation

IAM Best Practices for API Security

Identity and Access Management play a crucial role in API security also and the typical IAM best practices listed below also apply. Threat mitigation strategies and tools to defend against common API-specific attacks should be actively used, including the following best practices:

- *Least Privilege*: Grant only minimum necessary permissions for users/services for APIs access
- *Protect against broken authentication/authorization*: by using MFA, strong password policies, secure password storage, account lockout, secure session management, HTTPS/TLS, password authentication.
- *Centralized Authorization*: using RBAC or ABAC, enforce permissions based on roles and attributes. Only authorized users/apps can access and utilize specific APIs.
- *Secure API Keys and Tokens*: Treat API keys and access tokens as sensitive credentials, storage, regular rotation, and avoid hardcoding in applications. Implement short-lived tokens.

API Gateway Usage:

As said earlier, always use a secure API gateway to leverage the gateway to centralize authentication, authorization, rate limiting, policies and perform regular monitoring, auditing and alerting using API access logs and activity for suspicious patterns. Furthermore, validate and sanitize all inputs received to prevent vulnerabilities like injections.

It is important to protect the API Gateways from vulnerabilities, so it is crucial to regularly update and patch API components and infrastructure.

API Security Tools

Here is a quick summarized list of the API tools needed to be considered in the design and implementation:

- Access Control
- Threat Detection
- Confidentiality and integrity
- Audit Management

- Distributing multiple Scan Engines; this promotes fault tolerance and improves scanning performance while conserving bandwidth.
- Agentless operation scans, e.g., Nexpose scans, exclusively over the network while using common Windows and UNIX network protocols to gain access to systems.
- Assigning an asset group (a collection of assets) for scanning functions
- Security Console monitoring on a 24x7 basis.
- Devic asset discovery and inventory on a regular basis and reviewing it for anomalies.
- Vulnerability scanning and tracking and mitigating any identified vulnerabilities.

DDoS Attacks

Distributed Denial of Service (DDoS) attacks are caused by malicious actors who inundate and overload the servers with unauthorized calls to prevent the servers from servicing legitimate traffic. The types of overloads include the following:

- *Network resource overload* - exploiting a server vulnerability or inundating servers with requests. Or a threat actor consumes network resources by reflecting a high volume of network traffic to the target. The threat actor uses a third-party server (the "reflector") as an intermediary that hosts and responds to the given spoofed source IP address.
- *Protocol resource overload* consumes the available session or connection resources of target
- *Application resource overload* consumes the available compute or storage resources of target.

DDoS attacks need to be mitigated by understanding the type of the attack, the source of the attack, the cloud service provider capabilities and other protections as listed below:

- Understand critical assets and services within the organization. Confirm web application firewall (WAF) covers all critical assets and is configured in a Deny state.
- Understand how users connect to the network on-site and off-site via VPNs.
- Enroll in DDoS protection service such as via CSP and ISP,
- Understand CSP defenses and their shortcomings and the organization's role in additional security implementations.
- Understand the dedicated edge network defenses.

DevSecOps integration

DevOps has been in use for a long time to facilitate automating development and delivery of software in an agile mode. It breaks down the traditional silos between the coding and infrastructure teams to automate and integrate all development practices including coding, design reviews, QA and deployment. The pipeline for DevOps is typically known as CI/CD (Continuous Integration/Continuous Delivery) which provides for regularly merging code changes, automatically building, testing and deploying software. It also includes the process on Infrastructure as Code (IaC) for managing and provisioning infrastructure using code, thereby making the environment consistent. CI/CD requires continuous monitoring and feedback to achieve rapid improvements. CI/CD is used for small, frequent releases more often.

DevSecOps (Development Security, Operations) builds on DevOps by integrating security into every stage of software development lifecycle (SDLC) into the entire CI/CD pipeline through automation and collaboration

The Core Principles of DevSecOps are focused on ensuring all security aspects and implementing secure design throughout all phases of the SDLC. These core principles include:

- **Shift Left:** DevSecOps prioritizes incorporating security measures early in the development process, rather than as an afterthought.
- **Shared Responsibility:** It emphasizes shared responsibility for security among development, security, and operations teams.
- **Continuous Security:** Security testing and vulnerability analysis are integrated into the continuous integration and continuous delivery (CI/CD) pipeline.
- **Automation:** DevSecOps leverages automation to streamline security workflows and processes.
- **Collaboration:** It fosters strong collaboration and communication between different teams.

Implementing DevSecOps based on these principles helps reduce risk by integrating security early in the development process and integrating security throughout the lifecycle to reduce the likelihood of security vulnerabilities being introduced.

DevSecOps Left Shift

'If Shift Left worked for software testing and the technology stack in DevOps, it would surely work for security, too, right?' Not necessarily. Developers began voicing frustration when security testing tools were abruptly inserted into DevOps-style continuous integration pipelines. These tools — mostly legacy scanners like SAST, DAST, and SCA — that had previously been used asynchronously to test software assets were now being forced into the fast-paced, synchronous environment of DevSecOps software orchestration. The result? Cumbersome integrations, painfully long build and test times, and unexplained blocking failures.

To overcome that, DevSecOps requires integration of security tools to automate security workflows, including static analysis tools, dynamic analysis tools, and vulnerability scanners. Security testing is performed on a continuous basis through each development cycle at every stage of the development lifecycle, from code review to deployment. Vulnerabilities are identified, analyzed, and addressed throughout the software development lifecycle (SDLC). DevSecOps often implements security policies and standards to ensure that applications are built securely.

How DevSecOps Works

DevSecOps works through tools like *GitLAb, Veracode, Qualys, Snyk,* and *Container security–Aqua* among others. The following lists the kay functions performed by DevSecOps.

- **Integration of Security Tools**: automate security workflows, including static analysis tools, dynamic analysis tools, and vulnerability scanners.
- **Continuous Security Testing**: Security testing is performed at every stage of the development lifecycle, from code review to deployment.
- **Vulnerability Management**: Vulnerabilities are identified, analyzed, and addressed throughout the software development lifecycle.
- **Security Policies and Standards**: Implements security policies and standards to ensure that applications are built securely.

Using DevSecOps with GitHub

To integrate policy controls into CI/CD within GitHub, GitHub Actions and Open Policy Agent (OPA) can be leveraged to enforce security and compliance rules throughout your development lifecycle. This involves defining policies in code, using GitHub Actions workflows to trigger policy evaluations, and taking action based on the evaluation results.

Using DevSecOps with Azure

For Azure environments, Azure Policy can be leveraged to integrate policy controls into Azure DevOps CI/CD and implement it as part of release pipeline.

Use the *AzurePolicyCheckGate* task within a release pipeline stage to check for policy compliance before deploying changes to ensure your defined security and compliance policies.

- **Define and Assign Policies:** Create and assign policies in *Azure Policy* to define rules
- **Integrate with Release Pipeline:** In Azure DevOps, create or edit a release pipeline.
- **Policy Checks**: Add a stage in the pipeline where policy checks need to be enforced. Add the *AzurePolicyCheckGate* task to this stage.
- **Configure the *AzurePolicyCheckGate* Task:** Specify the *resource ID* or *scope* where the policy should be evaluated. Define the *policy definition ID* or *name*. Choose whether the task should fail the pipeline if a policy violation is detected.
- **Run the Pipeline:** When the release pipeline runs, the AzurePolicyCheckGate task will evaluate the specified resources against the policies.
- **Interpret Results:** If the policy checks pass, the release will continue.

Implementing Policy Controls into DevSecOps

Policy controls should be implemented through DevSecOps at the earliest. The key benefits of integrating policy controls include early detection of non-compliance, improved security and compliance, automation of policy checks, and reduced risk of deploying non-compliant changes to production.

Implementing Policy Controls into Azure DevOps

To integrate policy controls into Azure DevOps CI/CD, Azure Policy can be leveraged and implemented as part of the release pipeline. Specifically, the *AzurePolicyCheckGate* task within a release pipeline stage can be used to check for policy compliance before deploying changes. This ensures that the infrastructure and code adhere to the defined security and compliance policies.

Here is a more detailed breakdown:

- **Define and Assign Policies:** Start by creating and assigning policies in Azure Policy that define the rules you want to enforce.
- **Integrate with Release Pipeline:** In Azure DevOps, create or edit a release pipeline.
  - Add a stage in the pipeline where the policy checks need to be enforced.
  - Add the AzurePolicyCheckGate task to this stage.
- **Configure the AzurePolicyCheckGate Task:** Specify the resource ID or scope where the policy should be evaluated.
  - Define the policy definition ID or name.
  - Choose whether the task should fail the pipeline if a policy violation is detected.
- **Run the Pipeline:** When the release pipeline runs, the AzurePolicyCheckGate task will evaluate the specified resources against policies set for it.
- **Interpret Results:** If the policy checks pass, the release will continue to the next stage. If a policy violation is detected, the task will fail the pipeline, preventing the deployment. The security team can view the policy violation details in the release logs.

By using Azure Policy and the *AzurePolicyCheckGate* task, security teams can effectively integrate policy controls into the Azure DevOps CI/CD pipelines and ensure that their deployments meet their security and compliance requirements.

Implementing Policy Controls into GitHub DevOps

To integrate policy controls into CI/CD within GitHub, security teams can leverage *GitHub Actions* and *Open Policy Agent (OPA)* to enforce security and compliance rules throughout the development lifecycle. This involves defining policies in code, using GitHub Actions workflows to trigger policy evaluations, and taking action based on the evaluation results.

Here is a more detailed breakdown:

1. Define Policies in Code:

   - **Policy as Code:** Treat security policies as code, using a format like YAML or Rego (OPA's language) to define rules.
   - **Example:** A policy could enforce that a specific version of a library is used in code, or that builds are only triggered by authorized users.
   - **Version Control:** Store these policies in the repository alongside the code, allowing for version control, review, and collaboration.
2. Implement with GitHub Actions:
   - **Workflow Creation:** Create a GitHub Actions workflow that runs at specific stages of your CI/CD pipeline (e.g., pull request, build, deployment).
   - **OPA Integration:** Integrate OPA into your workflow, using the OPA CLI to evaluate policies against the relevant data (e.g., code, build artifacts, environment configurations).
   - **Workflow Steps:** Install OPA, Policy Evaluation and Action Based in outcomes shown in the next few bullets.
   - **Install OPA:** Install the OPA CLI as a step in the workflow.
   - **Policy Evaluation:** Use the OPA CLI to run policy evaluations against the data.
   - **Action Based on Outcome:** Take actions based on the policy evaluation results (e.g., fail the pipeline, report findings, update the code).

Examples of policy enforcement: include code vulnerability checks to identify vulnerabilities and enforce a minimum code quality standard, secrets management to ensure that secrets are not hardcoded in code by enforcing policies that check for sensitive information in the codebase, dependency management to enforce the use of specific versions of dependencies by using policies that check dependency versions and access control to implement access control policies to ensure that only authorized users can make changes to specific parts of the codebase or trigger certain actions.

It is important to ensure scalability in the design if many policies or repositories need to be integrated; consider deploying OPA (Open Policy Agent) as a service within the infrastructure (e.g., Kubernetes) for better scalability and performance and maintainability to peep the policies organized and well-documented to ensure easy maintenance and updates. Policies need to periodically and regularly tested to ensure they work as expected and cover all relevant scenarios.

The following lists some common tools and technologies used for policy management:

- **Open Policy Agent (OPA):** A powerful and versatile policy enforcement engine.
- **GitHub Actions:** GitHub's CI/CD platform for automating workflows.
- **Security Tools:** Integrate tools like SonarQube, Snyk, and other security analysis tools.
- **Policy as Code Formats:** YAML, Rego.

Integrating policy controls into the CI/CD pipeline can ensure that the code adheres to organizational standards, reduces risks, and improves the overall security and reliability of the software.

The DevSecOps Pipeline

The following diagram shows the DevSecOps CI/CD cycle. The steps in this diagram include the following:

- **Testing** – Dynamic application security testing (DAST) and interactive application security testing (IAST) can simulate real-world attacks and analyze app behavior at runtime. These tools help discover issues that static analysis might miss, such as logic flaws or insecure runtime behavior, giving a more complete view of the app's security posture.
- **DAST** (Dynamic Application Security Testing): Simulates attacks on a running application (without access to code) to find runtime vulnerabilities.
- **IAST** (Interactive Application Security Testing): Combines elements of both by monitoring application behavior in real time during testing to deliver more accurate, context-aware results.

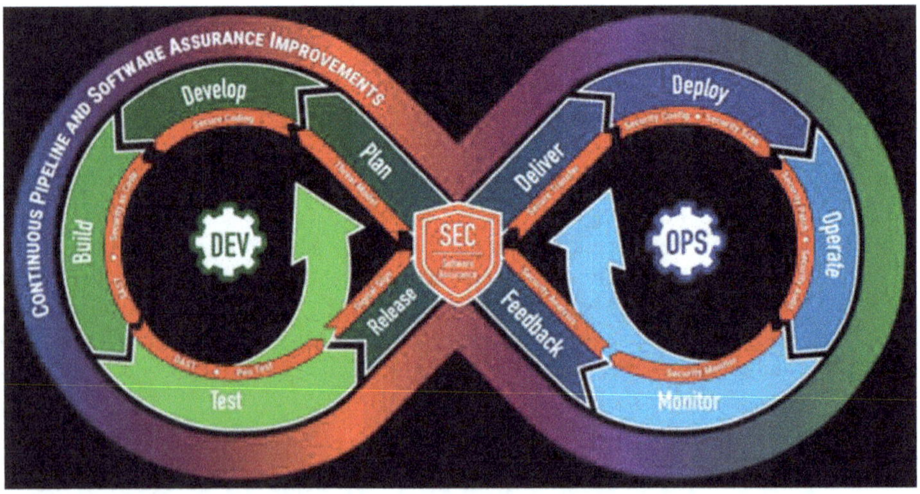

Source: Carnegie Mellon University:
https://www.sei.cmu.edu/blog/modeling-devsecops-to-protect-the-pipeline/

Figure 8-1 : DevSecOps Ci/CD Cycle

- **Releasing** – checks and gates must be present to make sure that if any vulnerabilities or security checks in earlier phases are missed, the deployment is blocked. This phase includes running final security scans, reviewing access controls, and checking audit logs.
- **Deploying** – it's essential to ensure that the pipelines include scripts or automation to enforce strong network security, proper policy configurations, access control mechanisms, encryption standards, and secure key management. **Scan for network policies and IAM roles** after each change.
- **Operating** – Once the deployment is live and starts receiving traffic, remember to continuously check for issues.

Follow these best practices:

- Choose tools that keep an eye on logging, provide intrusion detection, and generate real-time alerts to identify suspicious activity early.
- Teams should track system health, unusual user behavior, and any attempted breaches.
- Regular patching, updates, and incident response processes should also be in place to keep systems secure during ongoing operation.

Remember: SIEM solutions help here by continuously monitoring the logs and changes and by providing real-time alerts.

DevEx (Developer Experience)

DevSecOps improves the developer experience in the following ways:

- **Uninterrupted flow state**: Context switching is one of the biggest productivity drains for modern developers. Maximizing efficiency means allowing engineers to remain in a state of flow until they've fully solved a technical problem.
- **Limited cognitive load**: Developers need immediate access to all the relevant information necessary to resolve issues. Having to pause and research for additional context disrupts productivity.
- **Short feedback loops**: When additional input is needed before writing code, feedback must arrive in near real-time. Delayed feedback can lead to bad or insecure code.

With DevSecOps, three groups — Application Security (AppSec), Application Development (AppDev), and Platform Engineering (PlatEng) — share responsibility for managing software risk. The complexity of modern cloud-native software makes it impossible to fully assess risks without integrating insights from all three stakeholder groups. However, these responsibilities often overlap and are inconsistently defined, resulting in inefficient remediation processes and longer fix times

DevSecOps Tools

DevSecOps tools aim to integrate security practices into the software development lifecycle. Some popular tools include GitLab, Jenkins, SonarQube, OWASP Dependency-Check, Snyk, and Veracode. These tools cover various aspects, such as static analysis, dynamic analysis, software composition analysis, and container security.

- **GitLab:** A comprehensive platform offering Git repository hosting, CI/CD, and security features, covering the entire software delivery lifecycle.
- **Jenkins:** A popular open-source automation server for CI/CD, automating the build, testing, and deployment stages, ensuring security checks are integrated throughout the development lifecycle.
- **SonarQube:** A tool for build phase analysis, providing static code analysis and quality checks to identify potential security vulnerabilities.

- **OWASP Dependency-Check:** A tool for analyzing dependencies and identifying known vulnerabilities in open-source components.
- **Snyk:** A tool for identifying and fixing security vulnerabilities in open-source dependencies, helping teams mitigate risks associated with external components.
- **Veracode:** A static analysis solution for analyzing software libraries and identifying security vulnerabilities.
- **Container Security Tool:** Tools like Aqua Security, Sysdig, and Trivy are used to ensure the security of containerized environments, including scanning images and ensuring proper configurations.
- **Secrets Management Tools:** Tools like HashiCorp Vault, Conjur, and Bitwarden are used to manage sensitive information like passwords and API keys securely.
- **Dynamic Application Security Testing (DAST) Tools:** Tools like Fortify WebInspect, Pynt, and Acunetix are used to test applications during runtime and identify exploitable vulnerabilities.
- **Penetration Testing Tools:** Tools like Intruder and Burp Suite simulate real-world attacks to uncover vulnerabilities and provide recommendations for remediation.

Application Whitelisting

Businesses rely on a wide range of third-party applications. To ensure security, administrators use the approach of restricting the usage of any tools or applications only to those who are already vetted and approved. Organizations adopt this approach by delegating a system administrator or third-party application to manage the list of applications and enforce these restrictions. By blocking all unlisted programs by default, this method proactively prevents malicious software (including ransomware) from executing. Application whitelisting uses the Zero Trust principle, which holds that no resources within an organization may interact with the system without strict authorization.

Application whitelisting offers a high level of protection against zero-day attacks and malware because it doesn't rely on recognizing known malicious files, but rather on only permitting known good ones. Organizations define a list of authorized applications, libraries, and scripts identified using criteria such as cryptographic hash (file signature), digital signature/publisher, file path, file name, or file size.

Application Blacklisting, a less restrictive approach to whitelisting, is also used to prevent any third-party tools that are on the blacklist from running. However, blacklisting doesn't account for unidentified threats, sometimes resulting in a misleading sense of security.

The key difference between application whitelisting and blacklisting is that whitelisting follows a "Default Deny" approach, that is, all applications are blocked except those that are permitted. This is highly secure but requires more management, while blacklisting follows "Default Allow", that is all applications are allowed except what is specifically blocked. This is less secure as new, unknown threats can easily pass through.

Disk Encryption Tools

Disk encryption tools perform Full Disk Encryption (FDE), securing an entire disk drive including the OS, system files, and user data. This prevents unauthorized access if devices are lost or stolen

Windows comes with some built-in tools like Device Encryption and BitLocker with AES-128 or AES-256 encryption while the macOS has FileVault which encrypts the entire startup disk. Linux also provides a tool called LUKS for Unified Key Setup for managing volume encryption.

Third party open-source tools include VeraCrypt which can be used for creating encrypted containers or full partitions or NordLocker that provides file-level container encryption.

Anti-Malware Platforms

These platforms are security solutions designed to detect, block, and remove malicious software—such as viruses, ransomware, spyware, and Trojans—from computers, servers, and networks. Unlike traditional antivirus focused on known threats, these platforms use behavioral monitoring, machine learning, and sandboxing to identify evolving, zero-day attacks in real-time.

The following lists some examples:

- **Crowdstrike Falcon:** Endpoint protection platform.
- **Microsoft Defender/Antimalware:** Built-in Windows security.
- **Bitdefender:** Known for high detection rates.
- **Trend Micro Deep Security:** Focuses on server/cloud protection.

Application Security Monitoring tools

Application Security Monitoring tools operate “inside” applications to observe application and user activities and to identify anomalous behaviors.

For example, an Application Security Monitoring tool might detect:

- SQL statements included in data entry fields on a web form.
- Private data being sent over the Internet.
- A user logging on at 3:00 a.m. from an IP address that is not from the user’s home country.
- A query to download an atypically large number of records from a customer account database.
- A user in sales accessing an engineering database containing confidential intellectual property.

While some of these suspicious behaviors can be understood in purely technical terms (evidence of a SQL injection attack), others are meaningful only because they violate business norms (e.g. salespeople rarely access engineering documents). This ability to utilize business context is not easily available to security tools that operate “outside” of applications.

Application Security Monitoring tools also have several key advantages over the approach of writing monitoring code into individual applications:

- They incorporate the extensive knowledge and experience of the software vendor and the vendor's customers regarding attacks, abuses, and methods to detect suspicious activity.
- They can collect, normalize and log many types of application data, to compensate for limited logging built into the applications themselves.
- They can be deployed with legacy and purchased applications. There is no need to modify the applications or develop custom logs.
- They have well-designed methods for creating customized business rules.
- In some cases, they have out-of-the-box capabilities to interface with SIEM systems (discussed in the next section).

Combining Application Security Monitoring with SIEM

SIEM systems aggregate security and log data from many sources, including: routers, gateways and other network devices, firewalls, intrusion protection systems and other security solutions, databases, server and other system logs and directories, and identity management systems. SIEM systems can correlate these masses of data and alert operations and security personnel to probes, attacks, policy violations, unauthorized activities by insiders, and other indicators of security breaches.

Application Security Monitoring tools can feed event streams to SIEM systems, so application-related data can be correlated with network and security events and other systems data.

In fact, Application Security Monitoring tools and SIEM systems are an extremely powerful combination, because together they can identify subtle patterns of behavior that neither technology by itself could pinpoint.

The combination can be particularly effective when it takes advantage of industry- and company-specific business logic.

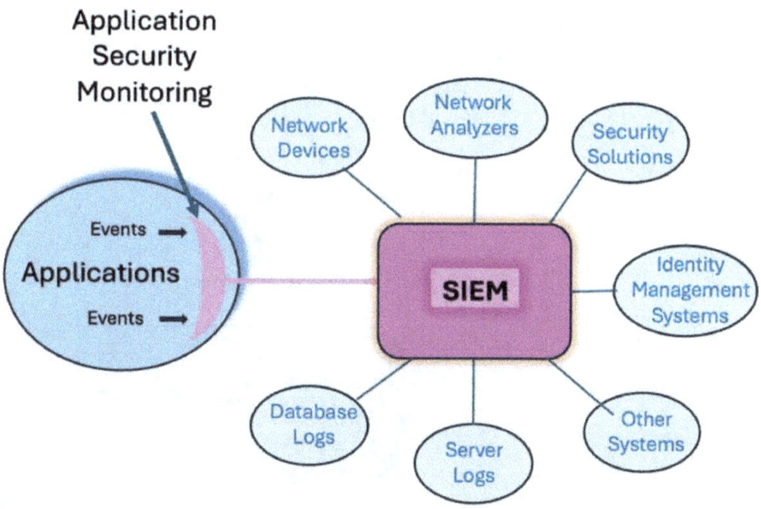

Figure 8-2 : Use of SIEM for Application Security

The movement toward increased application monitoring is being driven by the limitations of traditional perimeter and host security products, by the increased sophistication of hacker and insider threats, and by the challenges of providing security when parts of the infrastructure are located at SaaS and cloud computing sites.

But it also reflects the increased value that can be provided by utilizing a new technology with application security monitoring, particularly when combined with SIEM systems. The benefits include:

- Better protection against cyberattacks and insider security threats.
- Simplified compliance with government regulations and industry standards through better monitoring of application and user actions.
- The effective use of custom business logic and business context to detect fraud and sophisticated attacks targeting specific industries and companies.

For best practices it is important to have detailed awareness of the processes it should support, or the process improvements it could drive. Without the incorporation of targeted workflows, valuable incident information can be overlooked or mishandled because output is not directed to right audiences.

Information that lands in the wrong hands may be handled at less-than-optimal efficiency and tracked improperly for lack of automated handoff to helpdesk, engineering or other functional groups. Furthermore, indiscriminate data collection tends to be poorly documented and is not integrated with change management processes needed to ensure responsiveness of the SIEM to changes in the environment.

Ordinary IT environment changes – such as, operating system upgrades, the setup and tear-down of virtual machines, the implementation of a new patch management tool, policy changes to a firewall, or the upgrade of router software – can easily result in broken data collection processes, or SIEM correlation rules that are no longer accurate and relevant. The net result is an expensive undertaking that is not completely justified, leading to lost credibility for the original project advocates, and an unfortunate and unnecessary turn away from a very valuable technology. At best, the SIEM remains in use returning limited and decreasing benefits. In the worst case, it provides a false sense of security.

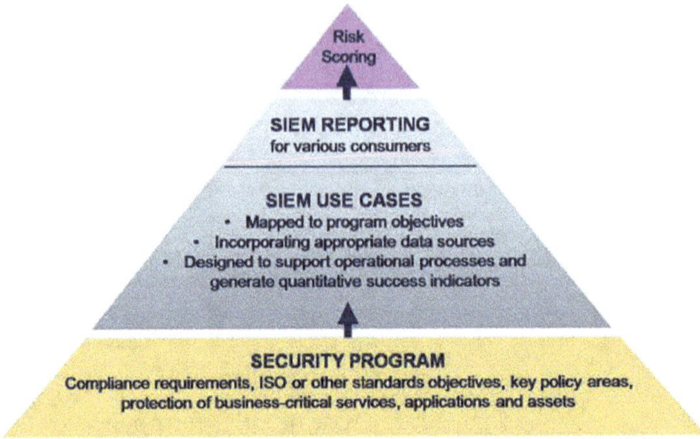

Figure 8-3 : The SIEM Security Program Pyramid

Perhaps the most unfortunate and least recognized shortcoming in SIEM deployments produced through this funnel approach is the inability to ultimately extend the SIEM beyond its traditional uses to directly address business needs. Advanced SIEM deployments have enormous potential to unify the efforts of security operations with business layers of the organization, enabling true and measurable alignment with the C-level objectives of the IT risk manager, CSO, CISO, CIO and line-of-business decision- makers. It can become:

- A central dashboard for ensuring business-prioritized allocation of limited security team resources.
- A platform for enterprise-wide monitoring and measurement of IT risk levels and improvements in security posture overall.
- A purpose-built engine for fraud detection and other advanced capabilities.

Use cases for real-time monitoring of complex, business-critical applications, services and transactions; and a central point of integration between security operations and other IT silos in the implementation of ITIL, ITSM, and other process-based improvements and capabilities.

Features	SIEM	SOAR	XDR
Primary Functions	Log management and analytics	Automation and orchestration	Unified threat detection and response
Data Collection	Logs from various sources	Data from integrated security tools	Data from endpoints, network and cloud
Threat Detection	Rule-based correlation	Depends on integrated tools	Advanced analytics and machine learning

Alerting	Generates alerts from log data	Automates alert response	Real-time alerting
Incident Investigation	Tools for log analytics	Case management for incidents	Integrated response capabilities
Compliance	Audit reports and logs maintenance	Com0liance through automation	May assist with compliance through integration
Scalability	Scalable for large log volumes	Scalable for automation workflows	Scalable across multiple security layers
Automation	Limited	High degree	Includes automation but less customization
Integration	Variety of data sources	Wide range of security tools	Natively with many platforms
User Interface	Dashboard for logs and alerts	User friendly workflow design	Simplified management interface

Table 8-1 : Comparison of SIEM, SOAR and XDR

While the vast majority of SIEM customers start with more traditional objectives for SIEM, a basic SIEM deployment done effectively from the outset lays a solid foundation for the SIEM implementation.

9 – Network Security

Securing the organization's network is important to prevent unauthorized access, misuse, theft, and damage to the systems and assets. Network security is achieved by using hardware, software, policies, and procedures to ensure confidentiality, integrity, and availability of network resources. It involves creating layered defenses to stop cyber threats like malware, ransomware, and denial-of-service attacks, securing everything from network infrastructure to user access.

Rigorous use of network security helps in threat prevention by blocking threats from entering the network. Organizations can achieve this by using tools like firewalls, intrusion detection/prevention systems, and antivirus software. Furthermore, good access control in managing who can access network resources through user authentication (IDs, passwords, biometrics) and authorization policies prevents unauthorized access and risks to the assets. It is also important to protect the sensitive data in transit and at rest through encryption and access restrictions, maintaining its integrity and confidentiality. Continuously monitoring the network traffic is essential to identity and to block suspicious activity using both manual and automated procedures to respond to incidents.

Layered Defense-in-Depth

Defense in Depth is commonly referred to as the "castle approach" because it is similar to the layered defenses of a medieval castle. Before an intruder scan penetrate a castle, the intruder is faced with the moat, ramparts, drawbridge, towers, battlements and so on. Once attacker breaches the outer walls, they may be faced with one or more inner security walls before they can reach the inner parts of the castle.

The modern digital world while revolutionized by how users access and use the data provided by the information systems is constantly open to attack. The range of attackers and the sophistication of attack technique vary only with the importance of the target system. To thwart these potential attackers, an organization needs to ensure that the appropriate levels of security are in place to prevent systems and networks being compromised. This may require multiple security techniques deployed across multiple layers to provide depth of data security needed for their business. While it may be impossible to protect against every possible attack that may occur, the defense-in-depth strategy may be the best option to successfully protect the organization against the most likely types of attacks. This is where defense-in-depth combined with a zero trust approach systematically applied to the organization's security architecture comes into play.

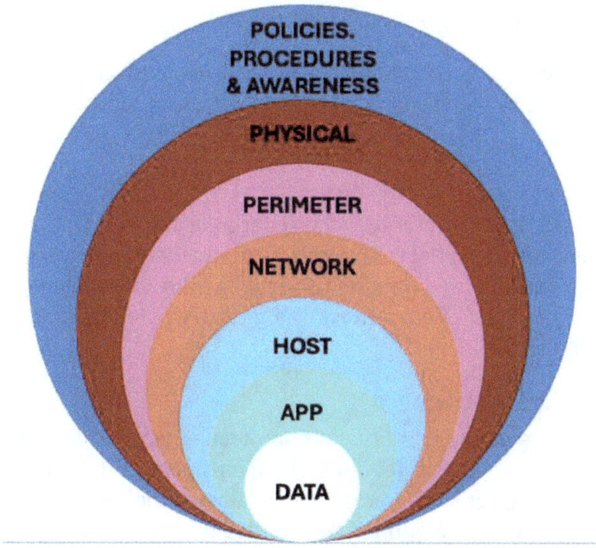

Figure 9-1 : Defense-in-Depth Security Architecture

Common components: Used for Defense-in-Depth

- **Firewalls**: Act as barriers between trusted internal networks and untrusted external networks.
- **VPNs (Virtual Private Networks)**: Securely connect remote users and sites.
- **Endpoint Security**: Protects individual devices like laptops and smartphones.
- Security Information and Event Management (SIEM): Collects and analyzes security logs.
- **Physical Security**: Controls physical access to network hardware (locked server rooms, biometrics).

Defense-in-depth uses layers of security measures including firewalls, secured gateways, authentication and intrusion detection systems, to protect internal networks not only from external attacks, but also from internal attacks from disgruntled workforce members or inadvertent exposure due to negligence.

This provides backup levels of security in case some security measures fail. The goal is to keep threat actors outside of the organization's network perimeter. So, if one defensive measure is compromised, another set of defense mechanisms can detect and prevent a breach attempt. By including redundancies and using security defenses across solutions, an organization can aim to close gaps in security and thwart potential attacks.

A layered approach to security can be applied to all levels of IT systems ranging from individual user laptops to thousands of servers in the data centers and extending beyond to the cloud environments. Note that not only does defense-in-depth protect an organization's sensitive data assets from external threats, the practices applied also protect their assets from insider threats.

Elements of defense in depth

New security products continue emerging to protect networks and systems. Here are some of the more common security elements found in a Defense-in-Depth strategy:

Network Security Controls

The first line of defense when securing a network is the analysis of network traffic. Firewalls prevent access to and from unauthorized networks and will allow or block traffic based on a set of security rules. Intrusion protection systems often work in tandem with a firewall to identify potential security threats and respond to them quickly.

Antivirus Software

Antivirus software is critical to protecting against viruses and malware. However, many variants often rely heavily upon signature-based detection. While these solutions offer strong protection against malicious software, signature-based products can be exploited by intelligent cybercriminals. For this reason, it is wise to use an antivirus solution that includes heuristic features that scan for suspicious patterns and activity.

Analyzing Data Integrity

Integrity of data, while in storage or in transit, is critical for every business. Data integrity can be managed in several ways. These include:

- Using checksums associated with stored fields. A checksum is a mathematical representation of the size of the file and any changes in the checksum while in storage or in transit can flag a loss of data integrity.
- File provenance (the source of its original location), the frequency of its use, checks against a known list of viruses and other malicious code.
- If an incoming file is of a type or nature completely unique to the system, it may be marked as suspicious.
- Data integrity solutions can also check the source IP address to ensure it is from a known and trusted source.

Behavioral Analysis

File and network behaviors often provide insight while a breach is in progress or has occurred. If behavioral analysis shows unexpected activity related to the use of the data, it could indicate a firewall or intrusion protection activation. Behavioral analysis picks up on the change from the norm and can either send alerts or execute automatic controls that prevent a breach from continuing any further. For this to work effectively, organizations need to set a baseline for "normal" behavior.

Defense-in-Depth vs. Zero Trust

Zero Trust is based on the concept of “never trust, always verify.” This cybersecurity framework is based on the idea that no entity – inside or outside of a network – should be implicitly trusted. Everything and everyone need to prove who they are and that they have the right permissions to access the target resource. In short, they need to undergo continual authentication, verification and authorization to keep access to applications and data.

What is the difference between Zero Trust vs defense-in-depth?

The main difference between Zero Trust and defense-in-depth security strategies is that Zero Trust never implicitly trusts users inside or outside network perimeters, whereas with a defense-in-depth security strategy, users within a network are usually implicitly trusted but controls are applied nonetheless to ensure they have the proper credentials to access data.

While Zero Trust aims to prevent attackers from the outset, the defense-in-depth strategy simply aims to delay the attack by increasing the number of barriers an attacker must overcome to get to the secured data within the security perimeter.

Benefits of Defense-in-Depth

The main cited benefit of a defense-in-depth approach is through layered security. If one part of an enterprise fails, then other networks and platforms are kept safe. To build it effectively, an organization must consider their strengths and weaknesses and add layers where a breach is most likely. This redundancy helps to ensure that a single point of failure won't be the sole factor in a successful breach. By layering perimeter defense with a defense-in-depth configuration, threat actors must clear multiple defenses which slows down threat advancement and adds complications to unauthorized data access or exfiltration.

The design of a Defense-in-Depth security architecture requires some key considerations that need to be front and center as part of the design effort. The architecture will be addressing a continually growing attack surface and will need the flexibility to manage that. Also, users bringing their own devices and potentially applications that must be administered effectively need to be very carefully managed. With the many layers, threat identification and management can become tedious and complicated as total visibility is addressed across the organization. Integrating a wide range of utilities and tools with existing ecosystems can require a lot of attention on an ongoing basis.

Best Practice for Protecting Workstations

With users, especially those working remotely, management of their devices and access rights and permissions is an ongoing challenge. The security architecture must address all aspects of user identification and access management. Key considerations for security architecture for workstations include the following.

Remove Local Admin Rights

Microsoft Windows, macOS and Linux administrator accounts open the door for threat actors. These privileged accounts are used to install and update workstation software, configure system settings and manage user accounts. Bad actors often leverage them to disable antivirus software or disaster recovery tools, and to launch ransomware and other types of malware. What rights they should have needs to be carefully evaluated and then minimized to what they really need.

Enforce Least Privilege

Users often have a legitimate need to perform an action requiring administrative privileges. Best-of-breed endpoint privilege managers allow elevating user permissions to perform certain specified tasks, based on policy, without requiring end-user action or help-desk intervention. By enforcing the principle of least privilege — giving end users and applications the bare minimum set of privileges needed to perform their jobs — workstation vulnerabilities can be mitigated and the security posture strengthened. Using a jump server to elevate user accounts to privileged accounts is worth considering. Leading endpoint privilege managers integrate with privileged access management (PAM) solutions to safeguard administrative passwords and strengthen workstation security.

Institute Application Control Policies

Application control is fundamental for protecting against malware and other threats. Many endpoint privilege managers support "allow listing" and "deny listing" functionality to explicitly permit or block known applications. The difference between a good application control and a great one is the ability to create comprehensive rules for applications that can be allowed and how they can be used.

Secure and Rotate Workstation Admin Passwords

Administrative accounts are a favorite target for threat actors. Even when local admin rights are removed from users, compromised admin accounts can still be used to launch attacks. Good admin password hygiene is essential, and policy-based governance is the best way to ensure good hygiene. Password must be rotated (changed) on a quarterly basis. A PAM solution can be used to safely store passwords in a secure digital vault to prevent theft and rotate them automatically.

Deceive Threat Actors and Detect Them Early in the Attack Chain

Best-in-class endpoint privilege managers support privilege deception functionality to help lure and throw off would-be attackers. They allow creating fake "honeypot" privileged accounts with alluring usernames like "admin2" and intentionally weak passwords like "admin" to reel in and block adversaries at the point of entry. The endpoint privilege manager will generate an alert to let you know when you've lured an attacker.

Proactively Monitor Privileged Workstation Activity

Many endpoint privilege managers provide monitoring and reporting capabilities to help track privileged workstation activity, identify suspicious behavior, and streamline compliance audits and forensics investigations. Most include canned reports that can be sued to easily identify which workstations and applications are protected, as well as the specific privilege elevation policies and business rules being enforced. Leading endpoint privilege managers generate detailed event messages whenever a policy is invoked and include dashboards and tools for observing and exploring policy-driven management.

Zero Trust Network Architecture

The National Security Telecommunications Advisory Committee (NSTAC) Report on Zero Trust and Trusted Identity Management defines Zero Trust (ZT) as "a cybersecurity strategy *premised on the idea that no user or asset is to be implicitly trusted. It assumes that a breach has already occurred or will occur, and therefore, an entity should not be granted access to sensitive information by a single verification done at the enterprise perimeter. Instead, each user, device, application, and transaction must be continually verified.*"

Zero Trust Overview

The concepts of Zero Trust were developed at Forrester Research in 2008. At that time, network perimeter-based security approaches were dominated by a trust model, which designated the external interface as untrusted and internal interface as trusted. But this trust model was recognized as cause for many data breaches resulting in the more granular security controls decoupled from the model of trust.

Organizations need to place a strategic emphasis on adopting Zero Trust as a transformative approach to cybersecurity. Organizations need to develop and implement a culture of Zero Trust and realize it as a strategy that truly and meaningfully transforms cybersecurity outcomes through a series of policy actions.

Defense-in-Depth works on the principle that users inside the network perimeter can be trusted but uses multiple layers to delay attackers or inadvertent damage by assuming breaches can happen. Zero Traut moves away from the "trust but verify" model to a "never trust, always verify" model. No user or device should be automatically trusted, regardless of whether they are inside or outside the network perimeter. Instead, it requires continuous verification and authentication for every access request, emphasizing strict access controls and least-privileged access.

The following lists the key tenets of the Zero Trust Network Access model:

- **Least-Privileged Access:** In this approach, the users are granted only the minimum level of access needed to perform their tasks, thereby limiting the potential damage from a compromised account or device.
- **Continuous Monitoring**: By continuously monitoring user activity and network traffic, any potential threats can be detected and responded to in real-time. Security policies are adapted as needed.
- **Assume Breach**: Using abundant caution implies assuming that the network has already been breached so that the focus can be on protecting critical assets and data, rather than solely relying on perimeter security.

Based on these key tenets of Zero Trust Architecture, many technologies and tools are used to achieve ZTNA in practice including the following:

- **Least Privilege**: Managing authorizations to only grant access to specific resources required for a specific role of the user. Escalation of privilege is limited and controlled, and any grants are revoked as soon as they are no longer required.
- **Identity and Access Management (IAM):** IAM play a very important role in ZTNA. Strong authentication methods like multi-factor authentication (MFA) and single sign-on (SSO) are crucial to verify user identities and must be used.
- **Dynamic Access Control**: Malicious actors are prone to changing their identities and behaviors so it is critical to continuously evaluate user and device behavior to determine if access should continue to be granted or revoked, even after a connection has been established.
- **Network Segmentation**: This divides the network into broad zones such as departments to reduce the attack surface. It typically uses hardware firewalls, VLANs, and Access Control Lists (ACLs) to limit access and prevent lateral movement.
- **Micro-segmentation**: This creates highly granular and isolated segments for individual workloads. The blast radius for a breach and potential damage can be reduced by dividing the network into smaller,

isolated segments that limit the impact of a breach and prevent lateral movement.

- **Security Groups**: These are dynamic, identity-based collections of users, devices, and applications used to enforce granular access policies, granting least-privilege access to specific resources rather than broad network segments, based on continuous verification of user identity. They act as a crucial component for granting access control and managing traffic based on device and application in a segmented network.
- **Endpoint and Device Security**: Ensures that all devices accessing the network are secure and compliant with organizational policies.
- **Data Protection**: Encrypts sensitive data and implements access controls to protect it from unauthorized access.
- **Prevent lateral movement:** Strong authentication is used to meet the Zero Trust requirement for verification of every access request, regardless of whether it originates from inside or outside the network. Technologies used include network segmentation, security groups, and password management.

The following are the key best practices driving Zero Trust in an organization:

- Use progress metrics for Zero Trust to drive accountability for strategic implementation.
- Establish a working group to develop Zero Trust maturity models for the organization
- Clarify the alignment of Zero Trust with regulatory standards that are required to be followed.
- Establish funding for Zero Trust implementation, and the teams within the organization are funded under this plan.
- Ensure that the Zero Trust capability applies to on-premises as well as cloud environments.
- Develop organizational policies, standards and procedures that must be complied with and rigorously followed by the entire workforce.
- Develop training and outreach to promote Zero Trust.

The traditional, centralized, 'castle and moat' security model is ineffective in modern decentralized environments in the current era of decentralized and distributed cloud computing and the remote workforce, where only a few organizational assets and users still reside inside the "castle."

Zero Trust is a holistic enterprise security strategy that encompasses cloud/multi-cloud (all service models), on-premises/hybrid systems, internal and external partner/stakeholder and user endpoints (organization-managed and BYOD endpoints), and is inclusive of operational technology (OT) and Industrial Control Systems (ICS) and Internet of Things (IoT). Consequently, Zero Trust has been compared to a mountain that must be climbed one step at a time, i.e., implemented incrementally and preferably in a risk-based manner. These principles are a common theme in CSA ZT guidance.

NIST SP 800-2007: Zero Trust Architecture

NIST SP 800-2007 defines Zero Trust as "a cybersecurity paradigm focused on resource protection and the premise that "trust is never granted implicitly but must be continually evaluated".

The Zero Trust Architecture provides the definition and framework for the key tenets as well as a roadmap to migrate and deploy Zero Trust security concepts to an enterprise environment. This is the basis for many other federal Zero Trust guidelines.

The key tenets under the Zero Trust Architecture include:

- All data sources and computing services are resources.
- All communication is secured.
- Access to resources is granted on a per-session basis.
- Access to resources is determined by dynamic policy.
- All assets are monitored and measured by the enterprise.
- All authentication and authorization are dynamic and strictly enforced before access.
- Information about assets, network infrastructure and communications is collected and used to improve security.

Integrating Zero Trust with IAM

Integrating Zero Trust with Identity and Access Management (IAM) and security tools involves using IAM as the foundation for implementing Zero Trust principles, such as continuous authentication and least privilege access, supporting Zero Trust concepts like multi-factor authentication (MFA) and risk-based authentication (RBA). Furthermore, security tools like SIEM and UEBA can be integrated with IAM to enhance threat detection and response capabilities within a Zero Trust framework.

Zero Trust for Security Operations Control

Zero Trust relies on strict and continuous verification and validation for every person, device, or entity attempting to access network resources. The primary goal is to prevent successful breaches or corruption of data, applications, and business-critical systems from attacks and exploits. The principles in Zero Trust listed below are designed to reduce exposure and unauthorized access across the threat landscape.

- Multi factor authentication (MFA)
- Policy of least privilege.
- Micro segmentation

Zero trust starts with verifying and validating users' identities such that the security architecture needs to be able to block or allow access based on a verified user and the implementation needs to be able to verify user identity everywhere throughout the security architecture where the system can block and allow access.

Applying zero trust to applications require a very similar approach but the identity of users trying to access applications needs to be addressed as also validating access between applications and workloads, and validating the transactions to ensure the content access related to applications is not malicious regardless of where these applications are on premises, in a private cloud, or public cloud.

The same rigor should be applied when looking at infrastructure by validating the identity of users connecting to the infrastructure and continuously discover and monitor all Internet connected assets and changes to existing assets.

SoC plays a key role in Zero Trust as described below:

- Continuous verification of Zero Trust policies
- Identifying gaps in the Zero Trust posture
- Limiting attack impact through automated enforcement
- Speeding investigation with automated threat data collection
- Continuous discovery of critical assets

Modern security threats are evolving at a faster pace while SOC is built around legacy security information and event management (SIEM) and does not necessarily provide a flexible and scalable solution that keeps pace with digital transformation, cloud initiatives, and advanced attack campaigns. SoC challenges lack of visibility and context, increased complexity of investigations, alert fatigue and noise from a high volume of low fidelity alerts generated by all systems.

A key component of rearchitecting the SOC for zero trust is to ensure that security teams are leveraging machine learning to its full potential to augment and complement humans in security. Advanced analytics and AI can significantly reduce the amount of time that teams spend processing massive amounts of data in the enterprise to come up with critical security insights. By automatically detecting anomalous patterns across multiple data sources and automatically providing alerts with context, machine learning today can speed up investigations and remove blind spots in the enterprise. Machine learning techniques provide for integrating the data, analyzing it, and automating human decision making by enriching incident data and automating system level actions workflows and decision making.

CISA Zero Trust Maturity Model

Adapted from NIST 800-207, The CISA (Cybersecurity and Infrastructure Security Agency – a US federal agency under DHS) -- Zero Trust model (ZTMM) is defined as providing a collection of concepts and ideas designed to minimize uncertainty in enforcing accurate, least privilege per-request access decisions in information systems and services in the face of a network viewed as compromised.

Its key pillars include identity, device, network/environment, application and workload, and data. Other cross-cutting foundational elements include visibility and analytics, automation and orchestration, and governance.

Sophisticated threat actors are increasingly adept at exploiting any exposed technical or human vulnerability in modern, highly distributed enterprise networks that often heavily leverage Internet connectivity. Successful cyberattacks generally exploit trust in some manner. Trust, when misplaced, becomes a vulnerability that must be actively managed and minimized. With Zero Trust, all network connections and packets are considered untrusted and are subjected to the same rigorous verification processes. The trust level is defined as zero, hence the term Zero Trust.

Implementing Zero Trust

The following describe the key steps for implementing Zero Trust in an organization.

Step	Activities
Define the Protect Surface	Identify the all of the desktop and data -as-a-service components and other endpoints internally and externally that need to be protected. This is the protect surface.
Map the Transaction Flows	Understand how the networks work by mapping the transaction flows to and from the protect surface, including how various service components interact with other resources on the network. These transaction flows help determine where to place proper controls.
Build a Zero Trust Architecture	Design your Zero Trust architecture, tailored to the protect surface(s) determined in steps 1 and 2. The way traffic moves across the network specific to the data in the protect surface should determine the design. The architectural elements cannot be predetermined, though a good rule of thumb is to place the controls as close as possible to the protect surface
Create a Zero Trust Policy	Instantiate Zero Trust as a Layer 7 (application) policy statement. Define the details for who, what, when, where, and how of Zero Trust policy writing to determine who or what can access your protect surface when and how. Consider both person and non-person entities.
Monitor and Maintain the Network	Inspect and log all traffic, all the way through Layer 7 (application). The telemetry from this process helps prevent significant cybersecurity events and provides valuable security improvement insights over the long term. As a result, each subsequent protect surface can become more robust and better protected over time.

Table 9-1 : Implementation Steps for Zero Trust

Automated Moving Target Defense.

Automated moving target defense (AMTD) is an emerging concept developed and championed by Gartner. Security Products and Services that employ AMTD technologies to raise the cost for attackers by orchestrating controlled change within IT environments to proactively disrupt attacks and confound breach activities.

AMTD approaches should be designed to be threat-agnostic and be able to address all types of cyberattack threats. AMTD-infused solutions should, therefore, be able to provide organizations with protection benefits by turning the tables on adversaries and rendering a large majority of malicious tactics, techniques, and procedures useless.

As part of the AMTD approach, Gartner has also defined the concept of Continuous Threat Exposure Management (CTEM), a systemic approach to continuously refine cybersecurity optimization priorities. A CTEM cycle includes five stages: scoping, discovery, prioritization, validation and mobilization as described by Gartner in the diagram below.

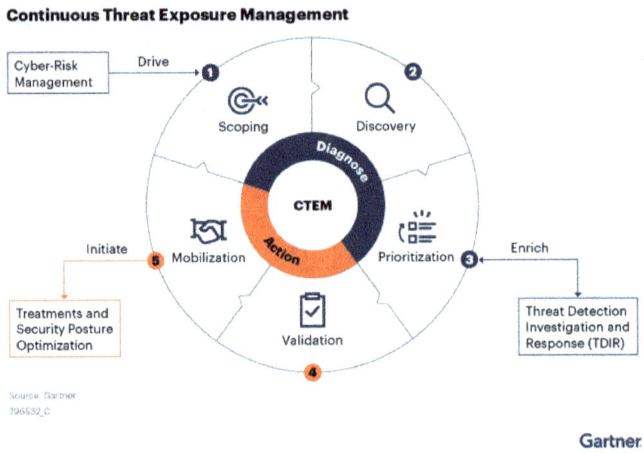

Source: Gartner

Figure 9-2. : The five Stages of Continuous Threat Exposure Management

This approach is used to design actionable security exposure remediation and improvement plans that business executives can understand, and that architecture teams can act on.

Adaptive attack protection is the driving approach for AMTD. For this to work, aggressive protection must be applied directly at the endpoints when an attack is detected and is in progress. In the event an attacker gains initial access to a device in the environment, applying these protections at the endpoints dramatically decreases the likelihood of the attack's success and provides defenders more time to neutralize it. In addition, defenders can also use defense measures, including blocking actions that may not inherently be malicious in an everyday context but are dangerous in the context of an attack.

According to Gartner, combining AMTD solutions at different layers of the technology stack provides security defenders with an effective 'defense-in-depth' strategy that significantly improves the overall security posture. AMTD includes proactive automation of cyber defense mechanisms to orchestrate movement or change in the attack surfaces, the use of deception technologies, and the ability to execute intelligent preplanned defensive posture and tools change decisions. This approach helps in automatically morphing system resources so that they cannot be easily targeted, and planting of decoy traps on top of morphed resources not only confuses the attackers but can help identify them and prevent future attacks. Any access to a decoy triggers a notification for reporting and visibility into the attack.

A variety of emerging security technologies are being designed to quickly pivot security programs and underlying technologies to increase the burden on attackers, forcing them to work harder or fail completely in their malicious efforts.

Currently, the technologies such as, detection-based next-generation anti-virus (NGAV), endpoint protection platforms (EPP), and endpoint detection and response (EDR/XDR/MDR) work by first detecting malicious files or behavior patterns and then responding to them. They are fundamentally reactive, but the AMTD goal is to be preventive.

Cybercriminals invest time and effort in fine-tuning their cyberattacks. They need to dedicate time and resources to gather the needed intelligence to be successful. AMTD's preventive approach is to defeat the value of the time and effort the attackers put into attack reconnaissance to discover vulnerabilities and the right way to exploit a victim's systems. AMTD methods like obfuscation and system morphing are particularly valuable in protecting against such highly targeted attacks. This preventive approach is especially effective in securing endpoints and server workloads—typically an organization's largest attack surface.

Many modern cyberattacks. are highly targeted and tailored to evade and bypass specific defense layers. The following diagram is Gartner's example of AMTD layered automation. Its focus is on three key steps:

1. *Identify Target Asset.* Determine what needs to be protected such as applications or data stored or in transit.
2. *Select Method/timing Interval.* Determine when automation is applied and the protocols that will be applied to achieve the planned changes for the automation.
3. *Automate Movement, Reconfiguration, Morphing or Encryption.* What components of the infrastructure, the operating systems, servers, and hardware resources will be involved in the automated reconfiguration of the environments (infrastructure and hardware) and movement of applications and data across them.

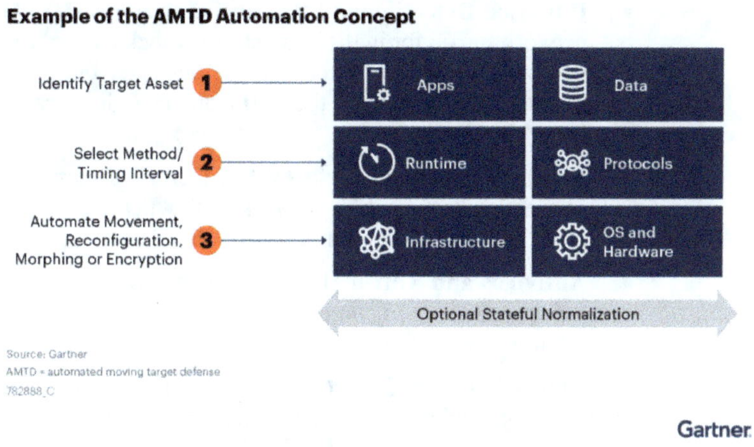

Source: Gartner

Figure 9-3. : Example of AMTD Automation Concept

The steps involved in this process include identifying target assets, selecting the morphing interval, and automating asset reconfiguration.

AMTD Approaches:

Some approaches used for defeating cybercriminals include the following:

- Enhance security for internet-facing applications by ensuring that every module loads at a random memory address each time the application starts, adding complexity to potential exploitation.
- The obfuscation of malicious code needs to be reversed (by a short initialization or loader routine) before it can run on the machine. This reversal process typically relies on specific operating system APIs, and attackers aim to avoid revealing this dependency right from the beginning as it can be an indicator of subterfuge.
- Use anti-malware scanning consistently.
- Create and enforce guardrails around code execution.
- Prevent Asynchronous Procedure Code (APC) injection.
- Utilize system functions at runtime which are not typically used by business applications.
- Introduce greater uncertainty and complexity for attackers by automated configuration changes.

Network Security Technologies

Many technologies play a crucial role in ensuring network security and they typically work in a complementary manner. These include:

- **Firewalls**: Barrier between a trusted network and external networks. Monitors, filters and controls incoming traffic based on rules – Fortinet, Palo Alto Networks Panorama
- **Intrusion Detection and Prevention Systems (IDS/IPS):** Monitor network traffic for malicious activity, block or alert on suspicious behavior. IDS is a perimeter device (analyzes but does not block traffic), IPS is in-line in the traffic and can block traffic. SolarWinds, Palo Alto Networks
- **Virtual Private Networks (VPNs):** Create secure, encrypted connections over public networks, allowing remote access while maintaining confidentiality. NordVPN, Proton
- **Antivirus and Anti-malware Software**: Detect and remove malicious software that could compromise the network. BitDefender, TrendMicro, Norton
- **Network Access Control (NAC):** Enforces security policies before allowing devices to connect to the network, uses authentication and device compliance checks. Fortinet
- **Data Loss Prevention (DLP):** Prevents sensitive data from leaving the network, often through monitoring and blocking unauthorized data transfers. Fortinet, Trellix.
- **Email Security**: Protects against email-borne threats like phishing and spam, often using techniques like filtering and encryption. MS Defender, Cisco Secure Email, Forcepoint

- **Application Security**: Focuses on securing applications and APIs from vulnerabilities that could be exploited to compromise the network. SAST and DAST penetration testing and SCA. Veracode, Qualys, GitHub Advanced Security, Checkmarx.
- **Web Security**: Protects against web-based threats, such as malware downloads and malicious websites, often using techniques like URL filtering and web traffic inspection. Splunk, Burp Suite, Wireshark, Forcepoint.
- **Wireless Security**: Secures wireless networks through strong encryption protocols (like WPA2 or WPA3) and secure authentication methods. Wireshark
- **SIEM (Security Information and Event Management):** Aggregates and analyzes security logs from various sources to provide a centralized view of security events and detect potential threats. Splunk, MS Sentinel,
- **Network Segmentation**: Divides the network into smaller, isolated segments, limiting the potential impact of a security breach in one segment. Cisco Secure Workload, VMware NSX, Akamai, Wireshark
- **Vulnerability Management**: Regularly scans for and addresses vulnerabilities in the network infrastructure and applications. Tenable, Qualys VMDR, Splunk,
- **Penetration Testing**: Simulates cyberattacks to identify weaknesses in the network security posture. Metasploit, Burp Suite, Qualys (handle multiple systems from a single console)
- **Micro-segmentation**: divides a network into isolated segments, even down to the individual workload or application level. allows for granular security controls to be applied to each segment, preventing threats from spreading across the entire network. Reduces attack surface, can be used with zero trust, Use Least privilege. SDN. Cloud based Firewalls, VLANs, WD-SAN (Western Digital Storage Area Network.

Network Security Groups (NSGs)

NSGs act as virtual firewalls for resources in a cloud environment. They control network traffic by filtering inbound and outbound connections based on defined rules. These rules specify criteria like source/destination IP addresses, ports, and protocols to either allow or deny traffic.

Intrusion Detection/Prevention Systems (IDS/IPS)

IDS (Intrusion Detection System); and IPS (Intrusion Prevention System) ; are cybersecurity tools that monitor network traffic for threats. The key difference between the two is that an IDS passively detects and alerts administrators while an IPS actively blocks malicious activity in real-time, making it a proactive defense. An IPS is typically deployed in-line in the main traffic flow for immediate intervention, unlike IDS which analyzes copied traffic in a separate area for processing. Both identify threats using signatures or behavioral analysis but have different response mechanisms, with IPS being more automated. An IPS can be potentially disruptive if it generates false positives and blocks packets of data.

IDS requires manual response by the security teams after the traffic is analyzed in an out-of-band copied area. Analyzing data in an out-of-band area helps avoid impacting network performance. An IDS is best suited for deep analysis, forensics, or environments where even minor disruption (from false positives) is unacceptable.

An IPS is similar to an IDS in terms of detection but provides added controls and automatically blocks, drops, or reconfigures traffic in real-time. Its placement in-line in the path of traffic allows it to intercept threats before they reach internal systems. It is best suited for environments needing immediate, automated threat containment. In that capability, it acts like an advanced firewall. Note that an IPS can block legitimate traffic through false positives and can be disruptive.

IDS/IPS Together (IDPS)

Many modern solutions combine both (IDPS), using IPS for active defense and IDS for deeper visibility, providing comprehensive, layered security.

Firewalls and Next-Generation Firewalls (NGFWs)

A firewall is a network security system acting as a barrier between trusted internal networks and untrusted external ones (like the internet), filtering traffic based on predefined rules and policies to block unauthorized access and threats. Firewalls are used to prevent malicious data from entering the network or sensitive data from leaving the network. Firewalls can operate as hardware appliances, software, or cloud-based solutions. Firewalls inspect data packets to determine if they are in compliance with the security rules and allow or deny them from passing through based on this assessment. Next generation firewalls can offer advanced features like deep packet inspection and application control, serving as a crucial first line of defense against cyberattacks.

How Firewalls Work

Firewalls monitor all traffic and inspect all incoming and outgoing data packets. They analyze packet content and details such as IP addresses, ports, and protocols and check them against the security rules and policies. If the packet content is compliant with the security rules, it is allowed to go through. If a data packet content is non-compliant with the security rules or is suspicious in some manner, it is blocked or dropped.

Next generation firewalls also have the capability for stateful inspection and can track active connections to ensure only legitimate responses are allowed back in.

Types of Firewalls

The following describes the different types of firewalls:

- **Packet Filtering**: Basic, fast filtering by IP/port by examining the header each data packet and allowing or blocking it based on predefined rules, typically checking source/destination IP addresses, port numbers, and protocols.

- **Stateful Inspection**: Tracks connection state for better security. It monitors each data packet and allows or blocks the packet based on predefined rules, typically checking source and destination IP addresses, port numbers, and protocols.
- **Proxy Firewalls**: Act as intermediary gateway between a private network and the internet, intercepting and inspecting all traffic at the application layer (Layer 7) to filter malicious content and enforce policies,.
- **Next-Generation Firewalls (NGFWs)** : Combine traditional functions with advanced features like deep packet inspection, intrusion prevention (IPS), and application awareness.
- **Host-Based Firewalls**: Software installed directly on individual devices (e.g., Windows Firewall on a laptop) to monitor and control its incoming and outgoing network traffic.
- **Network-Based Firewalls**: Can be a hardware device or software placed on a network's perimeter protecting an entire network by inspecting incoming and outgoing data packets and filtering them based on security rules and policies.

Next-Generation Firewall (NGFW)

NGFW is an advanced network security device that goes beyond traditional firewalls by combining stateful inspection with deeper packet inspection going to data beyond the headers into the actual packet content, application awareness, user identity control, and integrated intrusion prevention systems (IPS) to identify and block sophisticated threats hidden in legitimate traffic. They offer a comprehensive protection against modern cyberattacks like malware and exploits, not just port/protocol-based blocks. NGFWs are application aware and for example, can identity that the application is targeted to social media. They can enforce policies based on users and groups. An important feature provided by NGFWs is the capability to use cloud-based intelligence to identify and block emerging threats and can also block access to malicious websites. Furthermore, they can decrypt content in SSL/TLS traffic on the fly and perform deep inspection of even encrypted data.

Leading vendors of NGFWs include Palo Alto Networks, Fortinet, Cisco, Sophos, Juniper Networks, and WatchGuard.

Network Segmentation

Network segmentation: divides a large computer network into smaller, isolated sub-networks (segments or subnets) to enhance security, improve performance, and control traffic flow, preventing attackers from moving freely (lateral movement) if one part is breached, much like firebreaks in a forest. Each segment can have its own security policies, restricting access to sensitive data and containing threats, making it a crucial cybersecurity practice for protecting assets like customer data and corporate proprietary and intellectual property.

The tools used for network segmentation include firewalls (by acting as security checkpoints controlling traffic between network zones), VLANs, and Software Defined Networks (SDN). Additionally, traffic is controlled by implementing policies that dictate what traffic is allowed between segments. Security is enforced by preventing attackers from reaching critical assets in other segments if one segment is compromised. This ensures that the breach is contained within that one segment.

Network segmentation reduces the blast radius of a breach preventing malware spread. It also helps in improving network performance. By reducing congestion by separating network traffic and optimizing the bandwidth for the type of traffic. Segmentation further helps in ensuring regulatory compliance by isolating and protecting sensitive data. And it simplifies monitoring, troubleshooting, and incident response.

Some examples of network segments include:

- Employee networks vs. Guest Wi-Fi
- Production servers vs. Development environments
- Financial systems vs. General office networks

Network Access Control (NAC)

NAC is a security solution that restricts unauthorized users and devices from accessing a private network by enforcing policies that authenticate identity, check device compliance (like updated antivirus or patches), and authorize access levels before granting entry, acting as a digital checkpoint to keep networks secure and prevent breaches. It's a key part of a Zero Trust strategy, ensuring only trusted and compliant entities get network resources, from users to IoT devices, with dynamic control over what they can access.

NAC uses authentication as its foundation to determine who or what is trying to connect (e.g., username/password, biometrics, certificates) and verifies their authorization to determine what the authenticated user/device can access based on roles, location, and time. It also checks if the device meets security standards (e.g., up-to-date antivirus, no malware) known as *device compliance*. The use of *policy enforcement* determines if the user or device is allowed, denied, quarantined or restricted from access if it is a non-compliant device. It thereby prevents unauthorized access and blocks threats before they enter the network and also, at the same time, provides insight into all devices connecting to the network and ensures that the devices meet organizational security policies.

NAC supports Zero Trust and enforces the principle of "never trust, always verify" for every connection. Threat mitigation is achieved through NAC by limiting the spread of attacks by isolating infected devices. It controls who and what gets onto the organization's network by checking identity and security posture before granting access, and then enforcing policies to limit what they can do, acting as a central security guard for users and devices. It identifies users/devices, assesses their security health (antivirus, patches), authenticates them (login, MFA), and then authorizes access based on predefined rules (role, location), stopping threats like zero-day attacks and ensuring compliance.

SDN - Software Defined Network

Software-defined Networks (SDN) is an approach to networking that uses software to control and manage network devices, rather than relying solely on hardware-based configurations. This centralized control allows greater flexibility, programmability, and automation in managing and optimizing network traffic and resources.

SDN is typically implemented by separating the control plane (software) from the data plane (hardware) and then using a central controller to manage the network. This allows for centralized control, programmability, and automation of network configurations and policies through the control plane. SDN can be implemented using various models and tools, including Open SDN, API SDN, SDN Overlay, and Hybrid SDN.

SDN relies on network devices (switches, routers) that can be programmed to follow instructions from the controller. This can be achieved through software-based implementations of OpenFlow or other protocols. Applications interact with the SDN controller through a northbound interface, providing information about network needs and allowing for the implementation of policies. SDN provides a centralized point of control for network management, allowing administrators to configure, monitor, and troubleshoot the network from a single interface.

The following describes the key aspects for SDNs.

- **Separation of Control and Data Planes:** In traditional networking, the control plane (which determines how data is routed) and the data plane (which forwards the data) are tightly coupled within each network device giving limited control. SDN separates these planes, allowing the control plane to be centralized and managed separately by software. The control plane is managed by the SDN controller (software) and the data plane is responsible for forwarding packets (hardware).
- **Centralized Management:** SDN uses a central software controller that manages the network, enabling administrators to configure and manage network resources from a single point. Furthermore, they can change the network configuration at any time.
- **Programmability and Automation:** The separation of control and data planes enables SDN to be programmable, allowing network administrators to create custom network policies and automate network tasks.
- **Abstraction of Hardware:** SDN abstracts the underlying hardware infrastructure, allowing network administrators to manage the network without needing to be concerned with the specific hardware vendors or models.
- **Flexibility and Agility:** The ability to program and manage the network from a central point enables SDNs to be more flexible and agile, allowing businesses to quickly adapt to changing network needs.

SDNs can be used for a variety of applications, including scaling data center operations, deploying applications, securing IoT architectures, and enabling intent-based networking.

The core of an SDN implementation is the controller, which acts as the central brain of the network. It receives information from applications, defines network policies, and instructs network devices (switches, routers) on how to forward traffic.

Types of SDNs

The following describes the common SDN types:

- **Open SDN**: This approach utilizes open protocols like OpenFlow to communicate between the controller and network devices to program and manage network devices (switches, routers) from different vendors, offering flexibility, interoperability, and cost-effectiveness by avoiding proprietary lock-in. This allows a more open and standardized approach to SDN implementation.
- **API SDN:** In this SDN model APIs are the primary means of controlling the flow of data across network devices and it uses APIs to monitor and control network traffic, offering flexibility in managing devices with different protocols.
- **SDN Overlay:** This approach creates virtual networks on top of existing physical network (the "underlay"), allowing for flexible, programmable, and abstracted network services without changing the underlying hardware. This facilitates the creation of isolated and dynamic tunnels between devices. that This approach combines SDN with traditional networking protocols, allowing for a gradual transition to SDN in existing environments runs on top of an existing network.
- **Hybrid SDN:**. This is a network architecture that blends traditional networking with SDN principles, allowing for the coexistence and interoperability of both centralized, software-controlled functions and decentralized, distributed control, enabling gradual migration and leveraging existing infrastructure while adding modern agility. It's a pragmatic solution where some network traffic and functions are managed by an SDN controller, while legacy devices and protocols handle other parts, offering benefits like cost-effectiveness, flexibility, and simplified management for complex environments.

SDN Deployment

SDN virtualizes your network to abstract physical hardware network elements, such as switches and routers. Using SDN, you can dynamically manage your datacenter networking to meet workload and application requirements. Network policies can be implemented consistently, at scale, even as you deploy new workloads or move workloads across virtual or physical networks.

SDN can be deployed via VMM or PowerShell.

SDN VMM Deployment

The VMM fabric, within Microsoft System Center Virtual Machine Manager (VMM), refers to the unified, software-defined pool of computing, storage, and networking resources that the VMM manages as a single entity for creating private clouds and virtual machines. It integrates physical hardware like servers (Hyper-V), storage arrays, and network devices, and abstracts them into logical resources (host groups, logical networks, storage pools) that administrators can provision, manage, and scale. Deploying SDN in the VMM fabric provides the following functionality:

- Provision and manage virtual networks at scale.
- Deploy and manage the SDN infrastructure, including network controllers, software load balancers, and gateways.
- Define and control virtual network policies centrally and link them to the applications or workloads. When a workload is deployed or moved, the network configuration adjusts itself automatically. This is important because it removes the need for manual reconfiguration of network hardware, thereby reducing operational complexity while saving the organization's valuable resources for higher-impact work.
- Control traffic flow between virtual networks, including the ability to define guaranteed bandwidth for the critical applications and workloads.

SDN PowerShell Deployment

Deployment through PowerShell requires deploying all components using PowerShell scripts. The following lists the key advantages of deploying via the PowerShell:

- The use of a script reduces the introduction of manual errors and saves significant deployment time.
- If deploying using the script, the settings in the VMM console can be modified afterwards just as the SDN components can be deployed manually.
- Like the manual deployment, it provides the option of setting up a new management logical network and switch or to reuse an existing network and switch.
- If the script deployment fails, all the changed settings are rolled back so that the security team can start again.
- Deployment can be turned off for specific components. For example, if the network controller is already deployed, it can be configured to deploy SLB and RAS gateway only.

Other Technologies Used for SDN

The following describes other technologies used for SDN management.

- *Network Controller*: The network controller allows security teams to automate the configuration of their network infrastructure instead of manually configuring network devices and services.
- *RAS Gateway for SDN*: RAS Gateway (software based router) is a software-based, multitenant BGP capable router that is designed for CSPs and enterprises that host multiple tenant virtual networks using HNV (Microsoft's Hyper-V Network Virtualization technlolgy).
- *Software Load Balancing (SLB) for SDN*: SDN can use Software Load Balancing (SLB) to evenly distribute tenant and tenant customer

network traffic among virtual network resources. The Windows Server SLB enables multiple servers to host the same workload, providing high availability and scalability.

- VMM Load Balancer: System Center Virtual Machine Manager (VMM) supports the following two scenarios of load balancing:
  - Load balancing the external network traffic: This scenario includes load balancing the network traffic coming from an external network. Load balancing is done through a public Virtual IP (VIP). The workload VMs can be connected to a no isolation VM network or to a network virtualization enabled VM network.
  - Load balancing the internal network traffic (Internal load balancing): This scenario includes load balancing the network traffic of workloads in the VM network that is enabled for network virtualization. Load balancing is done through a VIP.

Network Address Translation (NAT) Setup

The following two NAT types are supported by VMM.

- **Outbound NAT** - Forwards the VM network traffic from a virtual network to external destinations.
- **Inbound NAT** - Forwards the external traffic to a specific VM in a virtual network.

10 – Cyber Threat Intelligence

Cyber Threat intelligence (CTI) is the processed, analyzed, and contextualized information about cyber threats. It includes potential attackers, their motives, their tactics, techniques, and procedures (TTPs), and the tools used by them. This information can help organizations proactively defend against attacks like ransomware or phishing. Organizations can become proactive rather than being reactive in implementing a preventive security posture to manage the threat. Threat intelligence is much more than raw data; it is actionable knowledge that enables better decision-making, risk management, and faster incident response.

Building threat intelligence starts with collecting data from various sources, including dark web forums, malware analysis, and security feeds and correlating and analyzing this data to determine patterns, identify indicators of compromise (IOCs), and reveal attacker tactics. By adding this contextual meaning to the data to potentially identify the source of attack, and possibly the malicious intent behind it, in addition to how the attack is carried out, the security teams have in their hands the key information to proactively prioritize threats and address security defenses strategically. This also provides insights for long-term security improvements and compliance.

The following is a sampling of the data collected for threat intelligence:

- Knowing a specific ransomware group that is targeting the organization's industry or business.
- Identifying malicious IP addresses or file hashes.
- Understanding the specific techniques a threat actor uses to gain access.

Threat Intelligence Tools and Platforms

Threat intelligence tools centralize, analyze, and operationalize threat data. The tools include:

- Specialized Threat Intelligence Platforms (TIPs) like Recorded Future, ThreatConnect, MISP which centralize, normalize, and manage threat data from many sources.
- SIEMs (Security Information and Event Management) such as Splunk, IBM QRadar) to correlate with internal logs for proactive alerting and automated responses.
- SOAR (Security Orchestration, Automated Response & Repair) platforms such as Splunk SOAR, Palo Alto Networks Cortex XSOAR, IBM QRadar SOAR, Microsoft Sentinel, and Rapid7 automate workflows across various security tools.

- EDR (Endpoint Detection & Response) platforms such as CrowdStrike Falcon, SentinelOne Singularity, Microsoft Defender for Endpoint, Palo Alto Cortex XDR and the unified security platform.
- XDR (Extended Detection and Response) platforms detect, investigate, and respond to threats *on endpoints* (laptops, servers) using behavioral analysis. They provide rich telemetry and remediation information.
- Network Security tools such as Next-Gen Firewalls (NGFWs) and Web Application Firewalls (WAFs) which block threats at the network perimeter.
- Malware Analysis tools such as Virus Total analyze malware to understand behavior and extract indicators of compromise.
- Open-source feeds like AlienVault OTX, AbuseIPDB, URLscan.io, Feodo Tracker, CISA KEV for specific indicators or security compromise. These tools help automate detection, enrich alerts, and enable proactive defense by connecting to firewalls, WAFs, and other security Network Security Tools:
- Dark Web Monitoring Tools such as Recorded Future help hidden forums and markets for leaked data or threats to brand/assets.

Threat Modeling and Hunting

Threat modeling is a proactive, structured process in cybersecurity for identifying, analyzing, and addressing potential security threats and vulnerabilities in a system, application, or network. By using system diagrams and hypothetical scenarios, it helps understand potential attack vectors and business risks, enabling teams to prioritize and implement effective security mitigations before an attacker can exploit flaws.

The key steps in a threat modeling exercise include the following:

1. Threat modeling starts by creating an abstraction of the system that includes the profiles of potential attackers, including their goals and methods, and a catalog of threats that could arise.
2. In addition, for threat modeling, it is important to identify the system's assets and data that need to be protected. These are used as flow diagrams or architecture diagrams that also visualize weak points.
3. Once this data has been collected the threat modeling teams need to get together to brainstorm what could go wrong by asking questions and analyzing the documented information for each identified "what could go wrong" issue by documenting potential threats, motivations, and methods attackers might use.
4. The team needs to further identify and mitigate vulnerabilities, and develop strategies and implement security controls to reduce or eliminate risk.
5. The information documented by the team on threat analysis, risks and mitigations needs to be shared with stakeholders.

The final part of this exercise is documenting a framework for understanding and prioritizing security risks.

Incident Response

Incident Response is the process used to detect, analyze, contain, eradicate, and recover from cybersecurity incidents like data breaches or cyberattacks to minimize damage, restore normal operations, and learn from the event to prevent future incidents. A documented incident response plan and a designated team, such as a Computer Security Incident Response Team (CSIRT), are crucial for effectively managing the chaos of an attack and protecting the organization's systems, data, and reputation.

The best way to manage an incident is to follow a documented incident response lifecycle framework plan that includes the following steps:

1. *Preparation*: Develop and document an incident response plan, train a team, and establish the tools and technologies to be used.
2. *Detection & Analysis*: Monitor the organization's systems to identify potential security incidents, analyze them, and document the results.
3. *Containment*: Take steps to prevent the incident from spreading and causing more damage. This could include isolating the affected systems (e.g. disconnecting them from the network or Internet), disabling disabling the compromised accounts, and blocking malicious traffic through firewalls and DNS. Preserve the evidence for eradication and recovery.
4. *Eradication:* Remove the root cause of the incident: the malware, and the compromised user account. Use the preserved evidence and balance immediate actions with long-term solution.
5. *Recovery*: Restore affected systems/services to normal operation and verify correct functioning.
6. *Lessons Learned*: Document the incident and response, identifying what went well and what could be improved, and update plans and procedures to enhance future preparedness.

Incident Forensics

Incident Forensics is the process of meticulously collecting, analyzing, and preserving digital evidence after a cybersecurity incident to reconstruct the event, identify its root cause, and understand the attacker's actions. It is a key component of Digital Forensics and Incident Response (DFIR), a discipline focused on gathering evidence for investigation and to stop ongoing attacks, contain the damage, and improve security for the future. The key steps for executing incident forensics include the following:

- **Evidence Collection**: Gather data from compromised systems, networks, and devices. Create forensic images as exact copies of the original data, to ensure the integrity of the evidence.
- **Evidence Preservation**: Isolate and secure collected data to maintain its integrity for later analysis and legal proceedings. Maintain the "chain of custody" and track who handled the evidence.
- **Data Analysis**: Examine collected evidence to identify indicators of compromise, malware, and other artifacts that reveal the attack's methodology and timeline.

- **Reconstruction**: Using forensic methodologies to piece together the events of the attack, determine the scope of the breach, and identify the vulnerabilities exploited by the attacker.
- **Reporting**: Document the findings in a comprehensive report that details the incident, the evidence collected and analyzed and provide recommendations for improving security.

Threat Modeling & Intelligence, Incident Response & Forensics Tools

A wide range of tools is available and in use for Threat Modeling, Threat Intelligence and Incident Response and Forensics. The following is a sampling of these tools:

Threat Modeling Tools

Microsoft Threat Modeling Tool and OWASP Threat Dragon, support methods such as STRIDE. The following lists common tools in use:

- Microsoft Threat Modeling Tool: A free, open-source tool to identify and mitigate security issues.
- OWASP Threat Dragon: open-source, web-based, desktop tool to create threat model diagrams and track threats and their mitigations.
- ThreatModeler: automated tool to scale the SDLC and integrate with DevOps workflows.
- IriusRisk: performs risk analysis, generates threat models for apps, expert questionnaires.
- SD Elements: policy-based automation for security requirements, threats, countermeasures.
- CAIRIS: comprehensive, open-source tool for the integrating requirements and security info

Tools for Threat Intelligence Platforms:

- Recorded Future, CrowdStrike, and ThreatConnect.
- SIEM (Security Information and Event Management): Centralize security logs/alerts from various sources, detect and analyze threats, filter through "alert fatigue" and identify actual incidents. Examples: Splunk Enterprise Security, IBM QRadar, ManageEngine EventLog Analyzer
- Security Orchestration, Automation, and Response (SOAR) Systems. SOAR platforms automate security workflows and can integrate with TIPs (Threat Intelligence Platforms) to share threat intelligence.
- Dark Web Monitoring Tools: scan forums, marketplaces, and social media for stolen credentials.
- Open-Source Intelligence (OSINT) Tools: gather data from public sources like blogs and news.

- Sandboxing Tools: analyze suspicious files or programs in an isolated environment
- MITRE ATT&CK: A globally accessible knowledge base of adversary tactics and techniques used to model and understand threat actor behaviors and to map security operations against these known threats.
- EDR/XDR (Endpoint/Extended Detection and Response): Continuously monitor endpoints for suspicious activity and provide the data needed to investigate and contain threats at the device level. XDR extends this by aggregating data across different security layers. Examples: CrowdStrike Falcon, and SentinelOne.

Additionally, tools aggregate information on known threats, vulnerabilities, and attacker patterns to provide context for incidents. Examples include: AlienVault and AT&T USM Anywhere.

Other tools in use are:

- IDPS (Intrusion Detection/Prevention Systems):
- Monitor network and system activities to identify and block malicious behaviors, preventing attacks from causing damage.
- Automate repetitive incident response tasks, manage workflows, and integrate with other security tools to streamline the response process. Examples: Cortex XSOAR by Palo Alto Networks, TheHive (open source).

Vulnerability Scanning Tools:

These tools identify vulnerabilities in systems and networks that attackers could exploit, allowing organizations to proactively address them before an incident occurs. Examples of these tools include comprehensive scanners like Tenable Nessus, Qualys, and Rapid7 InsightVM, alongside specialized web scanners like Burp Suite and open-source options such as OpenVAS

Forensic Analysis Tools:

These are tools or dedicated workstations for in-depth forensic analysis of disk images, memory, systems, etc. These tools collect, analyze, and preserve digital evidence from compromised systems to determine the scope and cause of a breach. Examples include SIFT Workstation (SANS Investigative Forensics Toolkit).

Other tools include:

- Open-Source Incident Response Platforms:
- Platforms for SOC teams to manage incidents, collaborate, and collect evidence.
- Tools for incident response (IR) and forensics include SIEM and log analysis tools (Splunk, Graylog), EDR/XDR platforms (CrowdStrike, SentinelOne), forensic analysis suites (SIFT Workstation, Velociraptor), network traffic analysis tools, threat intelligence platforms (TIPs), and SOAR platforms for automation and coordination. These tools gather

evidence, detect anomalies, provide contextual threat data, and streamline the investigation and response process.

- SIEM & Log Management Tools: these tools centralize and analyze log data from various sources Examples: Splunk, Graylog, IBM QRadar, Elastic Security
- Endpoint Detection and Response (EDR) & XDR: Provide real-time monitoring of endpoints, detect advanced threats, and enable deep forensic investigations on compromised devices. Examples: CrowdStrike Falcon Insight, SentinelOne.

Network Traffic Analysis (NTA) Tools:

Tools that capture and analyze network communications to identify anomalies, command-and-control traffic, or data exfiltration. Examples include NetFlow software, network traffic analysis tools, Apache Metron. Other tools include:

- Threat Intelligence Platforms (TIPs):
- Aggregate and correlate external threat data to provide context to ongoing investigations, helping to understand attacker tactics and identify malicious indicators of compromise (IOCs). Examples include ThreatFusion and ThreatConnect
- Security Orchestration, Automation, and Response (SOAR) Platforms:
- Automate manual tasks, orchestrate workflows, centralize case management, and coordinate responses across different security tools to improve efficiency and consistency. Examples: SOAR platforms.

Forensic Collection & Analysis Tools:

Specific tools designed to acquire and preserve digital evidence from compromised systems without altering the original data. Examples: include RegRipper (for registry analysis), Osquery (for OS-level queries)

Digital Forensics Tools

Digital forensics tools are software and hardware used to investigate digital devices, capturing and analyzing data for legal, security, or incident response purposes, with popular examples including Autopsy, Magnet AXIOM, EnCase, Cellebrite, and X-Ways Forensics, alongside specialized tools like Volatility (memory) and Wireshark (network) for deep dives into operating systems, memory, and network traffic. These tools help with data extraction, analysis of file systems, mobile devices, cloud data, and network packets, often featuring write-blockers for hardware and imaging tools to preserve evidence integrity.

Popular Digital Forensics tools include:

- Autopsy: A comprehensive, open-source platform with a GUI for analyzing hard drives and smartphones, built on The Sleuth Kit.
- Magnet AXIOM: Collects, analyzes, and reports evidence from computers, mobile devices, and the cloud.
- Cellebrite: Specializes in mobile device data extraction and analysis.

- EnCase: A long-standing, powerful commercial tool for computer forensics.
- X-Ways Forensics: Known for analyzing file systems, files, and disk images efficiently.
- Belkasoft X: A multi-purpose tool for computers, mobile, cloud, and memory forensics.
- Bulk Extractor: High-speed tool for scanning disk images for specific data like URLs and emails.
- Volatility Framework: Open-source tool for advanced memory analysis (RAM forensics).
- Wireshark: A widely used network protocol analyzer for capturing and examining network traffic.
- Mobile Forensics: Specialized tools (like Cellebrite, XRY) and methods for extracting data from phones.
- Memory Forensics: Tools like Volatility capture volatile data from RAM for real-time insights.
- Network Forensics: Wireshark and NetworkMiner analyze network packets and traffic.

11 – Endpoint Detection Response

Observability and Vulnerability are two key technology areas for ensuring cybersecurity protection in an organization's environments. Observability is the technology that helps the security team gain deep insights into their system's internal state from its external outputs such as logs, metrics, events and traces. Vulnerability management, on the other hand, is the continuous process of identifying, assessing, prioritizing and remediating vulnerabilities across the organization's systems to prevent breaches. Vulnerability management uses insights from their observability tools in real time.

The table below compares the two:

Topic	Observability	Vulnerability Management
Overview	Security Observability helps organizations better understand their overall security posture The three pillars of observability are logs (events), metrics (infrastructure, CPU and request latency), and traces (documented record of a series of causally related events on a network. These three data outputs provide different insights into the health and functions of systems in cloud and microservices environments. Observability offers a detailed view of a system's internal state from external outputs, essential for spotting anomalies that could signal vulnerabilities.	Vulnerabilities are weaknesses in system security procedures, hardware, design, implementation, internal controls, technical controls, physical controls, or other controls that could be accidentally triggered or intentionally exploited and result in a violation of the system's security policy. Also, broken authentication, SQL injection, Security misconfiguration, Cryptographic failure, Cross-site scripting and forgery, Exploits are the means through which a vulnerability can be leveraged for malicious activity by hackers; these include pieces of software, sequences of commands, or even open-source exploit kits. A threat refers to the hypothetical event wherein an attacker uses the vulnerability.
Tools	Dynatrace – Lakehouse, AI analytics, High availability Datadog – Small to large orgs, devStack, broad portfolio	Veracode – SAST – scan code for web apps Qualys - DAST– network security, assess on IP add Crowdstrike Falcon

	Splunk – Open telemetry support, ingestion analysis Cribl – small to large orgs, modular architecture New Relic – Telemetry data platform	AppScan – DAST– web apps/API, penetration test Prisma Cloud – ingests services and config data, IAM permissions
Comments	Display in Tableau or Google Chronicle which can ingest security telemetry data (from forwarders, ingestion APIs, integrations with Azure AD/Cloud APIs, and other tools	Vulnerability Assessment types: network, host-based, wireless network,

Table 11-1 : Comparison of observability and Vulnerability Management

Observability and Vulnerability tools help organizations in ensuring their *Cloud Security Posture Management (CSPM)* and *Security posture management (SPM).*

CSPM is an IT security solution that monitors cloud-based systems and infrastructure for vulnerabilities, compliance violations, and misconfigurations. CSPM tools automate the detection and remediation of these issues, providing visibility and policy enforcement to reduce risk. Tools include: CrowdStrike Falcon Cloud Security, and Aqua Real-Time CSPM.

SPM is a set of tools and strategies that help organizations detect and respond to threats that could affect their networks, devices, users, and data. SPM can help protect against a variety of threats.

Observability Management

Observability is a term used to describe the ability to understand a system's internal security state by analyzing its external outputs, like logs, metrics, and traces, to quickly diagnose issues and gain deep insights. This works in a complementary manner with monitoring tools, which are designed to check predefined conditions. Together they are used to determine the cause of a malicious attack, incident, or event on premises, in cloud-native environments, and hybrid environments. This observability approach ensures reliability, performance, and security of the overall system.

The security team can deduce the system's health and behavior by examining data generated by the observability tools without needing direct internal access to the systems' processes. Most applications are designed to create logs of their actions and status; observability tools are designed to collect metrics which are numerical measurements such as CPU and memory usage over time. *Traces* are used to track the end-to-end record of a single request's journey as it flows through complex, distributed systems, showing every step, service call, and component interaction, and is composed of spans (individual operations) to help pinpoint performance bottlenecks.

Observability helps in rapid troubleshooting to quickly pinpoint the root cause and in rectifying issues before they impact users. Another major benefit is understanding the weak links in the systems and points of exposure that must be cured for an improved security posture. Incidents in progress can be routed to the security operations teams for immediate containment action.

Observability Tools

The most common observability tools include Splunk, Cribl, Datadog, Dynatrace, and New Relic.

Splunk

Splunk works through a forwarder collecting data from remote machines and forwarding it on to an index. An indexer then processes that data in real time and stores and indexes it on the disk. End-users then interact with Splunk through the search head, which enables them to search, analyze, and visualize data.

Splunk works both as an observability tool as well as a vulnerability tool. Its features used for observability include unified monitoring across logs, metrics, and traces with capabilities for AI-driven root cause analysis, business impact correlation, and seamless integration, especially with recent enhancements like *OpenTelemetry* support and deep ties between Splunk Cloud Platform and Observability Cloud. Key features include streamlined alerts, automated troubleshooting, service mapping, and cross-platform visibility to detect and resolve issues faster across hybrid environments. It also allows repurposing logs from Splunk Platform within Splunk's Observability Cloud for unified views for reporting purposes.

The following describes the key features of Splunk used for observability:

Data Ingestion and Indexing:

- **Collecting Data:** Splunk gathers log data from various sources like servers, network devices, applications, and security systems.
- **Indexing:** The ingested data is then indexed, making it searchable in real-time.

Log Analysis:

- **Searching and Filtering:** Users can use Splunk's search language to query the indexed log data and filter specific events or patterns.
- **Visualization:** Splunk provides tools to visualize the search results, including charts, dashboards, and visualizations that help identify trends, anomalies, and potential issues.
- **Alerting**: Splunk allows users to set up alerts based on specific search criteria, which can be triggered when certain events or patterns are detected, says Splunk.
- **Security Threat Detection:** Identifying patterns and trends that might indicate security breaches, unauthorized access, or malicious activity.
- **Performance Monitoring:** Analyzing system and application logs to identify performance bottlenecks or anomalies.
- **Incident Response:** Quickly troubleshooting and resolving issues by analyzing log data to understand the root cause.

- **Log Observer Connect**: A robust, codeless interface for searching, monitoring, and analyzing machine-generated data, says Splunk.
- **AI/ML-driven features**: Service Maps and Trace Analytics provide actionable insights and facilitate quick troubleshooting.
- **OpenTelemetry integration**: Enables end-to-end observability, notes Splunk.

Compliance:

- Ensuring compliance with industry regulations and security standards by analyzing log data and generating reports.

Cribl Stream

Cribl Stream is a tool for collecting, processing, and routing data, offering flexibility in data transformation and routing. It allows users to ingest data from various sources, transform it using functions, and send it to different destinations. Key features include:

- **Data Flow:** Ingesting data from sources, processing it through pipelines, and routing it to destinations. For example, for AWS data can be collected from CloudLogs, CloudTrail, VPC and other services.
- **Data Transformation:** Using functions like mask, parse, eval, rename, and drop to modify data.
- **Data Routing:** Controlling data flow with routes, filtering and directing events to specific pipelines.
- **Monitoring and Validation:** Using tools like Datagen and Data Preview to test and verify data flow.

Steps for Using Cribl Stream:

- **Set up a Cribl Stream instance:** Organizations can start with a Cribl.Cloud account or deploy it on their own infrastructure.
- **Add a Source:** Configure sources to ingest data from various data sources using default or custom tiles (design patterns)
- **Create a Pipeline:** Define a pipeline with a series of functions to transform the data.
- **Add a Route:** Configure a route to direct data from the source to the pipeline, and then to the destination.
- **Add a Destination:** Specify destinations where the processed data will be sent. For example, it can be sent to Splunk, Tableu, and Google Chronicle.
- **Monitor and Validate:** Use the monitoring tools to verify data flow and performance.

Using Cribl with Splunk

Security teams can use Cribl Stream to collect logs also from a syslog server and other sources, parse them, enrich them with threat intelligence, and send the processed data to Splunk. Cribl is an extremely complementary solution to Spunk for enhanced data cleanup, analysis and classification, before sending it to Splunk thereby reducing Splunk costs.

Dynatrace

Dynatrace provides intelligent automation that adds context to logs and reliance on manual queries through several key technologies that are core to the platform including: Dynatrace OneAgent™, Smartscape, Davis AI, and Grail.

Dynatrace OneAgent

Dynatrace OneAgent automatically puts all logs in full context during the ingest phase. When OneAgent ingests a log into Dynatrace, it automatically discovers and associates the entire log context for a user. OneAgent enriches every ingested log instantly with various kinds of data, including the following:

- Host and infrastructure details which includes host name and type, Docker container names, Kubernetes namespaces, Kubernetes cluster names, and event types.
- Cloud platform details. For example, GCP instance name and ID, AWS region, AWS account ID, Azure resource name and ID, and database names.
- Web services details. For instance, how services are called and service names. OneAgent detects web services based on technology-specific frameworks.
- DevOps tools details. Including data from Ansible modules, Jenkins agents, Fluentd forwarders and aggregators, OpenTelemetry signals, service mesh sidecars, and so on.
- Application security data. Such as vulnerability status and business criticality, security context, severity level, affected entities, and new attacks.

Users can also create custom attributes to add to logs at ingest. Dynatrace OpenPipeline streamprocessing technology collects data from OneAgent, open-source collectors such as OpenTelemetry, and third-party tools, then filters and preprocesses that data to manage and reduce costs.

Dynatrace Smartscape, Davis™ AI, and Grail™

Another way Dynatrace automation decreases customer queries by 60% to 70% is Davis AI in association with Smartscape technology and the Grail data lakehouse.

Once logs with metadata are ingested into Grail, Smartscape topologically maps interdependencies of every entity within the entire IT landscape. There is no need to have to run exhaustive queries to determine time associations between distributed traces, user sessions, application events, infrastructure events, and logs.

To accelerate access to answers, such as when troubleshooting, Davis AI automatically establishes an operations baseline for user experience, applications and infrastructure. Then it automatically detects anomalies from that baseline, such as infrastructure failure rates, network retries, application performance response times, to name a few examples. This AI-powered alerting by Davis reduces alert storms and automatically adapts baselines in reaction

Datadog

Datadog's key features center on its unified observability platform, offering Infrastructure Monitoring, Application Performance Monitoring (APM), Log Management, Security Monitoring, and Digital Experience Monitoring, all unified by customizable dashboards, powerful alerting, AI-driven insights, and extensive integrations, providing real-time, end-to-end visibility across cloud, hybrid, and on-premise environments to troubleshoot faster and optimize performance.

The core observability features of Datadog are

- Infrastructure Monitoring: which collects metrics from servers, containers (Kubernetes), serverless functions, and cloud services (AWS, Azure, GCP) for real-time health checks.
- Application Performance Monitoring (APM): Traces requests across distributed systems, identifies bottlenecks, and optimizes application code and user experience.
- Log Management: Centralizes, searches, filters, and analyzes logs from all sources, correlating them with metrics and traces for faster troubleshooting.
- Digital Experience Monitoring: Includes Real User Monitoring (RUM) for front-end insights, Synthetic Monitoring for proactive testing, and Session Replay.

Datadog also provides many security and compliance features including:

- Cloud Security Posture Management (CSPM): Datadog monitors cloud configurations for risks and compliance.
- Cloud Workload Protection: Detects threats and vulnerabilities within cloud workloads.
- Code Security: Offers Static (SAST) and Runtime (IAST) analysis for secure code.

Datadog provides customizable dashboards & visualizations for creating unified views of metrics, logs, traces, and more for tailored monitoring and proactive alerts for issues, powered by AI for intelligent anomaly detection. In addition, it provides service maps and infrastructure maps that help visualize dependencies and communication flows in your system. The AI and Machine learning features are applied across the platform for anomaly detection, root cause analysis, and LLM observability.

New Relic

For observability New Relic provides a unified platform for full-stack visibility, using AI for insights, supporting OpenTelemetry, offering developer-friendly tools, and providing cost optimization. These are all available for collecting logs, metrices, events and traces data for deep monitoring from frontend to backend, infrastructure, and AI/LLM applications. This helps the security staff to achieve faster issue resolution and proactive management. New Relic can identify vulnerabilities in code and dependencies. It can provide integrations for custom workflows and CI/CD embedding. It also provides tools to embed observability in development.

The full-stack visibility provides a unified view across apps, infrastructure (including Kubernetes and cloud), databases, and user experience. AI and machine learning assist in root cause analysis, proactive insights, intelligence alerting using anomaly detection.

Data can be ingested from any source using Open Telemetry, ensuring flexibility.

Vulnerability Management

Continuous vulnerability management includes technologies and workflow required for controlling and removing vulnerabilities. The objectives of vulnerability management are to maintain a database of the computers and devices of the organization's network, its hardware assets along with a list of installed software, and its software assets.

The primary function of vulnerability management is to identify and fix faults in the installed software that affect security and enable the effective mitigation and management of security risks. Vulnerability Management tools can alert security teams on additions of new devices, ports or software to the databases. This allows an analysis of the changed attack surface and to detect successful attacks. It can also help understand the most effective workflow for patching and updating the devices to thwart attacks (such as malware, bots and so on). Based on the information provided by the vulnerability management tools, security teams can change the software configuration to make systems less susceptible to attack.

It is important to use the data provided by the vulnerability tools to document the state of security for audit and compliance with laws, regulations and business policy. Key functions of vulnerability tools include:

- *Asset Discovery* -- what assets (such as servers, desktops, copiers and mobile devices) are running on the organization's network including uncovering forgotten devices. The security teams also need to identify the people who are responsible for maintaining these assets.
- *Assessing the security status* -- vulnerability scanning feature of the vulnerability tool is used for finding and fixing the vulnerabilities in the organization's computer systems. The security teams can perform an assessment and can also perform a one-off scan for a snapshot or scan that runs repeatedly on a periodic basis (say daily or weekly), allowing the security team to track the speed of applying patches and software updates and to assess how your security status is improving. This level of assessment provides you with more information that is useful for effective VM.
- *Analyzing the scan* – the teams can use the scan results to identify the types of vulnerabilities and check sites for documented vulnerabilities such as the Common Vulnerabilities and Exposures (CVE) website, the National Institute of Standards and Technology's (NIST) National Vulnerability Database which also adds severity scores and detailed information for each vulnerability, The United States Computer Emergency Readiness Team (CERT) Vulnerability Notes Database, the Exploit DB database that collects Proof of Concepts for vulnerability exploits and the vulnerability tool's vendor website for their knowledgebase gleaned from its ongoing research and development efforts.

External Attack Surface Management (EASM)

EASM involves a systematic approach to identify, assess, and manage vulnerabilities and exposures across an organization's digital footprint. It helps organizations maintain visibility into potential entry points for attackers, including web applications, network infrastructure.

Figure 11-1. : External Attack Surface Management (EASM) Steps

The previous diagram describes the range of capabilities required for an EASM. The primary goals are early detection, minimization of downtime, avoidance of regulatory fines, and protecting brand reputation. The diagram following describes the functions of a continuous scanning platform complementing EASM.

EASM uncovers hidden risks and reveals unknown assets (shadow IT) that internal teams might not know about, but attackers can see. It provides proactive defense and helps organizations get ahead of attackers by finding and fixing vulnerabilities before they are exploited. Additionally, it reduces attack vectors and actively shrinks the digital perimeter by managing and securing public-facing entry points.

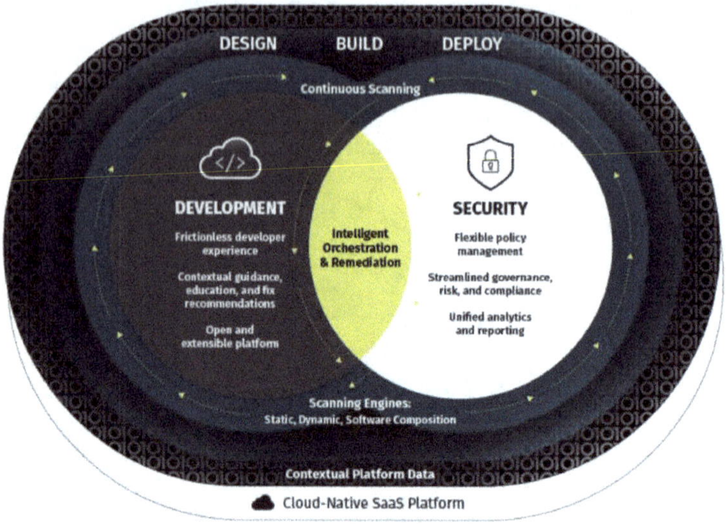

Figure 11-2 : Continuous Scanning Platforms

Primary challenges include the evolving threat landscape, interoperability and integration of security tools and platforms, regulatory and standards compliance, scalability and privacy concerns.

Vulnerability Management Tools

The following lists some common tools used for vulnerability Management

CrowdStrike Falcon	CrowdStrike Falcon excels with real-time threat detection, cloud-native flexibility, and seamless integration, enhancing endpoint security and management.
Darktrace	Darktrace excels in AI threat detection, real-time monitoring, and autonomous response, offering seamless integration and an intuitive interface. Darktrace / NETWORK uses a unique Self-Learning AI engine that learns what is normal behavior for an organization's entire network, continuously analyzing, mapping and modeling every connection to create a full picture of your devices, identities, connections, and potential attack paths.
Nessus	Remote security scanning tool, which scans a computer and raises an alert if it discovers any vulnerabilities that malicious hackers could use to gain access to any computer you have connected to a network. Tenable Nessus Agents help you address the challenges of network-based scanning, specifically for the assets where it's impossible or nearly impossible to collect information about your organization's security posture consistently.
VectraAI	Offers advanced detection and incident response capabilities, focusing on known and unknown threats across cloud, identity, SaaS, and on-premises environments. Its AI-powered solution goes beyond basic threat detection—leveraging behavior-based analysis and Attack Signal Intelligence to provide real-time insights into attacker methods. Vectra's platform unifies XDR with traditional

	network detection and response (NDR), helping teams detect, investigate, and respond to complex attacks efficiently.
SentinelOne	Singularity platform combines endpoint detection and response (EDR) with extended detection and response (XDR) to protect various devices and environments. This AI security software safeguards against ransomware, malware, and other advanced threats while allowing automated threat hunting and incident response actions.
Microsoft Defender	Provides capabilities for real-time asset discovery, risk assessment, and built-in [remediation of vulnerabilities and misconfigurations across various platforms, including Windows, macOS, Linux, Android, and iOS
Microsoft Copilot	Virtual assistant that streamlines your security workflows and protects your software. The AI analyzes vast amounts of security data, identifying patterns and prioritizing threats in real time. After that, it summarizes incidents and recommends response actions
Splunk SIEM	While Splunk SIEM is not a native, standalone vulnerability scanner, it is heavily used for vulnerability management and prioritization. Splunk's data-powered platform with assistive AI capabilities offers unmatched, comprehensive visibility by seamlessly ingesting, normalizing, and analyzing data from any source at scale. It can monitor, detect and investigate threats with speed and accuracy.

Table 10-1 : Sampling of Vulnerability Management Tools

SIEM

Essential capabilities of an analytics-driven SIEM are:

- *Real-time security monitoring and analysis*: detect and respond to threats fast.
- *Cloud security*: detect and respond to threats across hybrid, cloud and multi-cloud environments.
- *Incident response*: identify incidents when they occur, and track, route and annotate events.
- *Threat intelligence*: access curated, in-product security research on existing and emerging threats.
- *Incident investigation and forensics*: optimize threat hunting, reduce the volume of alerts and increase true positives.
- *Advanced and insider threat detection*: exponentially improve detection success, freeing up time and resources to zero in on complex, high-fidelity threats.
- *Compliance*: unify the three pillars of compliance — process, technology and people — through greater visibility across systems and processes.

The following able is a list of common tools for SIEM:

CrowdStrike Falcon	CrowdStrike Falcon excels with real-time threat detection, cloud-native flexibility, and seamless integration, enhancing endpoint security and management.
Darktrace	Darktrace excels in AI threat detection, real-time monitoring, and autonomous response, offering seamless integration and an intuitive interface. Darktrace / NETWORK uses a unique Self-Learning AI engine that learns what is normal behavior for an organization's entire network, continuously analyzing, mapping and modeling every connection to create a full picture of your devices, identities, connections, and potential attack paths.
Nessus	Remote security scanning tool, which scans a computer and raises an alert if it discovers any vulnerabilities that malicious hackers could use to gain access to any computer you have connected to a network. Tenable Nessus Agents help you address the challenges of network-based scanning, specifically for the assets where it's impossible or nearly impossible to collect information about your organization's security posture consistently.
VectraAI	Offers advanced detection and incident response capabilities, focusing on known and unknown threats across cloud, identity, SaaS, and on-premises environments. Its AI-powered solution goes beyond basic threat detection—leveraging behavior-based analysis and Attack Signal Intelligence to provide real-time insights into attacker methods. Vectra's platform unifies XDR with traditional network detection and response (NDR), helping teams detect, investigate, and respond to complex attacks efficiently.
SentinelOne	Singularity platform combines endpoint detection and response (EDR) with extended detection and response (XDR) to protect various devices and environments. This AI security software safeguards against ransomware, malware, and other advanced threats while allowing automated threat hunting and incident response actions.
Microsoft Defender	Provides capabilities for real-time asset discovery, risk assessment, and built-in [remediation of vulnerabilities and misconfigurations across various platforms, including Windows, macOS, Linux, Android, and iOS
Microsoft Copilot	Virtual assistant that streamlines your security workflows and protects your software. The AI analyzes vast amounts of security data, identifying patterns and prioritizing threats in real time. After that, it summarizes incidents and recommends response actions
Spectrum	"CA Spectrum," now known as "DX Spectrum," is a Broadcom product that is a services and infrastructure management system, monitoring the state of devices, applications, host systems, and connections, and collecting status information like faults and performance data.

Table 11-2. : Sampling of SIEM Tools

Endpoint Detection and Response (EDR)

EDR is a crucial cybersecurity technology that continuously monitors devices (endpoints) like laptops, phones, and servers for malicious activity, detects threats like ransomware, and provides tools for security teams to investigate and quickly respond to contain and eliminate attacks, offering deeper protection than traditional antivirus. It works by collecting and analyzing endpoint data, using behavioral analysis to spot anomalies, and automating responses to block threats before they spread across a network, acting like security officers inside your digital infrastructure. EDR protects various devices such as securing desktops, mobile devices, virtual machines, and IoT devices.

EDR works through continuous monitoring collecting data on all activities such as (processes, network connections, file changes and also on all endpoints. Using data analytics and advanced AI with the EDR tools detect threats or suspicious patterns that signal malware, ransomware, or other advanced threats.

Investigation through EDR tools provides security analysts with rich context about an attack's lifecycle how it started, what it did, and where it went. The correlated and classified data from this analysis enables automated response to enabling automated actions such as isolating a device and setting up alerts, and guiding SOC teams through manual steps to mitigate the threat.

Response & Remediation enables automated actions (like isolating a device) and guided manual steps to stop and clean up threats.

EDR implementation starts by assessing goals, evaluating the current security measures and shortcomings such as and identity gaps. It requires setting clear objectives with a focus on specific risks and environments to be protected. Once a solution (cloud or hybrid) has been selected, and for agent-based solutions the team needs to install and configure agents on all endpoints. The tools need to be customized with appropriate detection rules, automated response policies, and then integrated with systems like SIEM and threat intelligence feeds. The tool is now ready for continuously collecting endpoint data (processes, network, files), using AI/ML to analyze for threats, triggering alerts, and enabling automated or manual response actions like isolating devices or removing malware, all while integrating with existing security tools for a comprehensive defense strategy.

The collected data can be further used for deep dives into incidents to understand attack paths and gather evidence. The data can be classified and sorted and stored for post-incident analysis and investigation and future use.

Extended Detection and Response (XDR)

While EDR focuses primarily on endpoints (devices like servers and end-user devices), XDR builds on EDR by extending visibility and response capabilities across networks, clouds, and other security layers for a much broader view

XDR is a cybersecurity solution that unifies and automates threat detection and response across an entire IT environment, collecting and correlating data from endpoints, networks, cloud, and email to provide holistic visibility, faster threat hunting, and streamlined incident response, moving beyond traditional tools like EDR (Endpoint Detection and Response) for broader protection.

XDR collects telemetry data including logs, alerts, and any relevant activity from a variety of security systems, including endpoints (such as laptops and servers), cloud workloads, email, and network traffic. This data can be viewed in a single, comprehensive dashboard for security events across the entire system spectrum. This data is then analyzed using AI and machine learning tools, correlated across devices to see patterns, and identify threats, even the advanced ones that are spread across multiple security domains and devices. An important aspect of XDR is its ability to automatically enable remediation actions such as blocking malicious threat actions and isolating devices to limit threat exposures.

XDR is implemented through a phased approach consisting of the steps: 1) planning, focused on assessing needs, setting goals); 2) deployment and at the same time integrating data from endpoints, networks, cloud, and emails; 3))analyzing and automating while correlating data with AI to find threats, automating responses like isolating devices; and 4) continuously optimizing the XDR process and tool, training staff, refining workflows, and implementing monitoring improvements to achieve comprehensive security visibility and faster incident response across the entire IT environment.

12 – Wireless Security and MDM

When data travels on public networks, it becomes vulnerable so that malicious actors have an opportunity to intercept sensitive information, steal identities, commit fraud, and disrupt services, leading to data loss and financial disruption of the business. Data travels to mobile devices primarily through radio waves in the electromagnetic spectrum and is typically transmitted between the device's antenna and a nearby cellular tower, or via Wi-Fi routers. Cellular data uses 4G/5G technology to send data packets to base stations, which connect to the internet via high-speed wired, or sometimes fiber/microwave, and backhaul networks.

Wireless Security

Protection of wireless networks and Mobile Device Management (MDM) are key to protecting data from unauthorized access, theft, or damage. It is important that many end-user devices are connected through wireless networks and are targets for malicious actors to intercept and exfiltrate data. Wireless security, implemented to protect wireless networks and data from unauthorized access, theft, or damage, employs methods like encryption (WPA2/WPA3), authentication, and firewalls to secure radio-transmitted data, preventing attackers from eavesdropping on, accessing, or damaging the network. Using Virtual Private Networks (VPNs) to create secure "tunnels" for data, is essential for protecting information over public Wi-Fi.

Mobile Device Management

Mobile Device Management (MDM) is an IT security and management solution that lets organizations secure, monitor, manage, and enforce policies on employees' mobile devices such as employee smartphones, tablets, laptops, and other devices. The core purpose of MDM is to protect the corporate network by securing and optimizing mobile devices, including laptops, smartphones, tablets, and Internet-of-Things (IoT) devices, that connect to enterprise networks. This security capability protects corporate networks while enabling mobile productivity by remotely configuring settings, deploying apps, updating software, and securing data. MDM ensures devices comply with company rules, offers remote lock/wipe, and manages everything from device enrollment to decommissioning, often as part of broader EMM or UEM strategies.

Besides boosting the security of business networks, it enables employees to use their own devices, rather than corporate-supplied devices, to work more efficiently and be more productive.

MDM software is part of the wider enterprise mobility management (EMM) family, which incorporates enterprise file syncing and sharing, identity and access management (IAM), and mobile application management (MAM). MDM, in the context of controlling PCs, is referred to as unified endpoint management (UEM), which enables organizations to manage all of their enterprise devices from one single location.

MDM relies on two separate components. The first is an MDM server management console, which is stored in an organization's data center and enables administrators to configure, manage, and enforce policies. The second is an MDM agent that receives and implements these policies on users' devices.

Policies are configured by IT administrators through the MDM server management console, then the server pushes the policies to the MDM agent. The agent applies the specified policies onto a device by using application programming interfaces (APIs) that are built into the device's operating system

BYOD (Bring Your Own Device)

The MDM and BYOD space can be quite complicated, with many technologies and solutions available for organizations to choose from. Bring Your Own Device (BYOD) is the concept of employees using their own laptop or mobile devices for work. Traditionally, it meant bringing a device to the employee's workplace or connecting it to a secure corporate network.

The launch of Apple's first iPhone in 2007 fueled the BYOD trend which placed more importance on effective MDM tools. The risks associated with the BYOD trend led to organizations implementing MDM software that helped their IT teams monitor, manage, and secure all devices brought into the workplace network. These MDM tools remain crucial to securing the workplace in the face of increasingly sophisticated and costly cyberattacks and data breaches.

As employees increasingly expect to be able to use their personal devices at work, organizations need to be able to secure those devices and keep their users safe. Some employees who want to use their personal devices at work will do so even if their organization does not have a BYOD policy, a practice also known as shadow IT. It is therefore vital for businesses to implement a strong BYOD policy that enables employees to use their own devices without creating potential gaps in security.

How MDM Works

The following lists the steps for implementing) MDM:

- *Enrollment*: Devices are enrolled into the system, allowing IT to manage them.
- *Policy Enforcement*: Rules are pushed to devices (e.g., strong passwords, app restrictions, etc.).
- *Remote Management*: IT can remotely update software, configure settings, and push commands.
- *Security*: It protects against malware, secures Wi-Fi/VPN, and can remotely lock or wipe lost/stolen devices.

- *Mobile Application Management (MAM):* Manages the distribution, deployment, and control of apps on mobile device restricting users from installing unauthorized apps.

To ensure security it is important to implement data encryption, malware protection, remote lock/wipe features. The devices need to be configured with automated setup of Wi-Fi, email, and VPN profiles. Remote bulk app deployment to mobile devices and updates to the devices is essential for managing mobile devices. All devices must comply with the organizational standards.

Enterprise Mobility Management (EMM) is a broader suite including MDM, MAM, and Mobile Content Management (MCM).

Unified Endpoint Management (UEM) is the capability to manage all endpoints (PCs, IoT, mobile) from a single platform.

Common Features of MDM Software

Some of the most popular features included in most MDM solutions are:

- Simple mobile device enrollment.
- Profile configuration and management.
- Mobile application management.
- Mobile security management.
- Secure content distribution and management.
- Remote troubleshooting of mobile devices.
- Mobile OS update management.
- Complete asset management.
- Conditional Exchange Access (CEA) for managed mobile devices (available only on-premise).
- Secure e-mail access and management.
- Containerization and BYOD management.

Common Capabilities of MDM Solutions

Most MDM solutions provide these common capabilities pre-built into the solutions.

- **Device inventory and tracking**:
- **Content access**: Content access means providing a connection to a back-end repository that employees can use to share or transfer content onto their devices. This includes providing content access to repositories like SharePoint or Documentum, while avoiding roaming download restrictions and enabling logs of which users access and download files.
- **Passcode Enforcement**:
- Remote service management:

- **Enterprise mobility management (EMM):** An EMM solution is a collection of policies, processes, technologies, and tools used to manage and maintain employees' mobile devices. An EMM suite enables organizations to manage mobile device usage and drive the secure use of devices on their networks and systems. For example, MDM software is frequently used in combination with security tools as part of a complete EMM solution.
- **Mobile Application Management (MAM):** Mobile application management) is a process that enables organizations to apply policy control functionalities to applications, which are managed by their EMM console. This is particularly useful if a device does not allow the management capability that an organization requires or if businesses choose not to install MDM profiles onto devices. Mobile application management comes in two forms:
- **Preconfigured application**: This is typically an application like a personal information manager for calendars, contacts, or email. It could also be a secure web browser provided by a third party or an EMM provider. A preconfigured application is set up to be managed and secured by the organization's EMM system.
- **Application extension**: The policies are applied to applications through an SDK or through a wrapping process.
- **Mobile content management**: Mobile content management is the process of enabling employees to access content via their mobile devices. This can be achieved through client-side applications, or secure containers, that enable users to store content on a mobile device. The EMM enforces security policies such as authentication, copy and paste restriction, and file sharing to secure the process. The user is then able to access applications like email or content from back-end repositories. Content can also be managed through push-based document delivery, which puts functions in place to control document versions, issue alerts to users when new files are added, or to flag upcoming content expiration dates.
- **Remote Monitoring and Management (RMM):** RMM enables IT service providers to monitor devices, endpoints, and networks remotely. It is also known as remote IT management, whereby a provider manages a fleet of devices across an organization or multiple companies.

Mobile Device Management Solutions Examples

Many third-party products are available for MDM and provide the most of features listed in the previous section. Some of these products include:

- Manage Engine MDM Plus: it is used to monitor, secure, and manage corporate and employee-owned (BYOD) devices including smartphones, tablets, and laptops.
- Fortinet: through FortiClient EMS (Endpoint Management Server) and integrations with FortiNAC to manage, secure, and enforce policies on mobile devices.

- Microsoft Intune: cloud-based UEM service with strong integration with Microsoft 365 and Azure AD, and so is ideal for enterprise environments.
- Jamf Pro: enables IT teams to automate the entire device lifecycle -- deployment, security, and management --using native Apple frameworks without needing physical access to device
- SOTI MobiControl: MDM and EMM solution designed to secure, monitor, and manage mobile devices, IoT endpoints, and rugged handhelds.
- Hexnode MDM: Cloud-based tool offering strong kiosk mode and security to manage, monitor, and secure corporate and employee-owned (BYOD) devices.
- IBM MaaS360: AI Driven MDM solution that allows IT teams to manage and secure devices such as smartphones, tablets, laptops, and IoT from a single console. It supports Android, iOS, Windows, and macOS, focusing on BYOD, security, and threat defense.

13 – Internet of Things (IoT) Security

Our physical world consists of a lot of devices that are connected as endpoints to a variety of networks. Many devices are connected as end points on the Internet and are used for a wide range of functions. IoT systems enable real time data collection, automation, and enhanced decision making thereby driving the efficiency and optimizing operations for the devices, machines, or the systems that they're attached to.

The IoT refers to a network of these physical object, the "things", embedded with sensors, software, and technologies that enable them to connect, collect, and exchange data with other systems and devices over the internet. These interconnected "smart" devices, range from home appliances and medical devices to industrial machinery. They facilitate automation, remote monitoring, and increased efficiency.

IoT enables devices to communicate and act autonomously, such as adjusting a thermostat, tracking shipments, or predicting maintenance needs in factories. The scope of IoT extends beyond traditional computers to include everyday objects that can now communicate without human intervention.

Major applications of IoT include: smart home automation using devices such as thermostats, lighting, cameras and appliances; industrial and manufacturing automation to guide predictive maintenance, and supply chain; wearable trackers for healthcare monitoring; smart city infrastructure controls that can include air quality control, traffic management, waste management, and so on: and agricultural efficiency by using smart farming tools to detect soil moisture, and crop growth for yield optimization; and logistics for tracking movement of raw material and finished goods.

IoT Security

Security of IoT systems is the practice of protecting internet-connected devices described in the previous section and their networks from cyber threats, unauthorized access, and data breaches, ensuring the compliance with the CIA triage (confidentiality, integrity, and availability) for these systems. The unique challenges that need to be addressed for IoT systems include weak default settings, limited processing power in the devices, and securing the devices, networks, and the data they collect, transmit, and store against being breached and exploited for data theft, operational disruption, or as entry points into larger networks.

IoT security requires protecting the physical device itself from attacks, including firmware vulnerabilities and physical tampering, securing the network and the communication channels between devices and servers to prevent eavesdropping or data interception. Data encryption is essential to ensure that sensitive data collected by devices is protected, both when stored (at rest) and when being sent (in transit). IoT also requires that devices are secured throughout their entire lifespan, from manufacturing to deployment, and in use.

Another major challenge for IoT devices is the geometrically increasing attack surface due to rapid growth in numbers and types of connected devices that, in addition to industrial machines, includes smartwatches, cars, home appliances and anything that can be automated in the real world. This creates numerous potential vulnerabilities due to physical and digital convergence. Many IoT devices lack robust built-in security, making them easy targets for attackers to compromise data or use them in botnets.

loT Gateways

IoT devices need to be connected to a variety of networks to operate. These connections are channeled through IoT gateways which include physical devices or software that act as central hubs, bridging and connecting IoT devices (sensors, actuators, and end devices) with the cloud or central servers. These collections through the gateways are used for collecting, filtering, processing, and securely transmitting data. The gateways assist in translating different communications protocols, and managing device communication to ensure efficient, scalable, and secure IoT ecosystems. It acts as the "entrance" for device data, allowing less complex, cheaper devices to connect and interact with the internet, and performs crucial tasks like data aggregation and edge computing locally.

The IoT gateways can connect IoT devices using a variety of protocols by automatically performing protocol translation and converting device-specific protocols into a common language such as MQTT (Message Queuing Telemetry Transport). MQTT is a lightweight, open-standard publish-subscribe messaging protocol designed for low-bandwidth, unreliable, or high-latency networks, commonly used in IoT and machine-to-machine communication for the cloud. The IoT gateway can filter out irrelevant data and aggregate the data from multiple sources before sending it. It also facilitates edge computing by performing local processing and AI and machine learning based analysis.

Tools and Technologies Used

Some common IoT hardware and prototyping Tools include the following:

- Microcontrollers/Boards: Arduino (for prototyping), Raspberry Pi (single-board computer), Tessel 2, and Flutter.
- Sensors & Actuators: Temperature, motion, gas, and light sensors that convert physical signals to digital data.
- Edge Gateways: Devices that connect, manage, and process data from sensors before sending it to the cloud.
- IoT connectivity using wireless: Wi-Fi 6, 5G, Bluetooth, Zigbee, etc. eSIM (embedded chips in devices for subscriber identity) for cellular connectivity.
- IoT Software & Platforms such as: AWS IoT, Microsoft Azure IoT, Google Cloud IoT, Oracle IoT, and Particle.

- Frameworks & Tools: Node-RED (visual programming), Eclipse IoT (frameworks), and Home Assistant.

Device Authentication Tools

For security, IoT devices must be authenticated and checked for authorization to ensure that only devices authorized to connect are allowed. IoT device authentication tools are technologies and methods used to verify the identity of devices attempting to connect to a network, ensuring only authorized, secure devices gain access. These tools, including digital certificates (X.509), cryptographic keys, tokens, and hardware-based solutions, prevent malicious actors from hijacking devices or data.

Key IoT Device Authentication Tools and Methods

The following tools are crucial for securing IoT ecosystems in any domains where IoT systems are being used for collecting data from devices and getting devices to perform specific tasks where unauthorized access can lead to significant disruptions or data breaches.

- *Public Key Infrastructure (PKI) & Digital Certificates (X.509):* The X.509 certificates are validated by establishing a chain of trust from the entity certificate on a device up to a trusted Root Certificate Authority (CA). This is the most common secure method where each device holds a unique certificate to prove its identity to a server.
- *Hardware Root of Trust (HRoT) & Trusted Platform Module (TPM)*: HRoT is a dedicated, tamper-resistant hardware component that forms the secure foundation for a device's security, anchoring trust by protecting critical processes like key storage, secure booting and attestation. This ensures that only authenticated software runs and safeguards sensitive data from malware and physical attacks. TPM chips are designed to securely generate, store, and manage cryptographic keys and sensitive data like passwords and certificates, ensuring the computer's firmware and operating system haven't been tampered with.
- *Access Tokens (OAuth/OIDC*): Unique tokens issued to devices by identity providers upon provisioning that are verified during each data transmission.
- *MAC (Message Authentication Code*): is a cryptographic checksum, or tag, created using a **secret key** and a message, verifying both the message's **integrity** (it hasn't been changed) and **authenticity** (it came from the expected sender). The sender generates the MAC (media access control, a data link layer sublayer (Layer 2) that controls how devices with 48-bit MAC addresses, access the shared communication medium) by appending it to the message, and the receiver recomputes it with the same key. MACs use symmetric keys (same key for sender/receiver) and are fundamental to secure communication protocols like TLS/SSL.
- *Device Provisioning & Identity Management*: Tools that manage the lifecycle of a device, including secure onboard, identity issuance, and configuration.

- *Protocols*: Specialized, lightweight, or secure protocols such as Lightweight Machine-to-Machine (LWM2M protocol, an Open Mobile Alliance for managing and communicating with resource-constrained IoT)devices, enabling efficient remote device management, data reporting, firmware updates and diagnostics over low-power network. TR-069 is another protocol used. It is used by Internet Service Providers (ISPs) to automatically configure, manage, and monitor customer home devices (like modems, routers, and set-top boxes) remotely through an Auto-Configuration Server.

loT Vulnerability Scanners

IoT vulnerability scanners are specialized security tools that automatically identify, analyze, and assess connected devices (e.g., cameras, routers, sensors) for risks like weak passwords, unpatched firmware, and open ports. They provide an attacker's view of the network to help secure IoT ecosystems by identifying vulnerabilities. These vulnerability tools discover IoT devices on the network, including manufacturer, model, and firmware details. They check devices against databases of known vulnerabilities, such as MITRE CVE (Common Vulnerabilities and Exposures) which is an industry-standard dictionary of publicly disclosed cybersecurity vulnerabilities in software and hardware. The MITRE CVEs also include firmware and potential zero-day exploits, and unsafe function calls. These scanners also check credentials and can identify weak or default credentials that could be easily exploited.

Vulnerability scanning tools can passively monitor traffic or actively probe devices for details. They scan the network to find connected IoT devices and their open ports. The scanning tools generate reports with actionable intelligence, listing vulnerabilities by severity and recommending remediation actions. They assist in meeting regulatory requirements and security standards.

IoT Vulnerability Scanning Technologies and Tools

Examples of IoT vulnerability scanning technologies tools include:

- Retina IoT (RIoT) Scanner -- a cloud-based security tool designed to identify, assess, and manage vulnerabilities in Internet of Things (IoT) devices like IP cameras, DVRs, printers, and routers. It provides an attacker's view of network risks
- Nozomi Networks – provide a suite of tools designed to provide visibility, security, and monitoring for Industrial Control Systems (ICS), Operational Technology (OT), and IoT environments. Their solutions combine artificial intelligence with network and endpoint analysis to detect threats, vulnerabilities, and anomalies.
- Check Point Software -- secures IoT environments using ***its*** *Quantum IoT Protect* solution, which provides automated device discovery, AI-driven risk analysis, and network segmentation to enforce Zero Trust policies. It protects against cyber-attacks, including, but not limited to, zero-day vulnerabilities, using network-level security gateways and, for embedded devices, lightweight Nano-Agents.

Firmware Integrity Checkers

IoT firmware integrity checking tools are security mechanisms that validate the authenticity, legitimacy, and untampered state of an embedded device's software. They use cryptographic signatures, hashing (e.g., SHA-256), and secure boot processes to prevent unauthorized code execution, ensuring only trusted firmware updates from manufacturers are installed. The bootloader verifies the digital signature of the firmware before allowing it to run, ensuring it has not been tampered with. Over-the-air verification ensures that the firmware received via remote, potentially insecure networks is authentic and intact before installation.

These checkers use cryptographic hashing which compares the firmware's hash against a known-good value to detect corruption or unauthorized modifications. These checkers also continuously validate the firmware code in memory to ensure that it remains unaltered during operation.

Hardware Root of Trust (HRoT) utilizes hardware security modules (HSMs) or trusted platform modules (TPMs) to protect cryptographic keys used for verification.

These systems prevent compromised devices from running unauthorized code, protecting against supply-chain attacks and unauthorized modification

Secure Communication Protocols

Secure communication protocols tools for IoT, such as MQTT with TLS, CoAP with DTLS, and HTTPS, encrypt data in transit and authenticate devices to prevent tampering, unauthorized access, and eavesdropping. These protocols ensure data integrity, confidentiality, and reliability, with choices often depending on whether the device requires low power (MQTT, CoAP) or high-bandwidth cloud connectivity (HTTPS).

Here is a quick review of the IoT communication protocols used for security:

- *Transport Layer Security (TLS) / Secure Sockets Layer (SSL)*: tools offers a robust encryption and authentication for securing TCP-based traffic (e.g., HTTPS, MQTT over TLS).
- *Datagram Transport Layer Security (DTLS*): tools provides TLS-level security for UDP-based, resource-constrained devices, often used with CoAP.
- *Message Queuing Telemetry Transport (MQTT) with TLS*: A lightweight publish-subscribe protocol ideal for low-bandwidth, unreliable networks, often secured with username/password and TLS.
- *Constrained Application Protocol (CoAP) tools with DTLS*: A RESTful protocol designed for low-power, lightweight M2M applications, using DTLS for security.
- *Advanced Message Queuing Protocol (AMQP)* tools: A reliable, secure, and interoperable messaging protocol often used in industrial or enterprise IoT, supporting TLS and SASL.
- *HTTPS*: Used for API-based, cloud-connected IoT devices, providing encryption through SSL/TLS.

- *X.509 Certificates*: Used for mutual authentication (mTLS), ensuring both device and server are trusted.
- *Protocols like OAuth 2.0* manage access control are used for authentication and authorization.

The choice of protocol depends on device capabilities (power, memory), network constraints (bandwidth, reliability), and the required security level. For example, MQTT is preferred for battery-operated devices, while HTTPS is better suited for devices with constant power and high throughput.

14 – Operational Technology

The industrial world uses a lot of industrial equipment such as robots, pumps, sensors, and valves. Unlike Information Technology (IT) that manages data, OT manages physical processes in sectors like manufacturing, energy, and transportation. Examples of these systems include Programmable Logic Controllers (PLCs), robotic welders, and traffic light systems

Operational Technology (OT) consists of hardware and software designed to detect or cause direct changes in, and controlling industrial equipment. OT priorities focus on system safety, reliability, and availability, rather than just data security. OT includes Industrial Control Systems (ICS), Supervisory Control and Data Acquisition (SCADA), and Distributed Control Systems (DCS) that automate tasks too dangerous or precise for manual operation.

Common OT applications) include controlling assembly lines in factories, monitoring power grids, managing water treatment facilities, and controlling HVAC systems in buildings. OT systems are increasingly connecting to IT systems and the internet for enhanced efficiency which raises cybersecurity concerns.

Industrial Control Systems (ICS)

Industrial Control Systems (ICS)) are integrated hardware and software, including SCADA, PLC, and DCS, used to monitor, automate, and control physical industrial processes, such as manufacturing, energy production, and water treatment. These systems manage critical infrastructure by receiving data from sensors, comparing it against setpoints, and managing actuators to maintain safety and efficiency. ICS consist of interconnected components, including sensors, actuators, controllers (e.g., PLCs), and human-machine interfaces (HMIs).

The following describes the most common ICS in use:

- *Supervisory Control and Data Acquisition (SCADA):* Systems that manage high-level, process-level supervisory operations.
- *Distributed Control Systems (DCS)*: Control systems used for large-scale, complex manufacturing or processing plants.
- *Programmable Logic Controllers (PLCs):* Small, rugged computers used for direct, real-time control of machinery.

These systems automate industrial processes, allowing for remote monitoring and control, reducing human intervention, and optimizing performance. These are most useful in areas like manufacturing, oil and gas, electric power, water treatment, and transportation sectors.

ICS systems act as the brains behind the industrial processes, managing everything from assembly line speed to power plants and robots. Due to their critical nature, these systems require specialized cybersecurity to protect against physical threats and cyberattacks.

SCADA Security

SCADA (Supervisory Control and Data Acquisition) Security is designed for protecting industrial control systems that manage critical infrastructure (like power grids, water systems, oil pipelines, etc.) from cyber threats, focusing on preventing unauthorized access, data breaches, or malicious control that could disrupt operations, compromise safety, or cause physical damage. They use measures like network segmentation, firewalls, and access controls. SCADA is essential for utilities (electricity, water), manufacturing, transportation, and energy sectors They monitor and collect real-time data from sensors and devices like programmable logic controllers and remote terminal units to manage remote control of industrial processes (pumps, valves, motors) from a central location.

They take on a special significance because attacks on utilities can disrupt essential services, posing risks to public safety. They also pose an operational risk of malicious actors attacking for ransomware, malware, and other cyberattacks that can halt operations, leading to costly downtime. In the case of utilities and factories, control by malicious actors can cause dangerous conditions, explosions, or even loss of life.

Common SCADA security measures used to ensure security include:

- *Network Segmentation*: Isolating SCADA networks from general IT networks to limit access from compromised IT networks.
- *Access Control*: Strong authentication and strict permissions so that only authorized users have access to the industrial OT systems.
- *Firewalls & Intrusion Detection/Prevention*: Monitoring and blocking malicious traffic at the perimeter and using IPS to prevent attacks at the perimeter.
- *Patching & Updates*: Regularly securing hardware and software and ensuring that the most recent security updates from the OT software vendors have been applied.
- *Monitoring & Logging*: Real-time alerts for abnormal activity which can be analyzed to deter mine what mitigation steps should be taken to harden security.

Device Hardening Tools

Device hardening is an IT security process that reduces the "attack surface" of a device such as a computer, server, or IoT device by eliminating vulnerabilities, closing unused ports, removing unnecessary software, and applying strict security configurations.

Device hardening tools used for OT include software utilities, configuration scripts, and frameworks used to reduce a device's attack surface by eliminating vulnerabilities, disabling unnecessary services, and enforcing security policies. Key examples include: Center for Internet Security (CIS) benchmarks which provide standardized checklists to secure OS, databases, and network devices; network hardening tools that disable unnecessary ports, protocols (e.g., SMBv1, FTP); Microsoft Group Policy Object (GPO) to centrally manage, configure, and secure Windows operating systems, applications, and user settings across a network; tools to enforce the principle of least privilege, removing local admin rights; application white-listing tools that allow only authorized applications to run; vulnerability scanners; host-based firewalls; and endpoint detection and response (EDR)

OT Threat Intelligence Platforms

Operational Technology (OT) Threat Intelligence tools are specialized solutions designed to collect, analyze, and disseminate information on cyber threats targeting industrial control systems (ICS), SCADA, and IoT devices. These tools provide visibility into malicious activities, vulnerabilities, and threat actor TTPs (tactics, techniques, and procedures) to protect physical, critical infrastructure.

The types of OT threat intelligence tools and components used can include:

- Specialized OT Monitoring/Detection Tools: that monitor industrial network traffic and sensor data in real-time to identify anomalies in PLC, DCS, and SCADA environments. Common tools in use include Claroty, Dragos, and Nozomi Network.
- Threat Intelligence Platforms (TIPs): systems that centralize, normalize, and analyze data from external feeds to provide actionable intelligence regarding specific threats to OT environments. Comon tools in use include platforms like Dragos and Nozomi Networks, framework-based tools such as MITRE ATT&CK for ICS, and intelligence feeds from Mandiant, CrowdStrike, and Recorded Future
- Vulnerability Management Solutions:) specialized tools that identify weaknesses in industrial hardware and software, often addressing vulnerabilities that lack traditional IT CVE listings. Tools in use for this include: Tenable OT Security, Forescout, and CrowdStrike Falcon Exposure Management
- OT-Specific Threat Feeds: real-time data streams focused on indicators of compromise (IoCs) related to industrial malware, targeted attacks, and exploit attempts.

These tools help organizations move from reactive to proactive security by providing context on threats before they impact physical operations.

15 – Popular Cybersecurity Tools

Cybersecurity tools are software and hardware solutions used to protect computer systems, networks, and data from cyber threats like malware, unauthorized access, and data breaches. These tools monitor systems and networks to detect threats and prevent attacks, respond to incidents, and help maintain security by performing functions such as detecting vulnerabilities in the systems and networks, data encryption usage, and managing user access. The following are some examples of common cybersecurity tools used by organizations to protect their networks and data assets:

- **Antivirus/Antimalware Software**: These tools detect, prevent, and remove malicious software like viruses, worms, and ransomware from systems and devices.
- **Firewalls:** Act as a barrier between trusted and untrusted networks, controlling incoming and outgoing network traffic to block threats.
- **Vulnerability Scanners**: Identify weaknesses in systems and applications that could be exploited by attackers. They can check databases of known vulnerabilities, detect unpatched software, misconfigurations, weak passwords, and open ports.
- **Data Encryption Tools:** Convert data called plaintext into unreadable format called ciphertext using a mathematical algorithm using a unique key, protecting its confidentiality even if it's intercepted during transit or at rest.
- **Intrusion Detection and Prevention Systems (IDS/IPS)**: Monitor networks and systems for suspicious activity, alerting administrators to potential attacks or actively blocking them. IDS tools are passive in that they detect threats in real-time and alert administrators while IPS tools operate within the traffic stream and actively block detected threats in real-time.
- **Identity and Access Management (IAM) and Privileged Access Management (PAM) Solutions**: Control and manage user permissions, ensuring that only authorized individuals can access specific resources. PAM is a subset of IAM that specifically manages and secures highly sensitive privileged accounts and their elevated access to critical systems and data.
- **Security Information and Event Management (SIEM)** Software: Collects and analyzes security data from various sources, helping to detect and respond to threats in real-time. These tools may use analytics, AI, GenAI and machine learning to correlate data, and generate prioritized alerts for potential attacks and anomalies.

- **Security Orchestration and Response (SOAR)**: integrate various security tools, automate repetitive tasks, and orchestrate coordinated responses to incidents. These tools streamline threat detection, analysis and response.
- **Virtual Private Networks (VPNs):** Encrypt data transmitted over networks, providing a secure connection for remote access and users. VPNs encrypt Internet traffic, hide real IP address, and tunnel a user's connection through a remote server. They help protect data being channeled through public networks.
- **Threat Modeling, Analysis, Threat Intelligence, Forensics and Incident Response and Management: P**rovide mechanisms for identifying risks of cyber-attacks, the potential malicious actor actions, the assets at risk, immediate mitigations, and implementation remediations:

These and other cybersecurity tools provide a diverse range of benefits to your organization that together help in establishing and managing comprehensive Security Posture Management (SPM), Cloud Security Posture Management (CSPM) and Data Security Posture Management (DSPM).

Importance of Cybersecurity Tools for Organizations

Cybersecurity tools and technologies are vital to protect against increasing cyber threats, safeguarding your sensitive data from theft and damage, ensuring business continuity and operational integrity, and preserving trust and confidence for individuals, businesses, and governments. They help prevent data breaches, identity theft, and help prevent or minimize financial losses due to a breach, while also enabling compliance with regulations and defending critical national infrastructure from attacks. A few key functions provided by cybersecurity tools include:

- Data Protection: Safeguards the confidentiality, integrity, and availability of data, especially sensitive data.
- Threat Detection and Prevention: Tools like firewalls, antivirus and anti-malware software, and intrusion detection systems are used to continuously monitor systems and networks to identify and block malicious activity including malware installation, phishing, and other cyber threats.
- Incident Response: These tools help organizations detect and respond to security incidents, minimizing the impact of a breach. They also provide forensic capabilities to identify and track potential attacks.

The impact of cybersecurity tools on individuals includes the following:

- **Protect Personal Data**: Cybersecurity safeguards personally identifiable information (PII), financial details, and other private data from misuse and theft.
- **Prevent or Minimize Financial Fraud and Identity Theft**: Tools like antivirus software and secure online platforms help prevent financial loss and the fraudulent use of personal information.
- **Ensure Privacy**: They help maintain personal privacy by securing online accounts and preventing unauthorized access to personal information.

The impact of cybersecurity tools on businesses includes the following

- **Protection of Intellectual Property and Sensitive Data**: Cybersecurity secures proprietary information, customer data, and trade secrets from cybercriminals.
- **Business Continuity**: By preventing disruptions from cyberattacks like ransomware, cybersecurity ensures that businesses can continue their operations without significant downtime.
- **Maintaining Customer Trust**: Secure systems build confidence among customers and clients, preventing reputational damage that can result from a data breach.
- **Compliance with Regulations**: Many industries have regulations requiring specific data protection measures. Cybersecurity tools help businesses meet these legal and regulatory obligations.

For Governments and National Security, the impact of cybersecurity tools includes the following:

- **Defense of Critical Infrastructure**: Cybersecurity protects essential national systems, including military operations, energy grids, and other government services from cyberattacks.
- **National Security**: Robust cybersecurity is crucial for national security, preventing foreign powers or malicious actors from disrupting or compromising governmental functions.

Cybersecurity Tools Areas

New cybersecurity tools, especially those driven by AI and GenAI keep emerging and existing tools number in hundreds, if not thousands. So, finding and selecting the tool most appropriate to meet your business objectives requires a lot of research and evaluation. Good common sources for this research for me, the author of this book, has been through participation in many virtual cybersecurity conferences run by FutureCon and ISC2 where a large number of tools vendors maintain virtual booths and follow-up with emails describing their tools in detail. This regular flow of information on new cybersecurity tools and upgrades to existing ones from this source has helped the author build up his Confluence library.

Here is a broad sampling of cybersecurity tools that I as the author have actually selected during the last 10 years and run Proofs of Concept (PoCs) on. Also listed below are other potential tools that the I as the author researched and even evaluated but did not necessarily run PoCs on.

Enterprise Cybersecurity

For IAM, PAM, CIAM, Identity Federation, RBAC/ABAC the tools that I ran PoCs on include BeyondTrust, OKTA, Ping Identity and Ping Federate, and Prisma Cloud. Other tools researched and evaluated include CyberArk, and One Identity.

GRC & Risk

For risk recording, assessments, standards and compliance and for driving the risk register, I evaluated AuditBoard and Archer and ran detailed PoCs on Archer for policies and standards management, compliance analytics and reporting, and for creating executive risk dashboards, audit evidence gathering and supporting auditor interactions (FFIEC, OCC, Reserve Bank). Other common GRC tools include ServiceNow GRC, and MetricStream.

Cloud Architecture and Security Tools

Include cloud-native tools for Azure (Microsoft Defender), AWS, and GCP and tools for on-premises to cloud migration, cloud identity management. Tools I ran evaluations and PoCs on Qualys, CrowdStrike, GitHub for IaC (Terraform), HashiCorp Sentinel Policy-as-Code, and Palo Alto Networks Prisma Cloud for fine-grain policy management and in-production compliance analysis. Other tools researched and evaluated include Orca Security, and Trend Micro.

Observability

These tools gives organizations a detailed real-time assessment of their security posture by collecting logs, traces, end-point security attacks, incident and alarms data, and other security event and incident related data to allow security teams to classify and correlate information from the various sources to create metrics, Tableau reports, and cloud-native publishing as well as immediate real-time alerts to security teams for follow-up action and address security weaknesses in systems. The tools protecting endpoints and networks are based on technologies such as IPsec, TLS 1.3, IDS/IPS), AppSec, and Zero Trust. I performed PoCs on tools including Splunk, Cribl, DataDog, Dynatrace, and evaluated Grafana. Also researched and evaluated SolarWinds, and AppDynamics.

Vulnerability Management

This is crucial for an organization's security posture so a thorough understanding of the cybersecurity tools for vulnerability management and rigorous management and use of these tools is paramount for ensuring prevention of attacks by malicious actors. The tools I have actually run PoCs on include BeyondTrust, Veracode, Qualys, Prisma Cloud. Also researched and evaluated Wireshark, and Burp Suite.

Threat Modeling, Threat Intelligence, Forensics & Incident Response

Collectively they help an organization's risk posture by providing security teams the mechanisms for identifying risks of cyber-attacks, the potential malicious actor actions, the assets at risk, immediate mitigations, and implementation remediations. The tools I have conducted PoCs on include SIEM tools like Splunk, Endpoint Detection and Response (EDR) tools: CrowdStrike Falcon, Threat Modeler. Also evaluated SOAR platforms and OWASP Threat Dragon.

Network and Zero Trust Application Security Tools

These tools, technologies and capabilities including PKI, IPSec, TLS 1.3, VPN/IpSec, biometric authentication, encryption at rest/in transit/use. Tools I have run PoCs on include Splunk, Cribl, OKTA. Other tools evaluated include Forcepoint and Zscaler.

Data security Tools

The regulatory requirements for maintaining and using consumer data for the financial, banking and brokerage firms and for large corporations include CCPA, GDPR, GLBA, NYDFS , SOX, PCI-DSS, and other Cybersecurity Regulations. Rigorous use of security measures ensured through these tools becomes critical for your organization if your organization is required o comply with these regulations. The tools I have run PoCs on include Fortinet, Splunk and Proofpoint.

Steps for Implementing Cybersecurity Tools

To implement cybersecurity tools, first, assess the organization's environment and risks, then establish a clear strategy, select appropriate tools, and configure them based on applicable regulatory cybersecurity standards and policies and frameworks like NIST, CSA, ISO27001, or data security standards such as GDPR, CCPA, PCI-DSS, etc. and others. Next, create implementation playbooks and provide training for the security teams managing the tools, and implement operational procedures for using the tools including ongoing continuous monitoring, analysis of data collected from the tools and reporting. Also develop plans for incident response and recovery, followed by ongoing refinement of the entire cybersecurity program. The key implementation steps are described in the following:

1. Plan & Prepare

- *Assess The Environment*: Conduct a comprehensive assessment of the existing technology, infrastructure, and digital assets to understand the current security posture and identify areas of weakness. Describe how the cybersecurity tool will operate within this environment and the expected results from its operation.
- *Perform a Risk Assessment*: Identify and evaluate potential cybersecurity risks, determine their potential impact, and create a risk management plan to mitigate them. Identify which risks will be addressed by the cybersecurity tool and how will the risk management be achieved.
- *Define Goals & Strategy*: Establish clear cybersecurity goals and develop a strategy to address current and future security requirements, considering the threat landscape. It is important to clearly understand and document how the cybersecurity tool meets the business objectives driving its acquisition.

2. Implement And Secure Systems and Networks

- *Choose a Framework*: Select and weave in a recognized cybersecurity framework, such as the NIST Cybersecurity Framework, to guide the framework implementation. Map the current security posture to the framework's core functions (Identify, Protect, Detect, Respond and Recover) and identify gaps where the cybersecurity tool can be leveraged.
- *Install & Configure Tools*: Install cybersecurity tools like firewalls, anti-malware software, and multi-factor authentication systems based

on the organization's strategy. An installation playbook is a good approach to ensuring that the operations team fully adheres to the operating requirements of the cybersecurity tool.

- *Configure Policies*: Establish and enforce strong cybersecurity policies for managing user privileges, data security, and network security. These are driven by the type of cybersecurity tool, so it is important to document policies applicable for the tool.
- *Provide Training*: Train employees and key personnel on cybersecurity best practices, including strong password usage, phishing awareness, and threat detection and how these apply to the cybersecurity tool being installed.

3. Monitor & Respond

- *Monitor & Detect*: If needed, implement continuous monitoring systems to check on the operation of the cybersecurity tool to detect suspicious activity and vulnerabilities by logging and analyzing network traffic. Different tools will have different needs in this area so this needs to be fully customized.
- *Manage Incidents*: If the cybersecurity tool identifies incidents, develop a comprehensive incident response plan to handle detected cyber events, including communication and mitigation strategies.
- *Plan for Recovery*: Failures of the cybersecurity tool in operation or observed risks or incidents identified by it require following established data backup and recovery plans to ensure critical information is safe in the event of a tool or system failure or data loss.

4. Refine & Improve

- *Test & Update*: Regularly test the reliability of the operation of the cybersecurity tool and ensure that it is correctly protecting the environment and identifying incidents and anomalies that need response and recovery to ensure security posture is maintained. Also create plans to improve awareness and highlight areas for improvement.
- *Continuously Improve*: Proactively refine the cybersecurity tool implementation based on lessons learned from the results obtained from the ongoing operation of the cybersecurity tool.

Aligning Cybersecurity Tools with Business Objectives

Business objectives are the driving incentive for the use of cybersecurity tools. The tools must align with the business objectives focused on protecting the organizations data assets, client and customer data privacy, and workforce privacy and credentials protection. Unauthorized, unplanned or unanticipated, or malicious exfiltration of data, at the very least can negatively impact the business operations and profitability but can even cause loss of reputation and regulatory fines.

Planning for acquiring a cybersecurity tool starts with formal documentation that includes the following:

- Business objectives and target deliverables that the tool must provide

- Type of deployment of the tools – within the organization's extended network perimeter or accessed on a third party-site from within the organization's network.
- Evaluation criteria – Tool vendor reputation and business stability, features and functions the tools provides, contract types and terms (e.g. site license, pay -per-use, registered or concurrent login-in users, national or global deployment regions, on-premises vs. cloud, etc.)
- Infrastructure and deployment requirements (typically a checklist, can be a spreadsheet)
- Feature requirements checklist (typically a spreadsheet).
- PoC test criteria and result formats (also typically a checklist).
- Post acquisition support contract terms agreement.
- Deployment contract terms agreement.

Types of PoC

PoCs can range from simple to very complex depending on the nature of the cybersecurity tool, the complexity of the tool itself as well as the deployment and integration complexity. The following is a sampling on increasingly complex PoCs:

1. A simple tool performing a very specific task and accessed as a SaaS product in the vendor's network and environment.
2. A cybersecurity tool deployment within the organization's extended network perimeter including the organization's cloud deployments and is tested for its effectiveness in meeting its stated functionality.
3. A complex tool that requires customization to meet the organization's business objectives and a custom infrastructure for installation and use. Testing includes performance test against a documented test plan and test data within a controlled sandbox (on-premises and cloud) with predefined test data.
4. A high-performance tool with an organization-wide impact that requires Installing and configuring the tool within a sandbox carved out of live production environment with a percentage of the production traffic copied to the sandbox environment to simulate real live production applicability of the tool. This is a very complex but a very powerful tool analysis methodology to check if the tool can scale up to the live production requirements and to gauge the cost implications of the infrastructure buildup.

Running a PoC in production environments is generally not considered good practice due to implications of production data corruption or customer data privacy concerns. But there are cases where such PoCs are really the only way to assess if the tool will, in fact, scale up to the production requirements and provide the performance for real-time actions. I have used this approach in a few cases. Two notable cases are described below.

1. Mobile Search Engine running on AWS. The challenge was to manage indexing inputs from up to 300 spiders running concurrently for searching the web for listings of hotels, restaurants, services of various kinds that mobile users wanted to search on, etc. The indexes created were used to

provide search results. Both of these tasks were very high intensity, and performance was key to ensuring integrity of the index data collected. Running PoCs in QA or non-production environments were inadequate to really assess how the product would hold up with hundreds of millions of on-line users. So. the approach I used was to create a parallel secure and restricted production environment that performed all functions including creating a duplicate index by copying a percentage (used 5 to 25% to get a real picture) of the production data into the production test environment. This provided really valuable insights into the deficiencies in the product that were prone to bottlenecks.

2. Another good example is a PoC I ran in 2023 to test a product called Cribl Stream. I researched several tools including Dynatrace and DataDog, and selected Cribl to augment Splunk to achieve significant cost reductions (almost 70%) for observability. I architected and designed the PoC and working closely with the Observability production services team obtained executive approval to fund and run an 8-month six-person team to build a comprehensive prototype to test Cribl. Another major challenge was to obtain approval to run the PoC in the production environment using real production data. The obvious security implications required senior executive approval to approve a plan to ensure rigorous access controls to ensure security and privacy of customer data throughout the PoC effort. As the PoC team, we collected logs from AWS (CloudWatch and Cloud Trail) from the production account into the Cribl AWS account, and using customized Cribl tiles, classified and correlated the data to identify attacks, the types of attacks, malicious actors, and also ran analytics. Not only did this help in feeding crucial information to Splunk for immediate protective response but also to the SOC team for follow-on actions. Summarized logs data captured through Cribl was forwarded for reports displayed in AWS S3, GCP Pub/Sub and Google Chronicle, and Splunk. Needless to say, the PoC was hugely successful.

Designing and Running PoC for Cybersecurity Tools

A PoC for a cybersecurity tool is a small-scale, controlled project that evaluates the feasibility and effectiveness of a security solution in the organization's unique environment. It helps validate vendor claims with real-world performance data before the organization commits to a major investment.

Phases of a cybersecurity PoC

A well-organized phased approach is crucial for the success of a complex PoC. The following lists the key distinct phases, which if executed well, can provide valuable insights into the product capabilities and its suitability to your organization.

Preparation: Define objectives and scope

Establish the problem: Clearly define the specific security challenge that needs to be solved. For example: "We need to improve our ability to detect and block phishing attacks" or "We need a more efficient way to monitor cyber-attacks and block them".

Set success criteria: Define what a "successful" outcome looks like. Metrics should be specific and measurable, such as:

- The tool must detect 95% of simulated phishing emails.
- The solution must generate and classify all end-point attacks and correlate them for publication in a daily report.
- Alerts must integrate with our existing Security Information and Event Management (SIEM) system.

Identify resources: Determine the team members involved (IT, security, end-users), the timeline for the PoC, approved budget and programmer resources, and required on-premises infrastructure or cloud resources.

Deployment: Create a secure test environment

Isolate the environment: Set up a temporary virtual or cloud environment (a "sandbox") that mimics the production environment as closely as possible without introducing risk to live systems.

Manage access: Implement robust access controls, including strong multi-factor authentication, and monitor all access to the PoC environment. Use the principle of least privilege, granting vendors only the access they need for a limited time.

Establish data controls: Use non-production data, and if sensitive information must be used, ensure it is encrypted. Contractually require the vendor to completely delete all data upon the PoC's conclusion.

Execution: Run tests and collect data

Simulate attacks: Execute predefined test scenarios to evaluate the tool's effectiveness against real-world threats. Common cybersecurity test cases such as:

- Phishing attacks
- Known vulnerability exploitation
- Distributed Denial of Service (DDoS) resilience
- Insider threat simulations

Involve end-users: Gather feedback from a small group of potential users to assess the tool's usability and integration into existing workflows.

Document observations: Record logs, system responses, and results meticulously for later analysis. Note any bugs or unexpected behavior.

Summary: Analyze results and present findings

Analyze performance: Compare the test results against your predefined success criteria. Did the tool meet expectations for detection, prevention, and response?

Report to stakeholders: Create a comprehensive report, use Grafana for showing real-time, technical performance, and use Tableau for interactive, polished dashboards for a business audience, that explain the findings and recommendations. Be transparent about both successes and limitations, and present options for enhancing the test and the tool usage.

Make a decision: Use the data to decide whether to proceed with a full-scale rollout, re-evaluate different options, or move to a pilot project.

Key differences: PoC vs. pilot

It is important to distinguish between a PoC and a pilot project. The table below describes the key differences between the two and why it is important to not let a PoC extend into an unplanned pilot. A complex PoC may take on some characteristics of a pilot. While a PoC is run in a sandbox environment, a pilot is typically run in real production mode.

Feature	Proof of Concept (PoC)	Pilot Project
Objective	Tests the technical feasibility of a concept in a controlled, isolated environment.	Tests the solution's performance and scalability in a realistic production-like environment with a limited scope.
Scope	Narrow and focused on core functionality (e.g., can the tool detect X type of attack?).	Broader, involving more features, users, and integrations with existing systems.
Environment	Isolated sandbox or test environment.	Controlled production environment or a replica of it.
Users	Often conducted by a small technical team; user feedback may be limited.	Includes a subset of end-users to test adoption and usability.
Outcome	Confirms whether the idea is worth pursuing.	Determines if the solution is ready for full-scale deployment.
Duration	Typically shorter (weeks).	Can be longer (months).

Figure 15-1 : PoC vs Pilot – Key Differences

Selecting Procuring and Implementing a Cybersecurity Tool

The success of evaluating, selecting, running PoCs, procuring, and implementing a cybersecurity tool depend on the rigorousness of the process used. The following sections elaborate on an organized stepped approach.

Step 1 – Establish the Business Objectives

Business objectives are driven by the business units responsible for the development and deployment of products. So, understanding their motivations and requirements for cybersecurity are paramount as a starting point. This process is formalized through obtaining product plans, features and functions and the deployment plan and documenting it from objectives perspectives. This documentation can then be presented to the key stakeholders in the business unit for confirmation so that the tools acquisition process can be delivered to meet these objectives. This step is also crucial in obtaining funding commitments for the tools acquisition.

Step 2 – Research and Identify Appropriate Tools Candidates

Next up is finding appropriate cybersecurity tools that meet the business objectives. A matrix with the requirements and the tools is an excellent way of researching tools that meet the general criteria for the business objective. The Vendor Evaluation Matrix (VEM) should include the requirements that cover the full gamut including:

- Core functions of the cybersecurity tool and its applicability to the business objectives
- Technologies used, including use of AI and GenAI techniques.
- Deployment approach – SaaS, on-premises, or cloud environments.
- Complexity of billing – site license, per registered or concurrent user, geographic regions, etc.
- Stability and reputation of the vendor including years in business, financials, and global footprint.
- Willingness to participate during the PoC and providing no cost implementation for the duration of the PoC; also a support plan including PoC design and deployment.
- Legal and business terms implications and sample contract.
- PoC and deployment roadmap that can be supported by the vendor.

Step 3 – Complete Requirements Checklist for Each Tool

For each of the selected vendors, fill out the VEM after researching all aspects about the vendor from the vendor documentation, search on Google on available content describing the tools as well its competitors and deployment experiences, and applicable Gartner Magic Quarter and other research. Summarize all collected data and enter the gist in the VEM. As a final step, make sure to have a column in the VEM with an overall compliance rating to show how well the tool meets the business objectives.

Step 4 – Conduct Vendor and Tool Evaluation Meetings

Vendor evaluation is a critical step in selecting a cybersecurity tool. Vendor evaluation starts with research on the vendor offerings and the business relationship potential as well as vendor's security and privacy compliance with not only the organization's requirements but also with applicable industry standards and regulations.

The next step is to prepare a Vendor Questionnaire (VQ), a detailed list of questions about the vendor product not answered in the documentation or the research, the vendor's business capabilities, typical vendor's contract terms, duration of the vendor's agreements, licensing terms, business practices, cost structures, and support plans.

Once a vendor has been selected as a potential candidate, send the questionnaire to the vendor and ask them to prepare a presentation to address the questions. Invite the vendor to a vendor meeting where the vendor has the opportunity to present and answer any questions. The meeting invitees should also be sent to your organization's legal, and vendor management teams, the business unit technical and managerial leadership, the QA team, the SOC and the DevSecOps team. Document the results of the evaluation and build up a score on each question as well as an overall score.

The final step in this process is to identify the top three vendors for a detailed evaluation discussion and follow-up on contract negotiation.

Step 5 – Conduct Contract Terms Meetings with Vendor, Legal, and BUs

Contract negotiations should start with the most highly rated vendor and should include legal, vendor management and business unit leadership. A draft agreement drawn up preferably by your legal team should specify the product specification, the deployment infrastructure requirements, the support plan options, the licensing terms, and pricing structure showing pricing incrementals with the growth of your organization.

Once the overall contract terms are finalized subject to a PoC, the PoC part of it is signed off by the four parties within your organization and the PoC contract itself is signed by vendor management.

Should contract negotiations fail, move on to the next best vendor selected and repeat the process until you have a signed-up vendor.

Step 6 – Document PoC Infrastructure Requirements and Acceptance Criteria

Based on the terms of the contract you can now document the PoC design specification, the acceptance criteria, and the detailed QA plan. As a next step establish the PoC team, start acquiring the product and start implementing the PoC infrastructure.

Step 7 – identify the Test Data Sources and Run PoC

Identifying the test data sources is important from a number of different perspectives including: where data resides and who has access to it, how is it being created in production, does it contain any sensitive data, and how will the test data be disposed of so that it does not linger in your network for potential future misuse.

Your security team is now ready to run the PoC and document the results against the acceptance criteria.

Step -8 – Present PoC Results to BUs, Legal and Architects

If the PoC successfully meets the acceptance criteria, the team leader can present the results to the executive leadership of the business unit, legal, vendor management and IT operations leadership.

Step 9 – Establish Procurement and Use Contract

The final step in the acquisition is to finalize the agreement including any changes required based on the PoC and have Vendor Management sign off on the Final Contract Agreement.

Production Deployment

The security team is now ready for deploying the tool in your production environment. Playbooks created during the PoC and upgrades to the installation and implementation documents will be used by the infrastructure operations team to deploy and operated the cybersecurity tool in production.

16 – Conclusion

With the increasing use of AI and GenAI not only in application development and application deployment and use, it's use in selecting resumes for hiring and for interviewing has become an increasingly complex challenge for all applicants at all levels of jobs. Job descriptions created using AI technologies cover the entire gamut of cybersecurity, cloud architecture, data security and governance for almost every job, asking for a candidate to be a master of all of these technologies. But the actual hiring has increasingly become skills based just-in-time hiring; that is, the focus is on a specific skill immediately required for a job. Resumes are rejected if that skill is not highlighted in the resume and interviewers reject candidates who do not demonstrate very recent hands-on and programming level competence in these skills even for architect and consultant level jobs. Overall capability, breath of knowledge and skills and professional maturity play a lower level of importance.

This book is intended for cybersecurity, cloud architecture, data security and governance professionals preparing for job interviews as well as new hires who need to rapidly come up to speed in a wide range of technologies and skills required immediately upon hiring. Given that singular focus in mind, this book focuses on breadth rather than depth so that as a candidate for interview you, the reader, have one place to learn all about standards, technologies and tools that you may be expected to answer questions on during an interview. It will also help you focus on parsing job descriptions quickly to identify skills you need to master rapidly in time to prepare for an interview.

The book covers a wide range of technologies broadly based on the requirements of businesses today. This book describes the core technologies required for most job openings.

Selection and implementation of cybersecurity, data security, cloud architecture and governance tools is by far the most common requirement. While large well-funded organizations have the financial and engineering resources to build their own custom cybersecurity tools, and many of them do where business objectives are not fully met by available third-party tools, in most other cases third-party tools provide an excellent option. Most well-known and heavily used third party cybersecurity tools have evolved over many years, fine-tuned by heavy in-production use and technology enhancements driven by the business needs of a wide range of their customers. They benefit from collective design enhancements driven by real customer needs. A well-thought-out analysis and rigorous organized evaluations, especially those driven through PoCs can go a long way in acquiring and installing the best-of-breed tools for your organization.

Given the wide range of international data security standards and practical limitations on compliance with all of them, organizations need to determine their geographical operational regions and the laws and regulations applicable to their organization. They have to then choose carefully which standards apply to their applications and determine which cybersecurity and data security frameworks they need to use and the certification steps for such frameworks. It is also important to prepare a consolidated list and specification document of all cybersecurity and data security controls derived from the standards that must be implemented and rigorously followed

AI has undergone dramatic advances and is now omnipresent in a wide range of applications and business domains. Its positive effects are being felt in our day-to-day lives. Generative AI (GenAI), a fast-emerging subset of AI which builds on the analytical capability of AI by creating new predictive content by extracting and building on patterns from existing content, is making a significant impact on enhancing cybersecurity. The dynamic destructive impact of AI has also been felt in the spate of AI-driven cyberattacks. The omnipotent capability of Generative AI to build fake content is being increasingly exploited by cybercriminals to attack systems ranging from financial institutions to large corporations, and even to governments at all levels. AI and GenAI technologies and the LLM architecture and uses are a common new topic in interviews as well as in most cybersecurity related jobs in organizations.

Zero Trust is another area that is being impacted by the use of AI and GenAI techniques. Zero Trust has its roots in the principle "Never Trust, Always Verify". The omnipotent capability of GenAI to analyze and predict has a broad impact on enhancing Zero Trust. The power of GenAI is being employed to contain and prevent cyberattacks through Zero Trust. It is important for your to learn about AI, GenAI and Agentic AI technologies and the frameworks that apply and then perform a deep-dive into each to determine all aspects of each framework that you need to prepare for an interview or to implement as part of your job

I hope you will find this book helpful in your hunt for a new job and also in ramping up in your job to become a well-diversified cybersecurity, data security, cloud architecture and risk and governance expert very quickly.

INDEX

A

D

E

F

G

K

L

M

N

O

P

Q

R

S

T

U

V

www.ingramcontent.com/pod-product-compliance
Lightning Source LLC
LaVergne TN
LVHW080036210926
848481LV00011B/3205